A *New Way* to Create
a Prosperous Business

The Upside
Within Reach

How to Find the *Best* Ways
to Boost Your Results

Drew Morris

Co-creator of *Chief Executive* magazine's Wealth Creation Index

EXECUTIVE EDITION

THE UPSIDE WITHIN REACH
How to Find the Best Ways to Boost Your Results
Copyright © 2022 Drew Morris

Lift Publishing™ (a wholly owned subsidiary of Great Numbers! LLC)
96 Rutledge Drive, Red Bank, NJ 07701
www.liftpublishing.com/contact-us

Cover design by Mary Schuck
Page production by Domini Dragoone
Editorial services provided by Natalie Horbackevsky and Lois Smith
Indexing by Rachel Kuhn

ISBN (print): 978-1-7361000-0-4
ISBN (ebook): 978-1-7361000-1-1
Library of Congress Control Number: 2022939224

Disclaimer

The Upside Within Reach is intended to guide readers in improving the financial results that their businesses achieve. The information presented is for informational purposes only and is the expression of the author's and others' opinions. The reader is solely responsible for any actions taken as a result of the book's contents, since the author is simply providing a framework to guide the reader's decisions, and the reader's execution of them. While every attempt has been made to verify the information presented in this book, the author is not responsible for any errors, inaccuracies, or omissions. Please consult a professional if you have any concerns or doubts regarding your actions. No liability is assumed for losses or damages due to the information provided.

Contents at a Glance

Contents

Chapter 7

Deftly Managing Costs 143

Chapter 13

Management Practices for Delivering the Upside 251

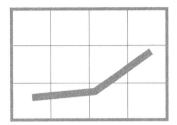

Preface

In the Summer of 1994, the potential of the business I was running began draining away, and I found myself looking for a better one.

On vacation one morning, in the surf off Cape May, New Jersey, waiting for a wave (we do a lot of that in NJ), the idea hit me that, "It's about results." That is, *better* results. Then I wondered, well just *how* do you do that?

I went looking for a way; one that would work for any (non-financial) business. After looking high and low, for many months, what I found were ways to cut costs, boost sales, and so on, but no overall *system* that would work for any business. Continuing to look, to this day, I still haven't found one.

So I made one, based on 25 years of research and more as a CEO, that I'll show you how to use in this book. It will answer the question:

What should I do to get my results up?

Simply, the idea is to first understand, down to your toes, *all* of the potential hiding in the various aspects of your business, and then, with eyes wide open, choosing to tackle those you see as the most rewarding and realistic. Those are *your best shots!*

If you use the *There's More! Framework* (depicted above) that we provide here, it will boost your results. It could also lead you to *pursue other rewarding businesses,* especially if the business you run now has been shuttered or traumatized by the Covid-19 pandemic, or if you're just starting one.

On a more personal level, working through all that's here will make you better at boosting results, because you'll gain a set of tools for doing so, along with the skills to use them. The wide world needs those who can create prosperity.

You won't find any miracle cures here, just a way to reveal where the untapped potential in your business lies, and to wisely choose what's worth harvesting. It's hard, enjoyable, rewarding work. But it won't magically reopen a shuttered business—more about that below...

If your business is doing OK, but you want it to be better, I invite you to work through the whole book.

If you need to pivot, or rescue your business, or if you're just starting one, please read the Introduction, then work through chapters 8 (Opportunities), 9 (Hungry Markets), 10 (Business Design), possibly 11 (Product and Service Design) and 12 (Innovation), the section of chapter 13 on Making Sage Decisions, and chapters 14 (Insight-Based Management), and 15 (Creating Your Prosperity Design), and use the *Let's See* decision-making tool that comes with the book to decide what to do.

Regardless of your situation, after you've worked with the book, I look forward to welcoming you to the book's Afterword. There you'll learn about the community we're working to create: of executives who use the book's approach, and contribute their advice and improvements, that you can become part of.

Because *There's More!*

—Drew Morris
2022

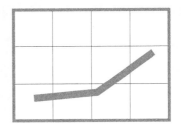

Part 1

The Core Concept, the Mindset, and the Skill That Drives Results

Tapping into the upside of a business is a powerful way to grow profits and revenue. Tapping the upside is also a core skill—that executives can hone, and use again and again, to boost results, and their own careers. That core skill requires a mindset we call *There's More!* It will power your pursuit of better results.

"It is not enough to do your best;
you must know what to do,
and then do your best."
—*W. Edwards Deming*

Introduction

In the best of situations, running a business is a fun, rewarding adventure. In others, it's not, *especially* when results are not where they need to be. That creates anxiety—and frustration.

Lackluster results impact everyone who manages a P&L:

- Business owners and entrepreneurs worry about losing their business (I almost did). In other cases, their business is declining, its markets are shrinking, or lenders are threatening to pull its credit lines. At the beginning, these people just wanted to build their businesses and sell them for a lot. But with down results, they're not worth a lot.

- When results are off, managing a corporate P&L is no picnic either. Many executives suffer from numbers stress, the pressure to make tough results targets that grates on both their health and their close relationships. They worry about getting fired, and they're frustrated, because they sure are trying.

In these situations, it's also likely that the boss, the investors, or owners are not happy. In the case of a large company, an activist could be circling, pressing for board seats or executive changes.

All of these executives or owners have probably tried some ways to boost results, but what they tried didn't live up to what they expected. Many are again trying to figure out what to do to get their business's numbers up and could be short of ideas.

This book is about one that will work—or nothing will—as we'll see.

A New Way for Your Business to Make More Money

Here we'll teach you a powerful *new way* to boost the results of the business you run, or want to run: creating higher profits, growing revenue, and crafting a more valuable business. You'll be able to use the skills you learn here again and again, making you more valuable, too.

How? Tap your business's upside. Every business has one. It's like a cache of buried treasure:

- Areas of your business where there's room for improvement, like more persuasive and sales-inducing advertising, and standout value propositions (so more people buy), customers' more positive attitudes about your business (so they buy again), strong brand promises, innovative pricing approaches, and others.

- Major initiatives such as: pursuing promising opportunities and hungry markets, crafting improved business and product-and-service designs, and creating new solutions to people's problems.

There's a lot you could do, which brings up the question of where to best focus your efforts. We've provided a way to figure that out: to find the handful of improvement efforts that are both achievable and that will give you the *highest* results increase in *your* unique business.

This will be an exciting, fun adventure that your entire team can rally around. But you might wonder, will tapping my upside matter?

The true story of two Fortune 200 CEOs...

Many executives rely on their skills in using tools like cost cutting to boost results. But using just that tool can make everything look like a nail. Which it's not. After repeated rounds of cost cutting, the tool becomes ineffective, because you run out of costs you can cut.

A single-minded focus on the cost-cutting tool also draws attention from other tools that can be used to grow the top line, and, for public companies, what the company is worth: its Enterprise Value (the amount needed to buy all of a company's stock at its current price, and to pay off all of its debt).

We've recently seen an extreme case of cutting costs in the cratering of Kraft-Heinz stock during the time that it was led by CEO Bernardo Hees (Spring 2015 to Spring 2019). Hees used Zero-Based Budgeting, an extreme cost-cutting tool, to the exclusion of other tools, which resulted in: the neglect of customers, sizable layoffs, which drained energy from the staff, and insufficient attention to marketing, hurting top-line growth.[1]

By contrast, during the same period, Best Buy, led by Hubert Joly, substantially lifted the company's value by using a broader set of results tools. They let him harness Best Buy's most appropriate upside elements. Among them:

- Its customer experience and value proposition (the ability for in-store customers to see, touch, and use the products Best Buy sells, to pick up online orders, to get help from a knowledgeable, attentive staff, and to get in-store repairs and technical support).

- Its pricing (a price-matching guarantee).

- Yes, its costs (supply chain, warehousing, real estate).

- Its opportunities (free, in-home tech consultations, tech-support contracts, including one designed for older adults).

- A store-within-store arrangement in which major vendors can showcase their products, drawing customers while lifting Best Buy's sales.[2]

Here's what came of both CEOs' efforts...[3]

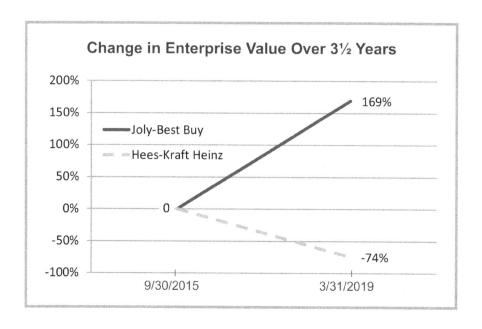

In the Spring of 2019, Mr. Joly transitioned to Best Buy's executive chairman as a hero. Mr. Hees was replaced.

*The Point: Use **all** of your applicable results tools to boost your results.*

This Book Will Help...

- Business owners, who want to prosper.
- Executives with tough profit and sales targets, looking for a way to meet them, and perhaps a way to the top.
- CEOs and their teams, who want satisfied investors and a company that's worth more.
- Entrepreneurs looking to create thriving, significant businesses.
- Anyone who aspires to one of these roles, including students with big plans.

The Upside and Your Business

Tapping your upside involves *closing* gaps like these:

- The gap between how you're often treated as a customer, and the treatment that would make you never want to buy anywhere else.

- The gap between an ad that makes you buy, and an ad that makes you laugh (but you don't buy).

- The gap between what you just bought being drop-dead easy to use, and one that's so confusing that you felt like screaming—with either outcome multiplied by what you tell other people.

- The gap in value between a business that's become a player in a growing, hungry market, and one that ignored that plum opportunity.

These gaps and others are where your prosperity is hiding.

You can take each gap's potential out of hiding by first realizing that it's there, figuring out *all* that its potential can contribute to your results, then making the promise of your most worthwhile and realistically addressable gaps show up in your financials. You'll find that there's a gulf between what most everyone gets from their business and what's *really* possible.

What About Your Business?

A business's performance on the activities that bring better results varies markedly. It's useful to understand how well your business is performing in the selected results-driving activities on the next page. Please take a minute to mark where your business is right now on each of the bars. It will give you a perspective as you work through what's to come.

This chart lists some ways to boost revenue and, with it, profit. To get a sense of how you can increase revenue, rate your business along the solid scales. Mark where you are now. Scores toward the left side of a particular scale indicate an upside inviting you to capture it.

Improve how prospects and customers *feel* about our company, brands and products/services, so they'll choose ours.	← We're widely disliked	They just love us →
Increase *how often* people buy.	← We do nothing about this	New uses, offers, events... →
Get more of them to *tell their friends*.	← We do nothing about this	Referral efforts very rewarding →
Beef up our *value proposition*.	← Unexciting	Gotta have it →
Make our brand promise *more compelling*.	← Lackluster	Ultra resonant →
Make our marketing *more persuasive*.	← Unconvincing	Prospects say, "That's for me!" →
Create a more powerful *business design*.	← Making money is hard	We're in a *great* business →
Find and serve *hungry markets*.	← We're fine as we are	Always on the lookout for these →
Seize our *opportunities*.	← We don't chase rainbows	This is job 1 →

In marking the bars above, you might have noticed some areas in which there's more you could do. Good. Keep in mind that it's also likely only a *part* of the full results potential of your business.

Let's go inside the upside, which can be better seen on what we call *The Upside Map*. We'll use a fictitious company, *Move It!,* a large, established provider of fitness gear and training aids, to illustrate.

In *Move It!'s* Upside Map, the lower portions of the bars (not to scale) represent the financial results of the business as it's now operating. Each bottom bar shows the (same) current financial results, with the potential gain its upside element can provide shown in the bar above it. The gains vary. And they're different for every business, because every business is different.

Clearly, there are a lot of things *Move It!* can do to boost its results, some of which will prove more appropriate than others. It's also possible that only some of an element's potential can be delivered, because some of the necessary actions don't make economic sense, or they require unavailable resources or skills.

Also notice that, for *Move It!*, the potential of squeezing costs out (6th bar from the left) and model management practices (2nd bar from right) have lower

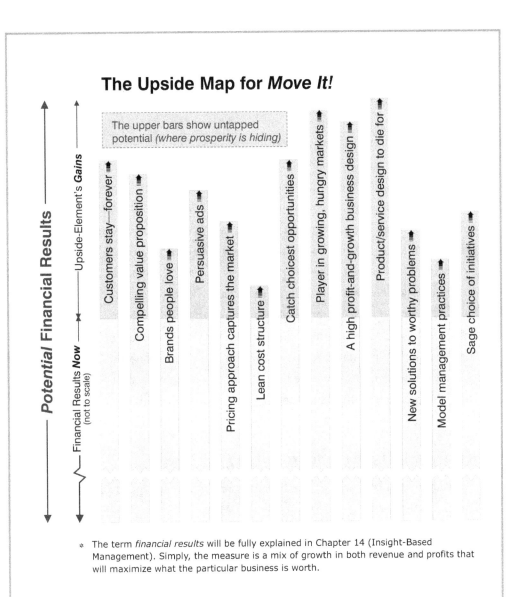

The Upside Map for *Move It!*

Potential Financial Results

Upside-Element's *Gains*

Financial Results *Now*
(not to scale)

The upper bars show untapped potential *(where prosperity is hiding)*

- Customers stay—forever
- Compelling value proposition
- Brands people love
- Persuasive ads
- Pricing approach captures the market
- Lean cost structure
- Catch choicest opportunities
- Player in growing, hungry markets
- A high profit-and-growth business design
- Product/service design to die for
- New solutions to worthy problems
- Model management practices
- Sage choice of initiatives

* The term *financial results* will be fully explained in Chapter 14 (Insight-Based Management). Simply, the measure is a mix of growth in both revenue and profits that will maximize what the particular business is worth.

potential gains than the others. That's because those areas of improvement have been well worked over, as is typical for most companies, so there's not as much potential improvement left.

The larger point is that *Move It!* still has a great deal of unrealized upside potential. And a mere 1% change in revenue or profit margin can move a public-company's stock.

The Upside Map is a way to see both the range of the upside, and the potential each element holds to possibly increase results. Most of them *have far more potential* than most everyone recognizes—people are either too busy or too distracted. We'll examine each element's potential in depth in the coming chapters, because you really need to understand how much of a boost each upside element can provide. To help you do that, we'll summarize the best thinking of a number of experts.

Finally, you can't and shouldn't pursue every upside element. You and your business simply don't have the bandwidth. You'll need to understand *which* of your upside's elements are best pursued, so you can make them happen and have their results show up in your financials. We'll call those your *best shots* (they're the X's on the map on the book's cover). We'll work through how to find them after we've assessed the individual upside-element's potentials.

The upside-element approach we've taken here, which we'll call the *There's More! Framework,* is a comprehensive process designed to maximize the value of a *single* business—one that sells a related group of products or services to a single market: people or businesses with a similar set of needs. To pick the business to work on (if you have several), first focus on one of the biggest, and one for which improving its fortunes will have a major impact on overall value.

Using This Approach Is a Skill

Outstanding athletes and accomplished people in all fields spend years honing the skills they need.

Yet for those who now run a business, or want to, there's a critical skill that's not even taught, much less honed, in business schools and executive-development programs (and I've been looking, since 1995).

That skill is boosting results—not just keeping the business going as is. Increasing results is *why* you're in your role. Boosting results is indeed a learnable skill, one that you can keep getting better and better at, like golf. Using this book's material will take your skill in boosting results from good toward great. Here's the core skill:

> *Surfacing all of the untapped potential of your upside elements, and then choosing which ones to pursue.*

Assuming that you get really good at it, what could that skill bring you in terms of career success, earning potential, and interesting opportunities?

Developing the skill of boosting results is about mastery—getting closer and closer to being truly outstanding. The thing that makes mastery so alluring is that you never get all the way there, but you can get pretty darn close, closer than almost everyone today. As in developing any skill—tennis, cooking, and any of the fine, martial, or performing arts—you'll have challenges and rough times, but when things go right, few pursuits are as satisfying.

Experts' Ideas—in a System

This book is a synthesis of original work and that of many others—*thank you!* We've provided summaries of their work, and recommended their original contributions, in our references. This is particularly true in the individual upside-element chapters. Extracting *all* of the potential value from each element draws on the work of Ken Blanchard (customers); the late Clayton Christensen (value propositions, business design, and innovation); Chip and Dan Heath (marketing messages, making sage decisions); Robert Kaplan and Robin Cooper (modern cost management); W. Chan Kim and Renée Mauborgne (market positioning); Rafi Mohammed (pricing); Michael Porter (business design); Adrian Slywotzky (creating demand), and others.

This book weaves their best ideas for improving the results from various upside elements into an integrated, actionable, overall *system* for boosting results: the *There's More! Framework*.

Why Should You Read This Book
(and do all the work it suggests)

In other words, what can come of your efforts?

- Your business will become more valuable. All who have an interest in its financial success will be happy. And you will get better at boosting results: worth more as an executive, with a stronger reputation. All because you have the necessary tools and you're getting good at using them.

- Your business and your company will obviously benefit from the improved results. Prosperity leads to a stable work environment, creating a platform for doing even better.

- You'll find out how good you can get.

- Your newfound skills could bring you a bigger future. You'll be seen as someone who has developed the insights and perspectives, and who's mastered the tools needed to handle tough results challenges. "Who they gonna call" when the next one rears its head?

- Best, you'll feel more "juice" flowing into your organization, and into yourself!

- And if you're not sure it's worth the trouble, consider whether your competitors are now reading this book—and acting on it…

Why I Wrote This

After a lot of searching through the business literature, I found myself frustrated that this obvious way to improve results was not widely recognized, codified, or practiced.

I also wanted to provide an honest, teachable way to increase results and create prosperous businesses. That also involved assembling, in one place, as much of the available wisdom about boosting results as I could.

How the Book Is Organized

We'll begin with the core concept—tapping your upside can boost your results. There's also a needed mindset—that there are better results to be had, but you have to look for how to get them. That's a skill that we'll help you hone in chapters 2–13. We'll explore what could be quick wins, then big initiatives—things that take more doing but that can bring breakthrough results. Finally, we'll guide you in figuring out your best moves to boost results, using insight-based management and its tools (chapter 14), and how to assemble those moves into *your* prosperity design (chapter 15).

Part 1—The Core Concept, the Mindset, and the Skill That Drives Results

We'll begin by showing how tapping into the upside of a business is a powerful way to grow profits and revenue. Tapping the upside is also a *core skill*—that executives can hone, and use again and again, to boost results, and their own career potentials. That core skill requires a mindset: *There's More!* It will power your pursuit of better results.

Part 2—The (Relatively) Quick and Easy Stuff

Here we'll pursue the upside elements within easy reach: creating zealous customers, powerful value propositions and brands, effective advertising, astute pricing, and that perennial favorite, cost management. Most of these are relatively quick wins.

Part 3—The Initiatives That Take More Doing

This part covers the big upside elements: capturing opportunities, finding hungry markets, market strategy and business design, product-and-service design, innovation, and management practices. Each can have a dramatic positive impact on your results, but they're major initiatives—consuming management time, considerable money, thought, etc.

Each of the chapters in Parts 2 and 3 include a Tapping Your Upside *exercise. These are sets of questions designed to help you think deeply about the chapter's topic, fully understand how your business can benefit from pursuing it, and figure out how you might go about doing so.*

Part 4—Your Best Results Moves: Insight-Based Management

There are so many powerful ways to boost results that you won't be able to tackle them all, nor should you. Depending on the business you're in, some won't amount to much of anything, while others will make it rock. In a different business, an entirely different set of upside elements would make it rock.

So we've provided a set of tools for wisely choosing the realistic upside elements that together will produce the best possible results for *your* particular business. It's a framework for doing so that we call *Insight-Based Management*. The idea is to first understand the type of performance (increased profit margins or revenue growth) that your investors, senior management, or a prospective buyer of your business, will value most. Then you'll be able to use the chapter's decision-making framework, the *Let's See* spreadsheet tool that comes with the book, to pick the realistic set of upside elements that will bring you the best possible results, and make your business the most valuable it can be.

Part 5—Your Prosperity Design

At this point in the book, you will have given your upside a thorough going over, and have a clear idea of the initiatives you want to tackle. In Part 5, you'll work through pulling those initiatives into a *prosperity design* for your business—a plan laying out which elements of your upside you're going to work on when, and how those initiatives will be integrated into your existing business and plans. The design will, by its nature, be a living, breathing creation, but capturing the starting version will serve as a springboard. The *There's More! Framework* will light a path for creating your design.

Using This Book

Getting the biggest results increase possible from working through the book will take a commitment of time on your part, or better, an unflagging, well-orchestrated group effort. Boosting results is the core of your role as an executive—very little is ultimately more important.

To have the best chance of delivering maximum results, give each of the upside-element chapters (2–13) a thorough going over, but, if possible, hold off on picking your best shots until you have a complete picture, so you don't slide right past your most promising upside element. Chapter 14, *Insight-Based Management,* will help you decide which elements are, in fact, those best shots, using the *Let's See* decision tool. By moving through all of the elements over a few weeks, or a month, perhaps two, you'll not unduly delay the benefits, nor will you miss the big one.

However, you might already be well aware of a quick win or two that you'd like to pursue, or are pursuing. In that case, you can work through the chapters about those quick wins, *then* tackle the others, but please read the rest of this chapter.

About the *Tapping Your Upside* exercises… They're opportunities to figure out what you're going to *do* as a result of what we've just covered. The intent is to get you to internalize the chapters' lessons, take a good hard look at how you and your business now operate, and *figure out how you're going to make things better*. These exercises will help to make your career. Do them.

What You'll Need (Later)

The book will walk you through the entire process of tapping your upside to boost results. To do so, you'll need to bring a few numbers-based insights to bear. This is done with the chapters' *Tapping Your Upside* exercises, and *Let's See*. Given good input, it will *reveal* your best shots.

You can download *Let's See*, and the book's tools and extras, by visiting: www.theupsidewithinreach.com.

You will also need:

- To pick a business to work on. If you have several, focus on one of the biggest, and one for which improving its fortunes will have a major impact on the company's overall value.

- A recent full-year P&L for that business, showing *operating results* (or projections, if you're just starting).

- Its full-year *unit* sales.

- A solid sense of how unit sales rise and fall when prices change in that business—fancy name: price elasticity. It's the percentage change in unit sales divided by the percentage change in price, and it's almost always a negative number (unit sales drop when prices rise).

- An estimate of the inflation rate.

We'll use the above in *Let's See* to calculate the profit and revenue gains that the various upside elements can bring. Chapter 14 is basically a guide to using that tool. Its *Tapping Your Upside* exercise is to use *Let's See* on the business you chose, above.

As you work through each of the upside-element chapters, do its *Tapping Your Upside* exercises and record your improvement estimates on the Upside

Element Assessment worksheet following the book's index. Now or later, you should also fill in your estimates of how risky and how doable pursuing that upside element is, what it will cost in terms of your capital and expense budgets, and what resources you'll need to pull it off.

Once you get to Chapter 14, *Let's See*'s THE CHOOSER worksheet will use all of that information to help you decide which upside elements are your best shots, so you can get on with planning how you'll pursue them and the results increases they'll bring.

Clearly, this takes work. It's also *why* you have your job: to create a prosperous business. It's the most important job in your business, and no one else has the wide perspective needed to tackle it. You can lighten the load by getting all the help you can from your team. Rowing together is great fun!

Now, on *to the beginning!*

"You don't have to look far to
see that things could be a lot
better, and the reason they
aren't is because no one has
thought about them enough."
—*James de Vries interview with
designer Marc Newson of Apple,*
Harvard Business Review [4]

Chapter 1

Leading Your Business to Better Results

Leading your business to better results requires a few steps:

- Being clear on what you want as the long-term outcome.
- Choosing the right results goal.
- Adopting the needed mindset.
- Doing the up-front work needed.
- Executing.

What Do You Want?

To get the most out of the efforts of everyone on your team, you should be crystal clear on the ultimate outcome you want, because it will influence the choices you make as you work through this book. Below are some possible outcomes. Choose the one that best applies, or create your own.

- You want to build a major business.

- You want to become one of the best results creators there is.

- You want to move up in your company.

- You want to pass on your business to the next person to run it, leaving it prospering at the transition. (Your successor might be another executive or a family member, if your business is privately held.)

- You want to sell your business for the most money possible.

- You want to build a great reputation, so that a bigger, more interesting future will *find you.*

Which of these did you choose? That decision will anchor everything you do.

What's the Right Results Goal?

With your outcome decided, your next choice is which performance goal will make your business the most valuable in the eyes of senior management, the board, the investors, prospective buyers, or you and your partners.

Should your goals emphasize revenue growth or higher profit margins? Startups often, correctly, focus on revenue growth, while mature businesses try to raise profit margins.

With that resolved, this book will show you:

- How to extract *all* of the results potential from each upside element.

- How to choose *which* elements of your upside to pursue, so your time is spent on maximizing the business's value, instead of on things that won't amount to much.

It all starts with a mindset.[5]

The Mindset You'll Need...

There are two crucial perspectives that will make your efforts successful. Neither is difficult to adopt; both, however, are necessary.

1. The Prosperity Perspective: *There's More!*

The *There's More!* perspective simply recognizes that there is indeed an upside in almost every business, and in every management team. There's always something better to tackle if what you're doing now isn't working out due to tanking demand, obsolescence, brutal competition, and so on.

The *There's More!* perspective will, over the long term, determine the level of prosperity your business achieves. If you're always looking for opportunities to boost results, you'll find them, as did Jeff Bezos at Amazon, among others. Some of these initiatives will have a modest impact, a few won't work, and some will be home runs.

But ya gotta look!

Looking means paying attention to what's happening in your industry and in the world; to trends; to shifts in technology, demographics, and culture; and to what you'll realize are enabling breakthroughs. So read, widely, and observe, closely, to uncover opportunities still not apparent to others.

2. The *There's More!* Cycle...

Let's say that this book helps you find a handful of initiatives (your best shots). You chose to improve your value proposition for customers, to give them a lower-friction customer experience, and to create a good-better-best-offering pricing approach. And you successfully pull off two of those three.

Do you stop there? Of course not. There's always, well, *more!*

Make another pass through your prospective upside elements. Now you know how. You've grown your skill at doing so. Identify new opportunities for improvement. Maybe it's time to look into new geographies, expand your product line or services, or apply that good-better-best approach to other offerings.

The point is that tapping your upside is not a one-and-done activity. It's *a process* you can and should use again and again as you lead your business to create ever better results.

Executing

From here on, your imperative should be to lead the discovery of the upside elements with the most power to drive your results, and to deliver on those you can.

As mentioned earlier, increasing results is *why* you're in your role. If you don't do that, who will? Your head financial person might not have the marketing background. Your head of marketing might come up short in financial analysis, and your head of product or service development might only want to get something cool out there. Someone needs to integrate and orchestrate your team's capabilities. Who'll do that?

Without you vigorously leading, this book is just, well, a book. It will just lie there quietly, resting—but the better results you want won't happen.

So, *will you?*

There are four things that only you, as the leader, can provide: intent, attention, constancy, and orchestration.

Intent

Intent is what drives an executive's vision of what his or her business needs to become. Earlier, I asked you to decide what you want. And critically, *why* do you want it? *What* are you trying to do?

How big is your dream? And are you wanting enough?

There's an order to these questions: the first is *why,* as Simon Sinek so well explains in *Start With Why.*[6] Being clear on *why* your business exists, its higher purpose, will propel it in the most energized and aligned way possible. And finding your *why* is possible for any business. Often, it's about serving, enabling, or presenting a line of offerings that enhances lives. There's also a recent *Harvard Business Review* article that provides examples of how purpose can also powerfully enhance a business's set of addressable opportunities and broaden its business design.[7]

Next comes the size of your dream. Is it, along with your *why,* big enough to inspire?

I completely agree that what you want should be an inspiring set of words, not a set of numbers. But if you have investors or lenders, or plan on selling your business sometime, tied to that set of words should be what you expect to come of those words in terms of profit and revenue numbers.

This book will provide two ways to help you decide whether revenue growth or higher profit margins will create more value, but it also depends, in a major way, on your reality: resources, offerings, markets, and competitors.

For now, the best intent you can have is to really *understand* the essence of your business, its customers, its markets, and *its upside*. That clarity will come as you work through these chapters.

Attention, Effort, and Organizational Energy (Juice)

Your efforts to tap the business's upside have to be viewed as an imperative throughout your organization. As the leader, you'll need to *keep your attention on it*. As wins emerge, enthusiasm will build, energizing your people. But you need to make tapping your upside crucial, at the outset and *from then on.*

Essential here is focus. One of the fundamentals of organization design is that what is operationally necessary always diverts attention from innovation and improvement initiatives, *unless* those initiatives are the sole responsibility of a dedicated team. It's not always practical to bring that about, but the leader's persistent, encouraging words and actions can prove vital.

Constancy

Constancy is important enough to merit its own section here. What would happen to your business's results if tapping its upside faded in importance, or was overcome by day-to-day demands? Sustaining initiatives can be hard. But the consequences of failing to do so are worse—the business can become unsustainable, creating personal financial risk; the activists can decide to come knocking; or management, or the board, can start looking for your replacement.

At some point, what you believed to be the best things you could do to improve results might not turn out to be possible or realistic, or to pan out. Your constancy in pursuing the best ways to boost results is essential. The specifics of how you get there need to be continuously observed and assessed, with your eyes and mind wide open, and the initiatives adjusted as necessary. An initiative-tracking system will be needed, and you likely already have one.

Orchestration

This is about who needs to do what. It's critical—you likely don't have time to do all that's involved in boosting results by yourself. More on this in Chapter 15, Creating Your Prosperity Design.

Your Role, and What Can Come of It

This book can't make you want what you really don't want. But once you see *how* you can boost results, you'll be more inclined to avidly pursue doing so—with a fresh dose of passion. Learning how to boost results requires:

- Adopting a perspective that lets you see, and appreciate, the full extent of the more obvious upsides, using the mindset: *There's More!*
- Committing to *hunt* for the harder-to-see upsides.
- Understanding what *the most promising elements* of your upside are— the biggest addressable gaps.
- Deciding *what to do* to deliver what's hiding in those gaps.
- Pulling off what's decided, *leading everyone* to do their parts.

In the process of finding and choosing among the elements of your upside, you'll gain the insights and perspectives and begin to get good at using the tools you can use to deliver on your upsides again and again, in future situations—a core skill for an executive with P&L responsibility, if ever there was one.

Springing Out of the Blocks...

Here's a true story about a freshman orientation speech in which the head of the student government upstaged a leading college's president. An incoming senior, she told of her experience the past summer traveling by bus, on a dirt road, through a tropical jungle, late at night, in a torrential rainstorm. She was the only white woman on the bus—and a little nervous. As luck would have it, the bus got stuck in the mud. In time, a group of men bearing rifles and bandoliers appeared. They boarded the bus and ordered all the men off the bus, and turning to the young woman said, "and you!"

The men herded the passengers behind the bus, and told them to put their hands on the bus.

After a pause that seemed like they were being given time to "say their prayers," out of the night, the men's leader boomed, "PUSH!"

And that was the young woman's message to the incoming class. *Push!*[8]

The assembly went crazy. Push is what had gotten the freshmen into this top-tier college in the first place. And they all had the sense that they were at the start of a dashing and bold adventure.

And so it is with you.

Push!

This book will help you and your team figure out ***where*** to push.

As described in the Introduction, we'll first go after quick wins: creating zealous customers, powerful value propositions and brands, effective advertising, astute pricing, and deft cost management.

Then we'll explore things that take more doing, but that can bring breakthrough results: capturing opportunities, finding hungry markets, business design, product-and-service design, innovation, and management practices.

Finally, we'll guide you in choosing the best things you can do to boost results, using the concept of insight-based management and its tools, and how to assemble those moves into *your* prosperity design (how you'll do them).

So those are "the places we'll go." Now you and your team can get behind your bus, and *push*—to best effect!

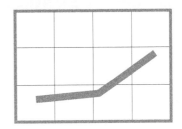

Part 2

The (Relatively) Quick and Easy Stuff

Here we'll pursue the upside elements within easy reach: creating zealous customers, powerful value propositions and brands, effective advertising, pricing, and that perennial favorite, cost management. Most of these are relatively quick wins.

Chapter 2

*Creating Zealous Customers**

Revenue. Without it, you don't have a business. Revenue comes from customers—who either buy what you offer, or buy from your competitors, giving them the revenue and clobbering your profits.

The cost of losing customers is made clear in the work of Frederich Reichheld, who wrote, in 1996, that the cost of disloyalty stunted corporate performance by 25 to 50 percent, and sometimes more.[9] He and his Bain & Co. colleagues also showed that a 5 percent increase in customer retention resulted in a 25 to 100 percent increase in the value of the average customer.[10]

This realization begat rewards programs, which do work but are essentially bribes. If companies stop funding the bribes, customers are left without a major reason to continue buying.

The approach we'll take here is different: create emotion-based loyalty, which can also be much less expensive and much more powerful. We see this in the behavior of consumers who flock to U.S. supermarkets like Trader Joe's. In the words of Mitch Goozé, president and founder of the Customer Manufacturing Group, "They don't have a 'loyalty program.' They have the Trader Joe's experience."[11]

---

* *Portions of this chapter are excerpted from the author's July/August 2009* Chief Executive *article. Used by permission*

Another zealous-customer creator is the legendary Wegmans.[12] Their company's driving force: "Every Day You Get Our Best." Whose job was it to create that driving force, and to make it the foundation of their culture?

So your job as an executive has a missionary aspect: turn your current customers into zealots—people who love your business. Do the same with your prospects—your competitors' customers. Because the strongest revenue per customer comes from the zealous: enthusiastic believers in your business and in what it offers. That's because zealous customers will be delighted to buy again, often without even considering the competition. They'll also tell others why they bought from you and suggest they do likewise.

Getting people to love your business is very different from rewards incentives. Creating the love, emotion-based loyalty, is achievable, but it does require leadership—particularly, the ability to inspire—see Wegmans, above.

Those few businesses that I recommend to others tend to be based on product designs that show a genuine care for the customer: Subaru (you know you'll get where you need to go, in any weather); ThinkPad laptops (design, quality, reliability), and the Japanese retailer Uniqlo's clothing (their clothes keep you warm, without reminding you that you're wearing them), and they provide a wonderful in-store experience (ready help from floor salespeople, and a moving-right-along checkout process, even on Black Friday).

There are also a handful of others, service businesses that I interact with personally, and feel zealous about.

One is R.W. Auto Repair, in Little Silver, NJ, started in 1978 by its owner, Bob Wichmann. He was recommended to me by my lead salesperson in 1984. Besides being knowledgeable, capable, honest, transparent, and wise, Bob really cares about his customers. I've found that his advice is always in our best interest.

In 2019, I was chatting with a local pharmacist and Bob's name came up. It seems that the gearshift on the pharmacy's delivery van had come off in the driver's hand. They towed it to the dealer, who estimated that the repair would cost $2,000. (The van wasn't worth that.) So they towed it to R.W., where Bob looked at it, inserted a screw to hold the gearshift, and sent the van off, no charge.

My now-retired lead salesperson also remains a customer. Thirty-five years of a healthy business in a community: a quiet, yet very loud, lesson...

If you're lucky, you might have a few of these businesses in your life. *Why* do you feel zealous about them? Can you use the same reason to create zealous customers for your business?

The upside element in this chapter is the difference between the revenue created by one-time, satisfied customers, and zealous customers. Its potential is substantial, or better. Consider:

- Are prospects more likely to buy from a firm they get enthused about?

- What's the additional revenue potential from the long string of repeat purchases that zealous customers make?

- How many new customers will you get as a result of your zealous customers' recommendations and general word of mouth?

Creating zealous customers is about first winning hearts, then minds. It's rooted in the customer's or prospect's *emotions*.[13] It's not at all about rewards programs. Nor is it even mainly about metrics like Net Promoter Score (what percentage of customers would recommend the business to their friends), which companies use to try to get their people to deliver solid service.[14]

It's more about creating a powerful emotional bond with customers—to have them feel that your business really cares about them, is trying to make things better for them, and is trying to do so consistently. The best examples I know of are the inspiring stories in Ken Blanchard's book *Raving Fans: A Revolutionary Approach to Customer Service*—too long to treat here, and better told in original form.[15]

Executives need to take the lead in creating those positive emotions—because every part of the company will have a role to play in bringing them about, and everyone will need to be clear on what they need to do. As we'll see, it's not a problem that can be laid in the laps of brand managers, the marketing department, or those responsible for customer service. It's a culture shift, if you're not yet there.

There are three prerequisites—necessary conditions—that have to happen in your business in order to evoke the emotions felt by zealous customers, and the revenue upside that will come from it. A business has to bring about *all three* of these necessary conditions, or the effort won't succeed to anywhere near the degree it can.

Necessary Condition 1: Simple Respect

The first thing that you need to do as an executive is to get your customers and prospects to believe that your business really cares about, and respects, them as people. Not wallets. For many businesses, this is a huge shift in the way they think and act.

All humans, when we encounter someone for the first time, make a near instant assessment of them, subconsciously. We want to know, to put it in the language of the sixties, where they're coming from. What are their intentions?

You can try this simple experiment with the next few people you meet for the first time and observe their reactions.

1. For some, show up wanting something from them. It could be a getting them to buy something, take a survey, go on a date, etc.

2. For others, show up expecting them to treat you like you're better than they are.

3. Finally, show up with the simple intention to be their friend. No agenda (other than to be helpful if you can), no airs, no judging.

What did you notice? Let's go through them:

1. We humans can "smell" someone who wants something a mile away. The problem is that because prospects perceive that you're up to something, they won't trust you, and rightly so. The relationship you want won't begin to form because of that lack of trust. Yet how often do businesses start a conversation with some form of, "Wanna buy this?" or a premature attempt to qualify the person as a legitimate prospect.

2. If you try to position yourself as better than they are, not only will the relationship fail to form, but they'll likely as not write you off as a jerk (more colorful words, and hand gestures, can also be used to describe this reaction). Yet how often does a business begin a conversation with some form of, "We are great, [big, famous, etc.] buy our stuff!"

3. When you show up without an agenda, or just wanting to help, the other person feels respected and at ease. They are *open* to a relationship.

One way to put a new relationship on this footing is to begin by alluding to a problem the other person might be facing.

Before anything else, we want to know whether the other party (1) believes that we're important, and (2) will treat us as such. Only if their intent is positive and the respect for us is there will we be open to the possibility of a relationship. Showing people that you think they're important and appreciated is powerful. *Examples:*

- If you've ever left a holiday tip (or a 6-pack) out for the trash collectors, you've no doubt noticed how everything you later need to dispose of, even if it's excessive, is taken away.
- A man was having a house built. Every few days, he would go see how it was going and bring coffee and donuts for the workers. Upon completion of the house, he remarked to a friend how many nice touches were in the house that he never expected, or paid for.
- A well-regarded, privately held firm that manages retirement accounts, untarred by financial-crisis debacles, noticed that in the first month of 2008's Great Recession, its call-center volume had spiked, because people were nervous. Some calls were dropped because of longer-than-normal wait times for a representative. But the firm had the account and phone numbers of those who had decided not to wait. They brought in their call-center staff on the weekend and *called all of those account-holders back.*

Most people who hear that story think it's wonderful. The sad truth is *that response should be normal.* Now what about the opposite of respect? We'll call it by its street name, "dissing."

This really happened to me. I stopped in to a Verizon Wireless store one day to try out some of their phones and to get my questions answered. There were three sales reps on the floor, all serving other customers. By interacting with one of their "floorwalkers," I put my name in their "waiting for a rep" queue, and my number in line showed up on a display board. I was 2nd in line. A few minutes later, I was 4th. When I asked the floorwalker what happened, he explained that "VIPs" (whoever they are) can jump the queue to get service. I had Verizon accounts for both residential and business service, and for wireless. What am I, chopped liver?

It would be hard to overstate the level of "grrr..." this induced. And it was *designed* to function this way! GRRRR!

Customer defections are a major, avoidable revenue leak.

Necessary Condition 2: Be "For Them"

Customers' feelings about the companies they do or don't buy from fall on what we'll call the *Passion-in-Customers Spectrum.*

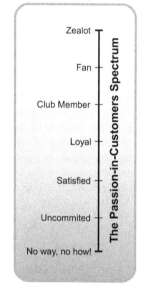

At the problematic bottom of the spectrum is a passion we've seen many companies evoke in customers: "No way, no how, will I ever buy anything from you again!" These are people who have been "dissed." Poster child: Dell's offshoring their tech support some years back.

Dell's senior management made what looked like a necessary decision from a cost perspective (cheaper PCs no longer permitted high-cost support).

What they didn't fully appreciate was that their customers thought they had *a relationship* with Dell. They liked the company and bought their products. And you'd get a lot for what you paid, even if there were some soon-to-arrive issues like key tops falling off.

Then Dell, by offshoring its support, badly, conveyed to its customers that they, and their technical issues, were not important. This included a support process, which someone actually designed, that drove Dell's technically troubled customers straight up a wall. Dell suffered "The Revenge of the Dissed," and its CEO at the time is now "former."

Worse, in May 2007, the then New York State Attorney General, Andrew Cuomo, sued Dell, claiming that, "At Dell, customer service means no service at all." According to *The New York Times*, Mr. Cuomo said that the suit was filed after talks with Dell executives *failed to resolve the issue* (a new high in lows in the annals of brand management).[16]

Once a customer perceives that they've been disregarded by a company, is it even possible to get them back? I haven't been.

At the next step on the Passion-in-Customers Spectrum are the uncommitted. These people have no strong opinions about your products, services, brands, or business one way or the other.

Further up the scale are satisfied customers. They have no unresolved issues and would buy from your business again. They've received good customer care, been treated fairly, and regard your offerings as a good value. But these customers might just "look at another provider" the next time they buy.

Moving customers to the next rung of the spectrum, loyal, requires that you create real loyalty. That springs from them liking and trusting your business.

Still further up the spectrum, we find the club members, the customers who take part in a like-minded *community* related to your business. An off-line example is the Harley-Davidson (motorcycles) Owners' Group (HOG). On-line examples include literary, product, and fan forums of all stripes, such as mugglenet.com for Harry Potter fans, which garnered 208,000 distinct visitors in November 2018.[17]

Communities work because people have an innate need to belong and contribute to groups they're passionate about. They'll join, and as long as their psyches stay entwined with the community, and your business doesn't do anything ultra-boneheaded, "they ain't goin' nowhere."

Higher still, we find fans—customers who will enthusiastically tell others about your business or what you offer.

Atop the spectrum are zealots—the highest level of customer passion. Zealots will enthusiastically recommend your offerings to any and all, and not even consider using a competing provider.

Beyond respect, what's the next thing you need to do to create those zealous customers?

For me, the key came while watching the film *The Mask of Zorro*. In the story, Zorro (a nobleman in disguise) foils the arrogant colonial governor's repeated attempts to kill, enslave, and abuse the peasants. They in turn were zealous (and then some) in their passion and regard for Zorro. The learning lies in *why*.

Zorro was **for them**. If you're poor, uneducated, oppressed, etc., it's easy to feel that nobody's *for you*. Zorro showed them through his actions that *they were important* to him, as was *making their lives better*. He cared deeply about them and their plight, and he put himself on the line.

The film makes vivid the enthusiasm that came back. It came back because it's so rare that anyone really gives a damn.

Lest you think that being *for them* only happens in movies, consider the recent case of the captain of the U.S. Navy's aircraft carrier, *Theodore Roosevelt*, Brett Crozier, who was fired for trying to protect his sailors.[18] And, if someone had to take the blame for writing the plea for help that leaked to the newspapers and got him in trouble, it would be only him: he wouldn't let his willing junior officers sign it as well, fearing for their careers.[19]

Creating the "For Them" Mindset: Some Dimensions of Enriching the Customer

The basic idea is well captured in the old saying, "I love you not only for what you have made of yourself, but for what you are making of me." What can your business do for your customers that they'll deeply appreciate and for which they'll want to freely reciprocate? Here are a few powerful ways to accomplish that. Visits to the websites of the companies we cite could be instructive.

Teaching

The American Girl historical character dolls (americangirl.com/discover/historical-characters) provide a deep emotional connection to the situations, challenges, and stories of young girls from various backgrounds living in (or coming to) America. The company has created a powerful social and learning community for these young people, and a deep, ongoing revenue stream.

Teaching and Protecting

You don't hear much good said about financial-services firms these days. One exception is T. Rowe Price (troweprice.com)—for two reasons: their efforts to educate prospective investors (kids included) and, based on many years of direct experience, I *know* they have my back. It has long operated with a squeaky-clean nose. When something (like a fund redemption) does go awry, one of their associates will grab onto the problem and ride it until it's resolved.

Tellingly, a few years back, T. Rowe Price's fund managers were working to ensure that private-equity firms didn't team up with a company's management to take it private for less than it was worth, leaving public shareholders (such as TRP's investors) the poorer.

Enabling

An oft-cited example of working to improve customers' lives is A.G. Lafley's legacy at Procter & Gamble (pg.com), in which P&G's people actually live with consumers so they can observe their problems and challenges in P&G's product areas and help to craft solutions. P&G's Children's Safe Drinking Water, and Live, Learn and Thrive programs are exemplary.

The outdoor equipment retailer REI (rei.com) is another classic practitioner of enabling the customer. On its website you'll find all sorts of outdoor gear, the sales pages for which are infused with quality advice for things like not breaking your neck, or getting buried in an avalanche. You'll also find a set of communities by activity.

Some enablers help customers show the world *who they are*. Target's (target.com), chic for less, is a good example of this approach.

Other enabler examples: Amazon (amazon.com)—easily finding what you want to buy, Google (google.com)—easily finding information, and the Firefox web browser (mozilla.org), which has gone all out to protect your privacy.

There's one other aspect of conveying to customers that you're really for them, best conveyed by this experience. We all have favorite foods. Many have brand names. These days the brand names compete with supermarket chains' store brands. Sometimes, in order to pump up their own brands' sales, the supermarket might stop carrying competing brands.

But customers might well wonder, "Whose need is being served here? The price might be lower, but I liked that non-store brand—*better!* Grrr!"

To clearly understand where a business is coming from, customers shouldn't pay any attention to its marketing messages. They can simply watch what it *does*. In the supermarket's case, what it did made clear whose side they were really on.

Necessary Condition 3:
Singing to Customers in Harmony

For the two previous efforts to be effective, it's necessary that a business, regardless of its size, give customers and prospects a *consistent* and positive experience.

The challenge is well illustrated by my experience as a Hewlett-Packard (HP) customer. Upon buying an HP All-in-One (a combination printer, copier, scanner, and fax machine) in early 2006, I was invited to enroll in HP's free online courses on both technical and general topics. I did, found them to be excellent, and took several.

So I loved HP. Until in early 2009, a flimsy plastic piece of the All-in-One's printing mechanism broke. Not only was the part impossible to replace—there weren't any, anywhere. After all, "The printer was more than 3 years old," I was told by HP support. Worse, the scanner and fax would no longer function if the machine was unable to print. Don't ask me why; I'm the now disillusioned customer.

The problem here was dissonance; various parts of HP were working at cross-purposes. The marketers and the training department wanted me to love HP. But the product was not designed to be repaired, nor was there an adequate supply of spare parts. It was also about as far from being sustainably "green" as it could be. There were other HP All-in-Ones in the electronics bin at the town recycling center, which is emptied weekly, so I guess I wasn't the only one.

The point is that unless the executive with "all the buttons" makes it crystal clear to everyone that product-design gaffes and other dissonance, e.g. lack of parts, are unacceptable, because they enrage customers, we'll continue to see customers like me moving from "zealot" straight down to "no way, no how" on the spectrum shown earlier.

HP needed to decide that it would serenade customers in harmony. Those voices could say, "We'll provide you with a quality product that will last and can be repaired; we'll provide training, and support along with it, and throw in some relevant education to boot." That message is internally consistent.

While every company needs to do this; few do.[20] There's that overlooked upside thing again…

In a large corporation, where the general managers, the executives who run the company's individual businesses, don't have "all the buttons," they and their division heads will have to enroll the CEO and their peers in getting everyone to "sing in harmony" to customers.

It won't be easy; just remunerative.

Pitching Versus Enriching— The Revenue Impact of How Your Business Thinks About Its Customers

The diagram below shows the typical way that a business goes about selling to prospects and customers. The prospect is treated as an *object who might buy*, rather than as a person. The business makes offers, often based on price, to someone who's emotionally unengaged. Note the thin lines leading to the revenue pot. We call this *pitching*.

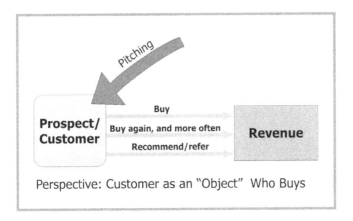

In the next diagram, below, we see an engaged, enthusiastic customer. She feels respected, and has gotten value from her purchases and experiences as a customer. She looks like a promoter of the company. Her feelings and their intensity are reflected by the wider arrows leading to the larger pot of revenue. This is the direct result of *enriching*.

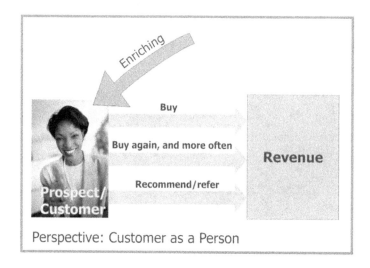

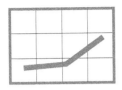

TAPPING YOUR UPSIDE:
Customers and Prospects

In this chapter, we've come to understand that creating zealous customers, and inducing prospects to join their ranks, requires that three things happen: respect, being *for them,* and singing in harmony. Take some quiet time to work carefully through how you'll accomplish them in your business:

1. **What would be the percentage increase in your revenue if every one of your customers never bought what you provide from another company?**

   _____

2. **What percentage of your current customers behave like that now?**

   _____

3. **What could you realistically increase that percentage to?**

   _____

4. **What would that realistic percentage mean in terms of:**

   Additional revenue? $ _____

   Increase in profit? $ _____

   Profit-*margin* improvement (profit/sales): Now? _____%

   If that realistic percentage increase happens? _____%

5. **If it seems worthwhile to work on this upside element, what specific things will you do to get your customers and prospects to**

believe that your business really cares about, and respects, them as people?

_____

_____

_____

6. **What will be your business's customer mindset:**

Its way of thinking about the customer that everyone in your business will need to embrace? To be ultra-clear, this is about what customers and prospects will come to believe about your business, based on their direct experience with it. It's not at all about what your business thinks they believe.

_____

_____

_____

_____

7. **Put yourself in your customer's or prospect's position and take careful notice of "where your business is coming from"—its attitude. What, if anything, needs to change?**

_____

_____

_____

_____

8. What, specifically, will you do for customers that clearly enriches their lives? See the examples of being "for them" earlier in this chapter.

_____

_____

_____

_____

9. How will your business make being "for them" happen? Who will do what?

_____

_____

_____

_____

10. What will you do to make sure that the message(s) you committed to sending to prospects and customers in the answers to questions 8 and 9 get delivered at *every* touch point? In other words, how will you make sure that your business "sings in harmony" to them?

_____

_____

_____

_____

11. What will you do to *continue to* enrich your customers, far into the future?

_____

_____

_____

_____

12. What is your hiring model for customer-facing people and their managers? What skills and personality characteristics do they need to have? How will you try to ensure this?

_____

_____

_____

_____

13. Same question as #12, for the company's customer-facing and marketing *leaders,* those who set the organization's "tone" with respect to customers?

_____

_____

_____

_____

UPSIDE ASSESSMENT: CREATING ZEALOUS CUSTOMERS

Roughly estimate what putting more effort into developing zealous customers will bring, and take…

Increase in:

Revenue _____ %   Profit _____ %

Profit-margin _____ %

Cost (expense-budget) impact _____ ($ or %)

Capital-budget impact _____ ($ or %)

Riskiness (0–9) _____ %

Likelihood of actually happening (0–9) _____ %

Absorption of:

Management time _____ %

Market-research/ethnographic resources _____ %

Customer-enrichment-program resources _____ %

Other resources _____ %

Enter the above into the Creating Zealous Customers row in the Upside Element Assessment Sheet, just before the last page.

And so, with plans for creating zealous customers in hand, we move on to equally powerful upside elements: your value proposition and the promise that is your brand.

Chapter 3

Honing Your Value Proposition— So More People Buy

Why should you craft the best possible value proposition for your business? Because a winning value proposition is one of the most powerful ways to *grow your top line*. And it's much more likely to make your business more valuable, in contrast to buying other companies, for example.

A healthy chunk of this chapter draws upon Michael J. Lanning's wonderful book, *Delivering Profitable Value*.[21] To quote Lanning, "An organization generates wealth and sustained growth *as a function of the value propositions* it delivers."

Another source, with what might be the best business idea of this century, is Harvard's late Clay Christensen and others' *jobs-to-be-done* concept, which we'll describe after laying some groundwork.[22]

A great value proposition is an almost universal prerequisite for a product or service to become a hit. The increase in business value that having a hit can bring is dramatic. Just ask Apple.

What Is a Value Proposition?

Value is what you get for what you pay. Both *get* and *pay* have facets that are not always fully considered by those assessing what they now offer, or deciding what they will offer.

When you buy some things, sure, you get the thing you bought. But you often get more than the thing itself. In many cases, what you get is the real reason you bought it in the first place. The rewards from having or using the product or service are almost always emotion-based. *Examples:*

- The psychic peace that comes from getting something you need, and getting it off your to-do list.
- Good feelings:
  - Your guide service helped us have a great time visiting this city (creating a pleasant, lasting memory).
  - Respect.
  - Happiness: "Your high-performance, reliable machines help us get our product out in high volume, with few problems, and made us heroes to our investors. (I might even get promoted, or a nice bonus.)"
  - Self-esteem: "I look great in this!" (So I feel better about myself.)
  - Enjoyment: "Your bagels taste fabulous!"
  - Self-expression: what this T-shirt, watch, car, club membership, etc. says about me.

And you pay, with money, of course. But you also often pay with things like:

- Hassle:
  - Assembly required.
  - Getting your purchase out of its packaging (while risking a trip to the ER).
  - Having to set up your new computer.
  - Transporting your purchase.
  - Learning how to use it.
  - Returning it if it doesn't fit, your life partner doesn't like it or feels you shouldn't have spent money on it, and so on.

- Effort: "It's such a long drive to that weekend getaway."
- Anxiety:
  - "Will I get a good job after borrowing all that money to get my degree?"
  - "I paid a lot for my seat at the championship tonight. What if my team loses, or the game is boring or lopsided?"
- Frustration: "I can't figure out how to work this thing."
- Danger: skydiving, etc. The thrill of flirting with disaster, and the satisfaction of emerging unscathed.

So, on net, your emotional sense of what you get has to exceed the sum of what you pay, to create enough value to induce you to buy. And, of course, people will differ on how valuable something is to them. The point is that the person crafting or refining value propositions, often someone in Marketing, needs to take the totality of both get and pay into account.

> **Please note:**
>
> Value does not mean cheap, or shoddy, as we might associate with a business called Vic's Value Furniture, or Ultra Used Cars. Our use of the word *value* has little to do with either. Value also doesn't mean high quality at celestial prices. Here's what customer value means in this book...
>
> If I *feel* that my experience, of buying and using some product or service, is well worth what I invested, I'm happy. So I'll say that its value is good, from my perspective as a customer. And as we've seen above, customer value can be, and often is, something intangible, such as not having to worry about it, its prestige, or the maker's reputation. But good value *never* leaves the buyer feeling that "I've been had."

A customer-value proposition, then, is the *experience* a business offers its customers.[23] For manufacturers, it includes price, *and* the other aspects of the customer's investment that are within its control, like guidance for using the product. For its retailers, the proposition includes whether there's frustration in the buying experience itself (long lines, clueless salespeople).

Good, and Not-So-Good, Value Propositions...

Good Value Propositions

There are a number of ways that a value proposition can be seen by customers as a good one. Here are a few:

Providing peace of mind regarding a purchase, like the lifetime guarantees on backpacks made by Jansport. The guarantee is that if the customer is *ever* dissatisfied with an item they bought, they can return it for an exchange or refund. Yes, really.

Creating confidence. Subaru, whose well-designed, reliable cars are able to get through most any kind of winter weather, gives drivers a strong sense that they'll get to work, or be able to pick up the kids, *no matter what.*

Enabling satisfactory purchases. Amazon's product-review system, which shows the good and the shortcomings of the items they sell, enables an informed purchase decision. That system is part of an extraordinarily well-designed online customer experience (though it lacks the ability to have a prepurchase conversation with an associate, or to physically get a sense of the intended purchase). Amazon does the best it can do in an intentionally hands-off situation, and compensates for the lack of hands-on with low prices.

Having many uses—the smartphone. The high quality now being built into smartphones allows people to stop needing or buying all sorts of other small electronic devices, such as music players, pocket cameras and video recorders, GPS devices, travel alarms, and watches. So the customer has fewer devices to buy, learn how to operate, remember to bring along, and charge.

Solving a problem—keeping warm in the winter (or excessive air conditioning), without clothing that weighs you down—from the clothing brand Uniqlo. Thanks to their underlayers and outerwear, you're warm and you don't notice why—you're just grateful.

Eliminating major hassles—the IBM 360. In the mid 1960s, IBM brought to market a line of computers that could be upgraded when a customer needed more power, without needing to rewrite their software so it could run on the more powerful machine. This capability was new at the time, and led to extraordinary sales, worldwide. The other thing that the 360 featured was the ability to run software written for customers' older, non-360 machines on the 360 itself, by using what's called "firmware" to emulate the hardware of the older machine.[24]

Providing a fun experience—a hiring model. Consider Southwest Airlines. They hire "people people," who like to have fun and interact with, and entertain, their passengers. Not very quantifiable, but who wouldn't like that, or allow it to sway their choice of airline?

Put more generally, the people who interact with your customers can be a substantial competitive advantage. Remember when you were young and had, well, a crush on the clerk in the local store? Any excuse to go there, right? Later in life, you go because you know you'll get expert advice from the salesperson at the shoe store and your feet will stop hurting. Or because you know you'll be made to feel like you (and the business you bring them as a customer) are appreciated, and you're respected.

Or because they'll get you in and out with no delays or hassles.

Or just because you liked how the receptionist (remember them?) answered the phone.

Mixed Value Propositions

Forcing tradeoffs—a good example is Starbucks: high-quality coffee, ambiance, free WiFi, bathrooms, along with mediocre food, high prices, and long lines.

Offering variety, with drawbacks—offering a broad selection can play a major role in a value proposition. For online retailers, an ultra-wide selection is a distinct competitive edge. In certain brick-and-mortar stores, coupling selection with the ability to browse is a major draw: think physical bookstores. Browsing in such a store is particularly valuable to certain book buyers: those very interested in a particular topic, and those who need to learn something about it. They can literally get a solid sense of a book in moments, something that can be very trying online, despite features like Amazon's Look Inside the Book. Downside for some, a plus for others: you have to go to the bookstore.

To try and counter that, the Amoeba Music store in Los Angeles, California, offers 300,000 titles, a passionate and highly knowledgeable staff, and personal shopping for requests received by phone or the web.[25]

Bad Value Propositions

Dell[26] and HP. Their offerings are often cheap, but to some, like this author, they have negative value because of design for obsolescence (as in the HP all-in-one case described earlier) and poor support. The personal price paid in wasted time, aggravation, and frustration is just not worth the initial savings.

"Sucker towels." Pictured at right, these patterned towels look interesting, but they're not very good at drying anything, because the valleys in the fabric that could be devoted to absorbent material don't have any. In other words, *they don't fulfill the basic function of a towel.* But a shopper taken by fancy patterns would be snookered into buying them, at least once. Reaction: *I've been had!*

What About Your Value Proposition?

Improving your value proposition matters mightily. Apple is an example of what having the best value proposition in a market can do. The business with the best value proposition captures the lion's share of the profits, and often, the revenue. The increased profitability comes about because only variable costs will increase as sales grow; fixed costs are, ideally, already covered. The higher the fixed costs, the more dramatic this leverage effect becomes.

Your business delivers a value proposition to your customers—even if you have no clue what it is at the moment. So let's get into figuring out how the customer experiences your product or service.

Value Propositions: The Whole Story

There are a number of players and parts in any value proposition: the person who needs (or wants) what you provide based on, say, its advertised value proposition, and often someone else, a gatekeeper, who will decide whether to go through with buying it. *Examples:*

Offering	Prospect (person who drives the purchase)	Gatekeeper (person who approves the purchase)
A child's toy, or phone	Child	Parent
An industrial tool	Factory worker	The manager; Purchasing
A new car	The driver	Sometimes no one—but it could be a leasing or finance company
An adventure vacation	A married person	Their spouse

Now let's look at the reasons behind these situations, because they're what lead people to buy what's offered—reasons you can and should address in *communicating* your value proposition—your advertising (Chapter 5).

Offering	Prospect (person who drives the purchase)	Gatekeeper (person who approves the purchase)
A child's toy	Child: *Fun! I'm cool!*	Parent: *I've decided that what my child wants is appropriate, and perhaps developmental (so I'm a good parent). And I get an emotional kick out of my child really liking the toy.*
An industrial tool	Factory worker: *This will help me work faster, make things easier on my hands, and I'll learn a new skill (and maybe get a raise).*	Manager: *I'll get higher productivity, less scrap, and a happier worker (at least temporarily).* Purchasing: *I need to cover my backside, so I need to get a good price, from a reputable company.*
A new car	The driver: *It meets my needs and shows people who I am.*	Sometimes no one—but it could be a leasing or finance company: *Got credit?*
An adventure vacation	A married person: *I'll have a lot of fun and make memories.*	Their spouse: *I need to research this, first.*

We see that many sales situations involve appealing to more than one party, and doing so for different reasons. And they involve addressing the concerns and objections of some of them. These considerations and others, as we'll explain shortly, go into the design of a value proposition.

A Value Proposition Is Not…

- About the business's products, services, strategies, resources, or processes.
- About the business's competitors.
- A mission statement (of the broad goals of the overall organization).
- A corporate-values statement.
- A set of corporate results targets.

- A vision statement for the business (except for one that says that the vision is to deliver the best possible value proposition).

- A value added (in, or to, the product).

- Arrived at by asking customers what they want, and doing what they ask without really understanding their problem(s).

That last one can cause an organization to miss a great opportunity, because of a phrase you often see on highway signs: "Limited Sight Distance." That is, few people are able to wrap their heads around whole new approaches to solving their problems. Before they were introduced, who would have thought that paper maps would be supplanted by expensive devices that provide turn-by-turn driving directions, that mobile phones needed built-in cameras, or that we could actually have clothing that doesn't wrinkle or stain?

The set of experiences that almost anyone will derive from an unfamiliar product or service is just too difficult for them to imagine. Instead, people will often tell you that they need what they think you want to hear, just like most politicians.

This holds true in selling to business customers, as well as consumers.

Related Entities

In addition to your customer and any gatekeeper, there are other parties that are *critical to actually getting what you offer to the customer.* Lanning calls them related entities. *Examples:*

- A consumer-products manufacturer selling through a retailer: The manufacturer has to motivate the wholesaler, the distributor, and the retailer before their product can land in the hands of the consumer. One easy way to do so is to generate strong demand from the customer, so that all parties in the distribution chain feel that the effort they invest will have a worthwhile return.

- A business that sells to another business: Heap Big Software, a provider of state-of-the-art, whiz-bang accounting systems, sells its software through independent resellers. Heap Big provides an extensive set of free migration tools that the resellers use to make it easier to convince customers to move up to Heap Big's software.

This is an example both of providing an attractive value proposition to the company buying the accounting system, and of motivating the related entity (the reseller), helping them to close more sales by lessening the conversion roadblock, and thus making more money.

- A medical-device manufacturer: Here's another type of related entity: regulators—for some, an ultra-critical intermediary. Without their consent to market your heart monitor, you don't have a business. Your Job 1 is to convince them of your product's safety and effectiveness. Even after they approve your product, you still need value propositions that will motivate the distributors, and the professionals who will prescribe your product, to do so.

Value-Delivery Systems

Together, the related entities for your business, and how they're orchestrated, form a *value-delivery system* (or VDS) for getting what you offer to your intended customers. While your value proposition gets people to want to buy what you offer, your value-delivery system makes it possible for them to do so. Obviously, both are needed.

It takes a lot of time and a major ongoing management commitment to create and maintain a value-delivery system. But it goes to the core of our responsibilities as executives: to create and deliver value to our existing and prospective customers, so they keep buying what we provide, and we have a strong top line.

Perspectives: On Value Propositions and Delivery Systems

As Lanning so well puts it,[27] "The business of the business is to deliver a value proposition to customers."

Lanning's position is that the business's executives have to take responsibility for choosing and continuously improving the customer-value proposition, and for getting all of the people in the business to embrace delivering it. This is not the common view. More often, the business is thought of as the collection of products, services, people, resources, etc.

That perspective is not helpful, because it doesn't encourage those in the business to rally around delivering the most valuable experience possible. And because of that common view, many businesses don't prosper to anywhere near the extent they could. (There's that foregone upside, again.)

Creating a value-delivery system is also a fundamental shift in how executives see their roles. In addition to coordinating the parts of an organization, and trying to make money, executives must establish and continuously reinforce the mindset that, "we as a business *are* a value delivery system." Everyone in the business, and those who partner with the business, needs to embrace that reality.

So the question is, how much of your upside gap could working on your value proposition and its delivery system fill?

Creating and Delivering a Winning Value Proposition

On to designing that winning value proposition, and creating the value-delivery system needed to get it in front of present and potential customers. (Chapter 5 is about *communicating* the chosen proposition, credibly and effectively, to those customers.)

Situations That Can Lead to a Strong Value Proposition

If your customer faces any of these problems, your company has an opportunity to develop a stronger value proposition for them:

- Being unable to afford a product or service. This is the need addressed by, for example, Costco, other big box stores, Amazon, and discount warehouses.
- Being unable to physically access goods or services, which led to Walmart's prominent presence in rural areas.

- Not having broadband internet access in remote areas, which companies are attempting to address with high-altitude balloons, satellites, and other solutions.

- Lacking the skill to build a website; solved for some with simple-to-use templates.

- "We'll do it for you" services like Task Rabbit.

A Reliable Approach to Creating Winning Value Propositions

Recent work by Harvard's late Clayton Christensen and others takes finding a superior value proposition out of the realm of winning the lottery and into a straightforward, learnable process.

The *value* to the prospective customer lies in satisfactorily handling *a job* the customer needs done in their lives. The *ways* the customer now has to do that job are either not very satisfactory or simply don't exist. But you can find these: see his *Competing Against Luck,* uncovering jobs.[28] *Examples:*

- Police forces and other first responders often need to light a wooded area or an accident scene, or respond to a night-time disaster call. The job they need done is to light the area, wherever it might be, and to keep the lighting on for as long as necessary. Pelican Products' portable remote-area lights nail that job.

- You just bought a new PC, and you want to migrate your existing applications and their settings to it—*without* reinstalling all of them from scratch, which could be a royal pain. Laplink's PC Mover product grabbed this job. It will move all or most of your applications, not just your data, and Microsoft's own software.

- Auto mechanics don't have time to go running around to get the tools they need for working on all kinds of vehicles. But then the Snap-on Tools van stops by…

Interestingly, the companies that first nailed these jobs to be done now seem to dominate those markets.

Christensen et al. also show how to find *the cause* of the job[29] so you can assess whether there's a stable reason for it: the likelihood that the cause will persist. It's been noted that causes of the job, as well as the jobs themselves, tend to be more permanent than the means of accomplishing them at a given point in time.[30]

Creating winning value propositions requires first *understanding* what a superior *experience* would be for prospects and customers. Doing so without kidding yourself requires *becoming* the customer: experiencing the reason they use what you offer in the first place, and their joys and particularly their challenges in doing so.

In his book *Demand*,[31] management consultant Adrian Slywotzky introduces the powerful concept of *hassle maps,* which capture those challenges, and which can help in coming up with ways to overcome them. In some cases, those inspired creations can markedly increase the attractiveness of a value proposition.

Examples of hassles include the things that the fictional creations on the television program *Star Trek* were designed to avoid: getting somewhere (transporter beams), preparing food (replicators), and finding out what's wrong after an injury and perhaps even fixing it on the spot, instead of a trip to the doctor or the hospital (medical tri-corders).

More earthly hassle examples would include: scheduling a business meeting (now somewhat ameliorated by software such as Microsoft Outlook), and doing your taxes (made easier by tax-preparation software.)

So what are the hassles, if any, involved in using what you offer? Do competing alternatives have them too? What about substitutes? What can you do about those hassles?

In *Blue Ocean Shift,* the authors W. Chan Kim and Renée Mauborgne have their own term for hassles: "pain points."[32] Their example: choosing a wine to serve guests (and for the corkscrew-less, opening it).

Addressing hassles or pain points can create markets, as we'll see in Chapter 9. Mainly, it creates a competitive advantage for what you now offer because of an improved value proposition.

The *Blue Ocean Shift* authors also provide several useful tools for formulating an improved value proposition.

Tool	What it Does	Pages in their book
The Eliminate-Reduce-Raise-Create Grid	This tool will help you see how to alter one or more of the popular value propositions in your industry to make them more attractive to prospects by taking one or more of the actions listed at left.	29, 35
The Buyer Utility Map	This 6 x 6 map shows 36 ways in which a business can improve its value proposition. You won't be able to say that there are no ways to improve the value you offer without really working through the map. Please see the book for explanations and examples.	147

Value-proposition design should also consider what present and potential competitors might do in the way of enhancing their own customer value and their experiences.

Perceived value is highly personal, because we each weight both the rewards and the other aspects of the investment through our own wants, likes and dislikes, and reality constraints like money and time. For example, certain rewards mean more to some of us; some of us are tight with money, others spendthrifts; some are early adopters; others don't want to have to learn anything new.

But given all this (and customization aside), we can design value propositions that appeal more strongly to significantly large groups of people who have similar wants, preferences, and constraints.

People assess a value proposition, consciously or otherwise, along five dimensions: the benefits of the product or service offered, its quality, the existing or potential relationship with the provider, the provider's brand, and the total investment (of money and the other factors mentioned earlier). While a business customer might judge this on a more formal basis than a consumer, the same criteria are used by both, if only subconsciously.

In an early paper,[33] the *Blue Ocean Strategy* authors, Kim and Mauborgne, recommend using what they call "value curves" to design a value proposition.

They suggest listing the things buyers would want in a column, and, along the bottom, how well a proposed value proposition would meet that want. Then plot how well your and your competitors' present and planned offerings meet those needs (you'll find an example of this in Chapter 9, Hungry Markets). Here are two useful refinements:

1. Understand which of these wants and concerns are: essential to deal with, somewhat important, or not worth worrying about.

2. In their *Harvard Business Review* article,[34] Anderson et al. point out that there are three kinds of value-proposition statements used in selling to customers, only one of which is effective. The first they call "all benefits," a.k.a. the kitchen sink. It simply lists every benefit that the product or service offers to customers. The next, called "favorable points of difference," lists the features and benefits on which the offering can be claimed to be superior (regardless of whether those points of difference have any value to the customer). Finally, they describe an effective approach they call "resonating focus," the one or two points of difference that the customer highly values. Of course, finding what will resonate requires research, as distinct from the first two approaches.

The Anderson article also introduces the concept of "points of contention," meaning that, in a given area, the business believes that its offering has an advantage, but the customer thinks that it's the same as what others offer. The point of contention could also be something that the business views as the same as competitors' offerings, but the customer believes that it's inferior. In both cases, educating the customer could make the business's offerings more attractive.

Characterize the things that buyers would want according to their importance to them, and apply the Anderson et al. criteria to the elements of your value proposition, then return to the Kim and Mauborgne suggestion, and decide which value-proposition elements can be:

- Dropped.
- Made less attractive (and less costly).

- Made more desirable.

- Added (something that's never been provided).

There is, of course, the famous *Blue Ocean Strategy*[35] approach of doing what no one else is, at least not yet—don't slug it out with competitors.

The steps in this section are laid out in a powerful, easy-to-follow way in the *Tapping Your Upside* exercise that closes this chapter.

Forging the Anchor of Our Value Delivery System: The Target Customer's Experience or the Job to Be Done

For starters, let's be clear on what an experience *is:* an event or series of events that happen in the customer's life as a result of the product or service your business provides to them, along with the consequence(s) of those events. *Examples:*

- Buying a book online.

- Purchasing a car.

- Having a memorable meal or vacation.

- Shopping for groceries.

- Picking up coffee or breakfast on your way to work.

- Having an in-patient medical procedure.

- Helping your customer compete. In a business, this would be something that would be of value to your customer's customers. (Focusing on this is one of the most powerful and easiest ways to have what you offer adopted.)

An Implied Assumption...

The section below assumes that the market you're serving or intending to serve is the best one available to you. That might not be the case, at all—see Chapter 9 on Hungry Markets. But assuming that it is, read on!

The experiences and their consequences should be *designed,* like that of the supermarket Wegmans,[36] and, ideally, be measurable. They can be tangible, or invisible, like a preventive-maintenance service that reduces unscheduled plant shutdowns. Price is one dimension of the experience, of many.

The value proposition for a different type of intended customer might need to be provided by a different value-delivery system, since *that customer might value different things.*

There is, of course, the "de facto" value proposition, the one that every business now delivers. That proposition is good to understand deeply, because doing so might lead to obvious or straightforward improvements.

Getting the Order of Your Value Proposition Steps Right

There are basically four things that have to happen, and in order, so that your business prospers from your value proposition:

1. Create a compelling proposition.

2. Create a powerful brand promise for it (or hitch onto an existing brand's promise).

3. Persuasively communicate the value proposition and brand promise through various forms of marketing: advertising, on-line discussions, and videos.

4. Quickly, yet carefully, pour customer feedback into the initial value proposition, so it grows more compelling.[37]

While the above sequence seems obvious, there are many examples of it being violated or ignored, with consequences like, and I quote, "Our advertising is not working. Fire the ad agency!" That's much more likely to be the result of starting with steps 2 or 3—putting lipstick on the pig, in other words, instead of taking the time to create a compelling underlying reason for customers to choose what you offer.

Choosing Your Value Proposition

The first issue for any business is the executives' *decision* to *choose* the value proposition they will deliver, rather than leave it unexamined or unchosen.

That begins with a look at what Lanning calls the "market space," the set of possible value propositions and value-delivery systems that the business could provide. These are the realms of opportunity for the business, or potential businesses.

> Work by Bain & Company provides a hierarchy of 30 distinct elements of customer value, some of which could, depending on the industry, grow revenue and/or increase customer loyalty. Not surprisingly, the most valuable element to pursue, across all industries, was quality.
>
> The Bain authors also provide, for 10 different industries, guidance on which subsets of these 30 elements best increase value.
>
> Finally, they suggest that someone in the business be responsible for designing (choosing and testing) the elements of value that a new or enhanced value proposition should include. For more, see: Eric Almquist, John Senior, and Nicholas Bloch, "The Elements of Value," *Harvard Business Review*, September, 2016, 47–53.

Before settling on ways to strengthen your value proposition, try to understand which of them will best increase the value your customers want to get, and which will maximize the business's value, so that what you do pays off. Often, these are the same because of the revenue growth that a great value proposition will create. Otherwise, choose the value element that will maximize the business's value once the options become clear.

As we said earlier, choosing the best value proposition you can offer requires *becoming the customer.* Doing so allows potentially valuable experiences to be discovered and competing alternatives identified and analyzed. It's about mutually beneficial cooperation with the customer.

This requires not market research, but really living the customer's life (even living *with* them, as P&G has sometimes done) until their problems are clear, and, ideally, *felt*. Doing so is not always easy, especially in business, but it can be done by convincing potential customers that it's in their interest to allow it. Having one of your customer engineers on-site for a time could spark improvements that would benefit both parties.

Lanning recommends creating in-depth narratives of both what the customer experiences now, and of what that experience could ultimately be. He gives, as an example, that of an unaccompanied woman who pulls into a service station to refuel her car at night in the rain. His vivid and detailed description of exactly what happens in a perhaps 5-minute actual activity (the base scenario) takes up two and a half printed pages. The second version, describing the best possible experience, is similarly detailed, and a big improvement!

Capturing this base scenario is one of the core responsibilities of the business. It might also be necessary to analyze the experiences of related entities and competitors in like fashion.

Another way to uncover the best possible scenario is to get your customers to tell you stories.[38] Traditional market research, in which you mainly get customers telling you what they think you want to hear, is useless. Sometimes you can just get a sampling of customers to tell you stories about how they actually use the product or service, then extract from this collection their hassles and what they would highly prize. For example, outdoor outfitter L.L.Bean works closely with customers, and employs independent field testers who literally live in Bean's boots, to make sure that its products remain leading edge.

"We get out into the field as much as we can … and do the same things that our customers are doing," explained Bean president Chris McCormick. "We use our own products so that we have a better idea of how they're performing. This practice helps us identify better with our customers' experiences and needs."[39]

Some companies encourage customers to use the voice recorders on their mobile phones to capture their experiences in various situations.

The best-possible-experience narrative, and the remaining hassles that emerge from all of this, are then used as a starting point for crafting the experience the business intends to deliver.

Crafting a high-value experience also takes knowing, specifically, what the customer's competing alternatives will be in the target time frame. Do they involve the competition, just the customer having available substitutes (instead of a heavy winter coat, a warm undershirt under a lighter jacket), or the customer doing nothing?

The chosen value proposition also needs to define the relevant market space, including:

- Who, specifically, the value is provided *for?* There is always an intended customer, perhaps a gatekeeper, and there could be related entities in the value-delivery chain. But choosing the intended customer is the first and crucial choice.

Lanning maintains that the intended customer is the person or organization for which the biggest increase in customer value can be delivered profitably.[40] This author disagrees.

My sense is that you should choose your intended customer to be the people or organizations for which the new or enhanced value proposition will bring the largest increase in *the value of your business.* In other words, don't spend time on things that might not amount to much in the grand scheme of things, even though somewhat profitable. We'll discuss what goes into determining the increase in business value in Chapter 14.

- Do you want to expand your overall market (by appealing to a new or adjacent customer segment)?
- What are the best competing alternatives from each target customer's perspective? These could be competitors' offerings, a substitute (for a writer, a substitute could be pen and paper in lieu of a laptop computer or, for anyone, taking available public transportation instead of driving), or it could be simply doing nothing.
- How will we win over the gatekeepers?

Use a wide-angle lens to assess competing alternatives. Maybe your product/service is inferior, or the same as everyone else's. But can it be made into a winning proposition?

For example, you could offer an "inferior," yet simple and inexpensive product, with all of the inessential features stripped out.

Or you could distinguish a commodity product like, for example, sand. You'd think that a company that delivers sand is pretty much like any other. Yet there's a sand distributor that charges premium prices for sand by delivering it:

- In the grade and color the customer wants.

- In the specific amount the customer wants.

- When the customer wants it delivered.

- Where on the property the customer wants it.

Is that sand a commodity? The company just went and created a superior value proposition that it could offer.

As Lanning puts it, "Where's the superior part?" Seek it out!

Also, you'll need to deliver the best possible value proposition, *but no more.* This is not about gold plating.

With all that as background, it's time to make some tentative choices.

- What specific experience will your business deliver to the customer (and the gatekeeper, if any)? What are its positive and its negative characteristics? How will delivering that experience impact other businesses within your company? When will its delivery begin, and how often will the proposition itself be revisited?

- What do you expect that the new experience will do in the way of increased profits and revenue (in rough percentages)?

- Next, the value proposition needs to be *economically* profitable—as defined in Chapter 14—and sufficiently so to markedly raise the value of the business and be worth the effort to create and maintain it.

- Finally, the business needs to *become the vehicle* for delivering (and communicating—Chapter 5) the offered experiences.

Crucial questions: Can your business really pull this off? What capability gaps, if any, will you have to address? How will you do so?

Another critical area is that the organization function *as an integrated whole* in delivering the offered experience. This is the antithesis of functional areas behaving like sovereign states—there's no room for politics. It's the senior executive's (not so easy) leadership job to bring this about. As Kevin Sharer, former CEO of Amgen, recounted:[41]

> *"After I became C.E.O., we probably replaced within a year most of the team, for a whole bunch of reasons. I remember when the new team was assembled, having a dinner and sitting around the table and saying: "You know, we're new, we're together, we all feel lucky to be here, but let me tell you something. I've operated in environments where there were master politicians. I'm not a bad politician myself. And so I can see it. And if any of you try to be politicians, I will know it, and I will fire you."*

The whole value-proposition-development process is: hard, labor intensive, and time consuming. And driving it is one of the most critical parts of your job as an executive. It's likely going to be a team effort. After the initial development, the responsibility continues: refining and evolving the experiences delivered.

Whose job will it be to first find a resonant value proposition or two? And who will be responsible for keeping them coming?[42] The job of finding resonant value propositions needs to be made the permanent, if not the full-time, responsibility of some key people. After all, there's little that's more important in terms of results and, ultimately, of wealth creation. For example, at Quaker Chemical, that responsibility rests with the chemical program managers, who work at their customers' sites (so they get to see, and experience, a lot of what their customers go through). More of us should be so lucky. Perhaps we should ask, with a good reason for the customer to do so in hand.

It should be obvious by now that done right, delivering a value proposition fundamentally transforms a business and how the people in it think about their roles—for the better. It requires organization-wide commitment; lip service won't begin to cut it. The commitment is *to live it*.

It starts with senior management, the questions they ask of the managers who report to them, and the results those managers are held accountable for.[43] Here are a few good questions:

- How well is our current value proposition working, i.e., what are the growth rates of both revenue and profitability?
- What are our competitors' comparable rates?
- How do we expect our and the competitions' growth rates to change in the next 12 months?
- Why? What are we going to *do* to bring about the change we want?
- What evidence do we have that what we're planning to do will work?

Lanning recommends that you repeat those questions, but ask for the answers from a 5-years-out perspective.

Mr. Lanning concludes his book with a section describing how Procter & Gamble approaches delivering customer value.[44] At P&G:

- Each brand is a value-delivery system, delivered by, in many cases, shared resources such as manufacturing.
- The brand manages the creation of a business plan, complete with, and in collaboration with, all of the needed resources to deliver the value proposition. The plan must then be approved by top management.
- Once approved, the business plan, not the players, governs. The brand managers are responsible for delivering on it, and for recommending future improvements to it. (Having *the plan* govern creates a business that succeeds or fails on its merits, not its politics.)

P&G uses rigorous financial criteria to judge how well a brand (a business) is doing, and the employees who influence its success are partly evaluated based on these criteria.

One thing this author takes issue with in Lanning's discussion of P&G is that managers are rewarded for achieving some expected return, but *not for exceeding it*.[45] The term *return* is vague, and therefore not useful as a measure.

Whatever it is, implicit in not exceeding it are a few things that might or might not be true:

- That whoever set the expected return got it right.
- That the revenue growth achieved by pricing so as not to exceed the expected return, will create more wealth than pricing for increased profitability—see Chapter 6.
- That managers can't find ways to reduce costs further, or make advertising more persuasive, increasing sales volume and overall profits.

If a giant global company like P&G can create and deliver on value propositions in this way, any business can, *if* it chooses to. It's one of the most wealth-creating (and fun) uses of executives' brains and talents.

In the next chapter, we'll dig into your brand, another powerful results booster. But before we go there, work through the exercises that follow to understand the specifics of how enhancing your value proposition can lift your results.

TAPPING YOUR UPSIDE:
Honing Your Value Proposition

About This Exercise

The goal here is to know how to really improve a value proposition for one of your *major* offerings. The approach is to do it, once. It won't be that easy. And at this stage, it shouldn't get your mightiest effort, because you might find an even better way to boost results in other chapters.

But honing your value proposition is one of the most powerful ways to lift results, so the exercise will be worthwhile. If there's someone who heads up the marketing or product-management areas of your business, it might be beneficial to ask them to participate in, or lead, the completion of this exercise.

The Path Through the Exercise

On the following pages, we've provided a worksheet, one that you can download and have others fill in*, that will help you structure your thinking about those your value-proposition touches, their wants and concerns, how your value proposition relates to them, and how it compares to those of the competition.

We'll begin by becoming very clear on the wants and concerns of the customer, the gatekeeper, the others involved in the purchase decision, and the related entities. And for each, we'll rank order their wants and concerns, then merge the ranked lists into one overall (re-ranked) list.

Next, for each element of your value proposition, you'll need to decide whether it's better than, the same as, or worse than the competition in the eyes of those making the buying decision.

Finally, we'll ask you to associate each want or concern with the value-proposition elements that apply, and to net out the better, same, and worse ratings for that want or concern. This will generate an overall rating on how what you offer fares.

---

* *The worksheet comes as part of this book's tools and extras, which you can download from www.theupsidewithinreach.com.*

That should provide a clear picture of where you are and what you're up against.

After doing this for the entire list of wants and concerns, you might see ways to enhance your value proposition. We'll ask you to carry out the better-same-worse exercise again with the elements of your enhanced value proposition.

On to the worksheet! We'll start with the first tab, shown below.

1. **After reviewing the Example columns (on the left), in the Your Offering columns (right), fill in the Who column, then what each of those you listed want. For each, rank them from strongest influence on the purchase decision to least.**

First tab

EXAMPLE: A CHILD'S PLAYTHING			YOUR OFFERING		
Individual Wants and Concerns (Ranked)			Individual Wants and Concerns (Ranked)		
Who	Rank	What	Who	Rank	What
Customer (school-age child)	1	Fun	Customer		
	2	Challenging			
	3	Cool			
Gatekeeper (parent)	1	Safe	Gatekeeper		
	2	Fun			
	3	Playable			
	4	Educational			
	5	Sparks creativity			

EXAMPLE: A CHILD'S PLAYTHING			YOUR OFFERING		
Individual Wants and Concerns (Ranked)			**Individual Wants and Concerns (Ranked)**		
Who	**Rank**	**What**	**Who**	**Rank**	**What**
Other (grandmother)	1	Customer would love it	**Other**		
	2	Safe			
	3	Educational			
	4	Price			
Related Entities (gov't consumer product safety agency)	1	Safe	**Related Entities**		

2. Next, merge the wants and concerns you've identified into the single prioritized list below and note any of them that various parties consider must-haves.

Second tab

Merged Wants and Concerns (Ranked Overall)						
		Must Have	**Whose Want or Concern?**			
No.	**What**		**Customer**	**Gatekeeper**	**Others**	**RE(s)**

Merged Wants and Concerns (Ranked Overall)						
		Must Have	**Whose Want or Concern?**			
No.	**What**		**Customer**	**Gatekeeper**	**Others**	**RE(s)**

As preparation for the next step, write out your customers' current experience with this offering in detail (shoot for at least a page), then continue below.

3. **Below, list and rate the elements of your value proposition from customers' perspectives.**

First, list all of the major elements of the value proposition you provide now, numbering them. As they occur to you, add any enhancements, identifying each with a capital letter, so you can easily tell them apart later in this exercise. It might well happen that enhancements will occur to you after you've gone through this entire exercise for the first time. That's to be expected, as the exercise is designed to help you see where you might be falling short of the highest customer value you can provide.

Third tab

YOUR VALUE PROPOSITION	Customer's Rating of the Value-Proposition Element	
Value-Proposition Elements Number exisiting elements; use A, B ... for *enhancements*	+ Better than the competition = Same as the competition – Worse than the competition	
ID	**What**	**Rating**

4. Finally, we'll line up your value proposition, and your contemplated enhancements to it, with the customers' wants and concerns. Start with your value proposition as it is now, the middle set of columns below.

Fourth tab

YOUR VALUE PROPOSITION VS. THE MARKET'S WANTS AND NEEDS, AND YOUR COMPETITORS' OFFERINGS

Merged Wants and Concerns			How Your Value Proposition Elements Address Customers' Wants, Concerns, and the Competition							
			Value Proposition Now				*Enhanced Value Proposition*			
No.	What	Must Have	Better ID(s)	Same ID(s)	Worse ID(s)	Net + = −	Better ID(s)	Same ID(s)	Worse ID(s)	Net + = −
1										
2										
3										
4										
5										
6										
7										
8										
9										

5. What did you learn from filling in those middle columns?

_____

_____

_____

6. Based on that, what value-proposition enhancements could you make? List them all.

_____

_____

_____

7. Which of these enhancements make financial sense (list their identifiers)?

_____

8. Which of these enhancements are realistic (identifiers)?

_____

_____

_____

9. Which of these enhancements could be delivered within a year (identifiers)?

_____

_____

_____

10. Which could be delivered within five years (identifiers)?

_____

_____

_____

11. Using the table below as a template, estimate the percentage revenue and profit increases, without double counting, that you expect to reap from each enhancement over time. In other words, *why* should you make the effort?

Enhancement ID	Time Frame	Revenue Increase (%)	Profit Increase (%)
	1 Year		
	5 Years		
	10+ Years		

12. What will you have to do to bring each of your related entities along regarding each value-proposition enhancement?

_____

_____

_____

_____

_____

_____

13. **Considering your business and all of its related entities as your value-delivery system, what orchestration will be necessary? In other words, how will you coordinate all of the moving parts?**

_____

_____

_____

_____

_____

_____

14. **Have everyone in your business write out the parts they'll play in the value-delivery system you're envisioning, and pull together their responses.**

a. Any gaps?

_____

_____

_____

b. Overlaps?

_____

_____

_____

UPSIDE ELEMENT ASSESSMENT: VALUE PROPOSITION

Please enter your estimates for the *overall* gains and challenges you expect to derive from your enhanced value proposition in the corresponding row on the book's Upside Element Assessment Sheet, just before the last page.

Chapter 4

Raising Your Brand's Power to Attract Sales

As explained in Chapter 3, your offering's value proposition can consist mainly of the reality of your product or service, its virtues and drawbacks in the eyes of prospective purchasers, and its price. The value prospects perceive also includes elements of your brand: whether the prospect trusts your business, whether they believe they can count on what you provide, and how your brand makes them feel.

Let's begin with, just what *is* a brand? Definitions vary; here's mine:

A strong brand is a concept, represented by words and/or a symbol, that people can embrace and that can come to mean something to them. Ideally, the brand represents a belief or principle they value and can attach themselves to, emotionally. It gives people a way to show the world who they are—for example, Apple fans, Harley owners, and buyers of designer handbags.[46] And it saves them time in deciding *which* product or service they'll purchase, out of a number of choices.

Brands make people think something is worth paying for.[47]

The strongest brands represent *a covenant* between the provider and the customer that what is offered will be as promised.

Of course, every brand does not click with every buyer. Most brands don't resonate with even a minority of prospects. Often that's because what the brand stands for is not compelling, or clear. Having a "so-what" brand is extremely expensive, in terms of lost revenue (and the attendant profits). But the loss is nearly invisible. It's almost as though thieves showed up, made off with your greatest treasure, and you never noticed. *And still don't!*

Why Brands Are Important, and Have a Huge Upside

For the seller of a product or service, a brand makes choosing what to purchase nearly automatic—once the buyer's habit becomes established. My brand of coffee, gasoline, detergent, personal computer, etc., is...

The upside: for the business that offers the brand, revenue becomes both predictable and dramatically higher than it would be if buyers actually made a choice of provider every time they bought.

Many brands allow people to project how they want to be seen by others, using the brand's perceived attributes (hipness, allure, tough guy) or associations (with sports figures or celebrities). Other brands represent a system of values or beliefs that people want to identify with. These psychological bonds can glue the buyer to the product or service. The resulting brand loyalty brings both repeat sales and positive word-of-mouth.[48,49,50,51]

Your business has a brand, unless you're just starting out. Every business does. Some executives are very clear on what their brand represents. And some are clueless about how their brand is perceived. But even if the brand is perceived as a good one, that perception can often be strengthened if the business's executives are aware of, and address, any flaws or hitches in what their business delivers.

The Promise a Brand Can Represent

Basically, a brand's promise is that *you'll get what you came for: what you wanted when you decided to buy from the company behind the brand.* For the companies below, their brand promise, a significant part of their value proposition, creates a substantial upside in terms of future revenue:

- IBM: unmatched technical depth and breadth; long experience in most industries; can count on.

- Southwest Airlines: customer experience.

- Apple: design, devices, and services that enable expressing creativity, "I'm hip!"

- Costco: a U.S. wholesale club known for low prices, a good customer experience, and a no-questions-asked return policy.

- Caterpillar: fast repair service; readily available parts—worldwide.

- Tiffany: the person that the purchase is for, is worth it.

Then there are lackluster brands—those with no promise. They don't seem to stand for anything. Businesses with lackluster brands do spend money on advertising—yet they seem to create "so what?" *Examples*:

- Hewlett-Packard: at one time, quality, innovation, and trust; now, commodity technology.

- A&P: a now-defunct U.S. supermarket chain, perceived as stuck in the past.

Finally, we come to wounded brands—companies that have betrayed their covenant with customers:

- Johnson & Johnson (a once-trusted health-care brand); now damaged in view of a 2009–2013 spate of quality problems:[52]
  - Concealing known hip-replacement-product defects, while continuing to sell them.[53]
  - Baby powder containing talc, which some studies have linked to ovarian cancer and which J&J kept quiet about, and recently pulled from the market in the U.S. and Canada.[54]
- There's also J&J's alleged role[55] in the opioid crisis.

These episodes are better associated with greed than good, although J&J did voluntarily pull its pelvic mesh off the market, after 53,000 lawsuits.[56]

- Goldman Sachs: another trust betrayal—selling customers securities they designed that were intended to fall in value, and for which Goldman paid a $550 million fine to the U.S. government.[57]
- Nokia: once known for innovation; more recently, failing to stay at the cutting edge of cell-phone technology.
- Dell: a lot for your money—*until* you need technical support.

These wounds can be very costly in terms of lost revenue going forward because customers no longer trust you, and for a public company, that can result in a battered share price. It's no surprise that the executives responsible for the wounding often wind up adding "former" to their titles.

Types of Brands

A brand can be associated with a product, or a company. Some product brands:

- Häagen-Dazs ice cream
- Pampers
- Apple's iPhone
- Microsoft Office

There are also very well-known corporate brands (that drive sales for multiple product lines because of the corporate reputation):[58]

- Apple
- IBM
- Tiffany

You tend to trust these businesses. That is, you generally assume that the business's product or service is good, because the people in the company are committed/talented, it is well managed, and they have processes in place that ensure that only high-quality offerings make it out the door. But a corporate brand's betrayal of trust, such as Volkswagen's emissions cheating, can negatively impact all of its products and product brands.

Both product brands and corporate brands can create new sales. A corporate brand allows multiple products and services to bask in the goodwill it creates. This leverage can dramatically improve the return on the investment made in the brand; however, if the product brand is not established as well, there are two potential downsides:

- It's much more difficult to sell a product, or product line, to another company when it's only associated with the corporate brand. Would Unilever buy "Procter & Gamble diapers?" Unlikely, but they would buy Pampers, a P&G product brand, under the right circumstances. So, failing to establish strong product brands can have a dramatic effect on what a product business is worth to a prospective buyer.
- The product's value proposition, compelling as it might be, is not given the prominence that could lift its sales.

A best practice would be to pour trust and dependability into both the corporate and product brands, and performance into the product brand.

The Biggest Problem With Branding

Implanting a brand in peoples' minds through advertising is expensive, and out of reach for some businesses. But it doesn't have to be.

Developing a Brand

There is a definite order to creating a brand. And spending money on advertising is clearly *not* the first thing to do.

A brand exists only in the heart (the emotions) of the prospect or customer. It needs to stand for something.

The first thing is to create a product or service that delivers a value proposition that customers will find attractive when it's experienced or described. And that great value proposition needs to be well delivered, time after time.[59]

Next comes the brand's promise—*choosing* the covenant with the buyer. *Example:* Back when IBM offered the ThinkPad brand of laptops (before they sold the brand to Lenovo in 2005), they positioned the laptops as "A better place to think." And arguably, they were:

- Shockproof hard drives that didn't get damaged if the laptop was dropped, so you wouldn't lose your precious thinking.
- Great keyboards, so you could capture your thoughts quickly.
- Solid construction, so you didn't have to waste your time getting broken parts repaired.
- Terrific technical support, by people who actually knew what they were talking about and who could be understood over the phone.
- Reliability: My previous ThinkPad was in daily use for 5 years, during which time, I only had to replace the fan.

And Lenovo has done a somewhat reasonable job of maintaining the Think-Pad brand's reputation for service.

With that example in mind, here's your first question: What attributes of your offering, or business, are the most emotionally resonant for the bulk of your customers and prospects?

What follows might help you choose a positioning for your brand. People want to know, "What will the brand do for me?"

- Show people who I am (another underlying emotional need this positioning targets is connection to the like-minded):
  - As a person: This is often done using what psychologists call "sweatshirt messages" that convey how we want to be seen by others. We all use our clothing, the décor of our living spaces,

our means of transportation (mainly cars), our lifestyles, our line of work, and our affiliations to show the world how we want to be perceived. *Examples:* cars (we variously buy Ford pickups, BMWs, Teslas, Hondas, and Hummers. The sets of buyers rarely overlap), clothing and "accessories" (high-fashion, hipster, preppie, tree-hugger), lifestyles (rebel—Harley, surfer—Billabong).

- As a member of a group: College students and alums, Fans of a sports team, rock band devotees (Deadheads).

○ Reinforce what I believe in, or represent my values.

- Habitat for Humanity, Friends of the Earth, Heifer International

- Religions

- Political parties

- Causes

○ Provide what I like, or need.

- A reliable car that can get through most any weather—Subaru.

- A tool that aging hands can grip—Oxo.

- *Knowing* what I'm buying—Amazon's reviews.

○ Excite me.

- Thrill me: Amusement parks, adventure vacations.

- Titillate me: Newsstand publications like *Cosmopolitan*, supermarket, and other tabloids, sold by what's on their covers.

○ Entertain me.

- Hit shows, movies, and music. Favorite bands.

○ Enable me

- Train me: Coaches of all stripes; personal trainers; fine and performing arts teachers; martial arts instructors

- Inform/teach me: News and special-interest books and magazines, nonfiction authors.

There's a sweet spot in all of this branding business: creating what in the rock-and-roll world are known as groupies. Some of these companies are obvious: Apple and Harley-Davidson come to mind. But it also can be done by business-to-business companies like IBM, and by smaller companies. One shining example is Big Ass Fans.[60]

They make, well, large fans, for industrial spaces that it would be impractical or inordinately expensive to air condition, like warehouses, assembly lines, and livestock barns. Their fans have high inherent utility, and quality. But the company went way beyond the product's inherent value in designing its value proposition...

They folded their outrageous *brand* into it, making the result dramatically more attractive. A bit of background...

Big Ass Fans' core buyer is a middle-aged guy who works in, or who is responsible for buying for, one of the types of spaces above. Most of these guys love sports and have a somewhat irreverent sense of humor, like the Parrotheads that swarm to Jimmy Buffett concerts. So what would appeal to a guy like that? Cheeky (sorry) humor and an association with a sports figure. The company signed former National Football League star William (Refrigerator) Perry as their spokesperson.

They started off building the brand by placing cards bearing Mr. Perry's picture, and, of course, one of their fans, in postcard decks mailed to industrial buyers. The card's main message: "Big Ass Fans: Savings Out the Wazoo!" When the recipient got over rolling on the floor laughing, he was hooked. "What a cool company! I'm there." As in, "I'm going to do my damnedest to support these guys. I love 'em. Why does everyone else who comes by to sell me somethin' have to bore me to death?"

So now, for the buyer, it's personal. Real personal. "I'm going to the Chicago Industrial Trade Show, so I can meet Refrigerator Perry, talk to these Big Ass Fan guys, and get some of the cool, logo'ed gear they hand out! My kids will love it. (And if we have a cooling problem down at the plant, I'll deal with that, too.)"

And there you have... *a whole different value proposition.* Great product, but a *towering* value proposition. Can you say, "The competition is helpless?"

Now Big Ass Fans' brand does *not* appeal to everyone. It's not intended to. There are some prospective buyers who profess to be offended by the company's

name, logo, and approach. The trade-off Big Ass Fans made in choosing its brand's position is simple. Strongly appeal to most of our prospective buyers, and piss off the rest—to create controversy, and more widespread awareness.

Finally comes associating the offering with the brand's promise.[61] As mentioned, this often consumes a fortune in advertising. But it need not…

We'll talk about this more in the next chapter, but here's an example. There's a company that makes high-performance dive suits for demanding customers like the U.S. Navy Seals. Their tag line:

If our name is on the suit, your diver will return.

That's a promise. More like a covenant! And one that, unlike a jingle, you only have to be exposed to once to want to buy, or at least learn more about, the product, assuming you're a dive-suit buyer. And the tagline is easily spread by word-of-mouth (a meme), and remembered.

As you can imagine, that tagline drives everything in the company: hiring, product design, production and testing, marketing, and sales. The covenant does have its costs, but it also has extraordinary emotional power:

- For the people in the company.

- For the specifiers and buyers of their products.

- For the divers themselves, and those responsible for their safe return.

So, what's the best way to build a brand? First, really sculpt the value proposition you intend to provide. Then, how can you make it about something more than the product or service, *and* something that will endure? How can you deliver it consistently? And how will you communicate the covenant it represents, with or without a big budget?[62]

Managing Your Brand

What to do with a brand varies by business, but every business needs to:

- Think deeply about what its brand *means*. The lack of a compelling and crystal-clear message means spending a lot on advertising, without the greatest return.

- Realize that cutting prices can weaken a brand.

Be *Consistent* About the Brand's Positioning

Simply said, don't slap the same brand on a bargain and a luxury product. Also inadvisable: using the same brand to appeal to markedly different psychographic groups.

Protect the Brand[63]

This seems to be a particular challenge for large companies. They need to do what I'll call:

Melt down the cannon, so you can't use it on your brand!

A few poster children among the major companies that have done this to themselves are Johnson & Johnson,[64] Volkswagen, and Wells Fargo.

Instead, you need to create effective ways to manage brand risk. Your business will make mistakes that impact your brand. Many are minor, and you can recover from them, such as when a celebrity spokesperson becomes controversial, or a product quality slip-up that's quickly corrected. But there are several, cardinal, brand sins:

- Having the same quality problem repeatedly, so customers figure that you don't believe fixing it is important,[52] or you're not acting out of prudence to protect them[53,54]—Johnson & Johnson.

- Dissing your customers (treating them like they're not important)—Dell (see Chapter 2).

- Making products that are not designed to last—HP (also in Chapter 2).

- Cheating customers (Wells Fargo—charging them for services they didn't ask for), and Volkswagen (selling cars that polluted more than the environmental tests on them indicated).

- Appearing slippery. I ordered a laptop computer case online; one made by a major manufacturer. At right is a portion of its (unreadable) guarantee. Would it make you want to buy from this company again?

Some of these stem from carelessness; others are deliberate. Forgivable? The sinners like to think so. The reality is that the propensity to forgive varies by person, by the mistake's severity, and whether it was deliberate.

A cardinal-sin perpetrator is much more likely to experience a lasting negative impact on their brand (and sales) than a business that just made an honest mistake, quickly owned up to it, then made things right for the affected customers. So how can you manage this? Say *NO* to:

- Doing things that matter on the cheap.
- Uses of the brand that it isn't really about, and that would dilute the brand's image. Examples would be Tiffany's selling costume jewelry, or Walmart selling ultra-high-end audio equipment.
- Lying to customers.
- Cover-ups.

And make sure that:

- Effective processes are in place to *manage* the delivery of the products and services the brand represents.
- The culture of your business values the sanctity of your brand above all else. As the leader, maintaining the brand in this paramount position is your leadership imperative, and unending reinforcement role.

Creating Success With a Brand

- Finally, for a brand, especially a premium brand, to succeed long term it must innovate (stay interesting), stay relevant, and represent a powerful promise.[65,66,67]
- Small or startup businesses should pursue the brand-management method we described in Developing a Brand earlier.

Discontinuing an Offering

Deciding to no longer offer something based on a newly emerged safety consideration is one thing. That's about managing the brand risk.

But deciding to discontinue something that some, or a lot of, customers highly value, based on its economics, could, and often does, fail to take into account the negative impact on the corporate brand, and the other revenue it drives.

Discontinuing an offering, a product, service, or even a TV show, can damage that brand, creating protests, bad publicity, and most important, a feeling that something that you came to love, or need, was not considered important enough by its provider that they would continue providing it. The anger that last one brings, springing from, well, "That business doesn't care about me!", can drive a stake through the sales of all of the business's other offerings. It's also been known to create an extremely emotional response, and we now live in the age of damaging viral campaigns. A good example is Johnson & Johnson's discontinued Rembrandt's Gentle White toothpaste, which was reported to be the only economical treatment for the pain of canker sores.[68]

What can a business do with a product they want to discontinue? They can sell it to a company with a less burdensome cost structure, better marketing, wider market reach, or just more attention to devote to the product. An example is Icy Hot, a topical pain treatment that's the only thing that works for some people. It was successfully revived, some years ago, under new ownership.

In some cases, it might also be possible to license the product, or just its formulation.

The Brand Upside

Near term, the upside has to be *the experience* you can provide to make your brand as engaging as possible. It's not simply about the product or service. It's also about all that you can associate with that product or service to create "gotta have it!", as we recounted for Big Ass Fans.

Longer term, from months to a year or more, the brand-upside opportunity goes beyond enhancing the experience. It begins with a serious look at the product or service offered, and folds in the improvements that can be made to both the experience and the promise, to create a more powerful brand.

We'll work on all of that in the *Tapping Your Upside* exercise up next.

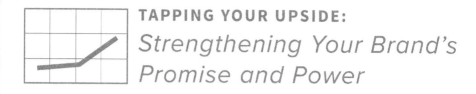

TAPPING YOUR UPSIDE:

Strengthening Your Brand's Promise and Power

1. Is there room in your market(s) for a more purchase-compelling

   brand? _____

2. What would its promise be? In other words, what is **the want** your promise could fulfill? It has to be something that would get the most people to say, *"That's for me!"* One way to tackle it is to list the positive and negative characteristics that your brand and competing brands have now.

Brand Characteristic	Your brand (+ -)	Competitors' (+ -)

3. The positive characteristics you want, but don't yet have.

   _____

   _____

   _____

3. The negatives you'd like to get rid of.

_____

_____

_____

4. Add to that your opportunities to seize and defend an attractive unoccupied position in the prospect's mind. (There will be more on this in Chapter 9, Hungry Markets.)

_____

_____

_____

5. How can your brand make a new and more powerful *emotional connection* with present and potential customers?

It's not mainly about goosing the ad budget, although that, too, might prove worth doing. Highly contagious word-of-mouth (buzz) is more effective, and way cheaper. How will you create that word-of-mouth in the real and digital worlds?

Your messages need to spring from an emotionally engaging *story* about the value you provide, and the values you stand for: a powerful brand essence, like the dive-suit company's.

Here are two more examples, from a corporate brand that seriously invests in creating goodwill, Procter & Gamble. One is its series of ads honoring the mothers of Olympians.[69] The ad's key: appreciation—for those who sometimes don't have their efforts and sacrifices adequately recognized. And every mother is a potential P&G customer. The strength of the emotional connection forged by these ads far surpasses that of most branding campaigns. Another example is P&G's suite of disaster-relief programs involving Tide, Duracell, and its pet-food brands. In March 2019, the *Tide Loads of Hope* mobile laundry vehicles provided free full-service laundry services to Nebraska residents directly impacted by the flooding there. Residents could bring up to two loads of clothes per household to be washed, dried, and folded free of charge. P&G also distributed free personal care and cleaning kits to those in affected neighborhoods and areas.[70,71]

Both campaigns demonstrate that the company's heart is in the right place—it cares—and with its disaster-relief efforts, P&G assumes the responsibility to help where and how it can. And each effort translates into "These guys 'get' me, they're on my side, and I'll buy from them." Even better, "These guys helped me; I'll help them back!"

6. *Why* should you create a bigger promise? _____

_____

_____

_____

7. With all that as context, your potential promises are:

_____

_____

_____

_____

_____

8. **For each potential promise:**

    a. Can you actually create offerings that will deliver on that promise?

    _____

    b. How likely is your new improved promise to work in the marketplace?

    _____

    c. Is it credible? _____

    d. Is it emotionally engaging for the buyer? _____

    e. Will it make your offering(s) stand out? _____

    f. How long will the effect of the new brand promise last? That is,

    will you be able to defend your brand's bond with that promise over

    the long term? _____

    g. What is establishing the new promise likely to cost? _____

    h. How much overall effort will it take? _____

9. **From that assessment, which promise(s) will you work on?**

    _____

    _____

    _____

10. **By what percentage range will your more purchase-compelling
    brand move the revenue needle?** _____

    (For both revenue and profit, below, include the increases that can
    come from being chosen by more customers for the first time and those
    that come from being chosen by all customers more often.)

    Revenue _____ Profit _____

11. **What will the profitability-increase-percentage range be?**

_____

12. *How* can your business create those increases *without* spending a
    lot of money?

_____

_____

_____

_____

13. **How will you know if the chosen changes are creating the result
    you want?**

_____

_____

_____

_____

(After all, if you get this completely right on the first try, you'll have
been both good, and lucky! So, watch closely and course-correct.)

14. **How will you keep an eye on whether your new brand promise is
    maintaining its purchase-compelling edge over time?**

_____

_____

UPSIDE ELEMENT ASSESSMENT: MORE POWERFUL BRANDS

Please enter your estimates for the *overall* gains and challenges you expect to derive from your enhanced brand in the corresponding row on the book's Upside Element Assessment Sheet, just before the last page.

Now that you've worked over both your value proposition and your brand for one offering, we'll next turn to how to *communicate* the results, so that people "get" them, and buy.

Chapter 5

Creating "I Want That!" and Triggering the Sale

Why This Is important...

One of the hard-to-recognize ways that people set their businesses up to fail is to have advertising that's less effective than it could be, sometimes accompanied by sub-par marketing and sales processes. Failing to get across to prospects *why* they should buy your product or service leads to substantial lost revenue, and its attendant profits. Unlike most costs, you can't see this money flying right past your business. You might not even notice it, much less do anything about it.

Unless, that is, you compare how your offering is selling versus its competitors. And unless you know whether your offering is taking an increasing share of the total market, month over month. When your offering is losing share, or it is simply not up to your reasonable expectations, next up is digging into why. It could be:

- How your value proposition stacks up to your prospect's alternatives. Does it need to be strengthened (Chapter 3)?

- Does your company have supply or demand-chain problems: "It's backordered," or "That dress is so last month," because of an inability to react quickly enough to a supplier hiccup or the winds of fashion?

- Do you have marketing or sales-force-related issues, or are there problems with the relationship and processes between the two organizations?

- Are your ads not reaching the right people? Do you have:

  - A clear picture of who your target prospect is?

  - A cost-effective way to get good prospects to raise their hands—one that actually accomplishes it?

- Is your prospect reacting to your message in one of these ways?

  - "I don't *care* about this. It's not relevant."

  - "I don't *understand* what's in it for me." (Confusion: the silent sales killer. Those who don't "get" why they should buy, don't buy.)

  - "I don't have a compelling *reason* to buy what you offer."

  - "It doesn't *excite* me." (Your message is weak. Have you clearly and in a short sentence or two spelled out how your product or service will benefit the prospect?)

If not, before you even try to fix it, do you know *why* people should buy what you offer, deep down? Really? What psychological or real-world reward do they get from doing so? And are you sure you've helped them to really "get" why they should buy, at the emotional level? (More on this later in the chapter...)

- Or is your prospect's sense:

  - "I don't like your *tone of voice*." (This means how you speak to me in print, television, or media ads, for example. You can be terminally annoying, sarcastic, smart aleck-y, condescending, superior, or insensitive, in any of these mediums.)

  - "I don't *like* what you or your business stands for." (I disagree with your position on gay rights, or the environment.)

  - I think you have a boring brand.

- Could be, too, that your prospects are not even *aware* of your message.

- Your brand is *wounded*—you have a history of quality issues or poor service, so I won't buy from you.

- Your business is not viewed as *trustworthy*.
- Are your messages appearing in the best places on a cost-effectiveness basis?
  - Are you exploiting all of the free and low-cost ways to get your message viewed by prospective buyers: articles? PR? social media? co-op advertising?
  - Could your offering serve as an element of an entertaining or educational online video, like BlendTec's famous "Will it blend?" series on YouTube?
  - Should your prospects be able to say that they see your message everywhere? Like Rosetta Stone.

How to Create "I Want That!"

At root, you want to create sales. Marketing comes first. After all, your product's value proposition and its marketing message have to overcome the prospect's often strong desire to hang onto their hard-earned money. Boiled way down…

> Marketing is getting your prospect to say, "Ooooo!"

Before that can happen, you need a message that will stir desire for what's offered in the prospect's heart. That is, your message must help *create demand*. Well, just *how* do you do that?

Creating a Compelling Message—Inducing *Want*

Below is a list of what Richard Ott, author of *Creating Demand*,[72] calls the Power Wants. Which of them can create demand for what you offer?

- Emotional stimulation, including excitement, love, laughter, and attraction.
- Psychological relief (from fear, pain, stress, anxiety, tension, anger, etc.). Take responsibility for providing that relief, e.g., lifetime guarantees.

- Higher status—prestige. The desire for admiration and respect is universal.

- What others want. This is also known as *demand contagion*. Can you create a buying frenzy, like those behind the "gotta have it" holiday toy every year?

Which of these can create the most demand for what you offer? And is there another that comes close?

Creating Attractors[73] From the Attributes of Your Offering

Attractors are what can make people comfortable with what you offer, or draw them toward it. *Examples:*

- Limited supply: Scarcity implies high demand in many people's minds. Recall, fondly or not, that those who played hard to get in their teenage years were often the most sought-after.

- Limited time: An ad that says "Sale ends Saturday. Don't miss out!" can get people to act.

- Distance: Appeal can be the lure of faraway lands, or proximity, "We're right around the corner!"

- Timeliness: An ad budget spent on frequent small ads, rather than fewer big ones could be more likely to trigger interest at the time the prospect happens to need what you offer.

- A deal on something expensive: A high price attracts by creating the perception of value. And offering a limited-time discount from that high price "for our best customers" can trigger a purchase. This approach is best used for infrequent purchases.

Now to the heart of the matter…

Creating "I Want That!"

A successful pitch…

> *In October 1917, during World War I, the U.S. government began to offer life insurance to those in the U.S. Army. The arrangement was that the soldiers would have to pay the low-cost premiums out of their own pockets—their service pay.*
>
> *As it happened, an Army platoon in Europe was preparing for an impending engagement with the enemy. Their newly minted lieutenant was trying to interest the soldiers in buying the life insurance, but the men were reluctant to part with the money they could spend on cigarettes, beer, or a visit to town.*
>
> *The lieutenant's pitch: "Look, men, if you buy the insurance and something happens to you out here, at least your families will get some money as compensation."*
>
> *It wasn't working.*
>
> *The platoon's sergeant, a Brooklyn native, asked the lieutenant if he could give it a try. His pitch: "Listen, you guys, it's like dis. If you buy the insurance, and you get killed, then the government, dey gotta pay. If you don't buy the insurance, and you get killed, then the government, dey don't gotta pay. "Now who d'ya think they're gonna send out there first?"*

How many of the soldiers bought the insurance?

They *all* did.

What did the sergeant do?

He "found the *buy* button" and pushed it. (Actually, he invited them to buy. More about this later.)

Which is harder: finding that button, or pushing it?

Clearly, it's finding. That's far from impossible, as we'll see. Engaging the prospect must start with *triggering an emotion*. The sergeant triggered the men's fear. Even in a business-to-business context, emotion plays a deciding role, like the '70s saying that "Nobody ever got fired for buying IBM." Other triggers:

- A picture of mouthwatering food.
- The knowledge that your loved ones will be protected—peace of mind, at least in theory, brought to you by the life-insurance industry.
- Ways to get ahead.

Without emotion, your pitch will be less convincing and compelling. This is why price-based pitches don't create loyalty, at least for people who haven't dedicated their lives (and their egos) to getting a good deal.

Often, it's the strongest emotion you can evoke that will wind up being the button. But you need to test this, as we'll describe below. For sparks that can help you find "the button," revisit the list of wants and needs that we laid out in the previous chapter, and work through this chapter's *Tapping Your Upside* exercise.

Once you have found what you believe to be the emotional reason for buying, you need to get it across—just right. Like the sergeant. *How* you say why people should buy matters—a lot.

Making the Message Believable

Sometimes you need to make the obvious (to you) value of what you offer explicit (to the customer). You might, for example, need to document the value your offering can provide. You can do this with stories (more on this in a moment), white papers, and case histories, or you can give customers value calculators or apps they can use to figure their own benefits, rewards, or savings.

Ways to Present Your Message

Invite, don't push. In Wharton marketing professor Dr. Jonah Berger's revealing new book, *The Catalyst*,[74] he explains why *telling* someone what to do, as ads often do, doesn't work. Even if what you tell them is in their own interest, and they know that, they still won't do it. They won't because everyone has a very strong need to show that they're their own person—that *they* are in control, not the advertiser. Not accepting what you're pitching is their way of showing it. They want to *decide for themselves* what to do. (You might have also seen this behavior in your kids.)

Instead, invite people to *decide for themselves.* The sergeant's approach was a bit like that, and the lieutenant's more like most ads.

Tell stories—that *engage.* The right story will create a "You had me at..." response. Here's what this means. When President Obama first met (now Senator) Elizabeth Warren, he mentioned that he wanted to talk with her later about predatory lending. When they sat down to discuss it, the President began to sell her on the role he wanted her to undertake. She interrupted him with the words, "You had me at predatory lending." (In other words, she shared his position on the issue, and his passion.)

Another wonderful example of this was Fiat-Chrysler's RAM trucks' "So God made a farmer" 2-minute TV ad shown during the 2013 Superbowl. The ad recited Paul Harvey's 1978 speech to the National Future Farmers of America convention on many of the trying and difficult things that farmers have to do, just to get through their days. It made vivid their challenges and through words and pictures brought about enormous respect for what they do. Only in the last few seconds was the truck shown. The you-had-me-at element is the respect for the farmer. The ad was viewed 18 million times on YouTube in the ensuing 10 days.[75] Seemingly, Fiat-Chrysler "got it." And presumably, any tradesperson who uses a truck in his or her work would feel the same. So the choice of which truck to buy was Dodge's to lose. And they did, shifting from heartfelt connections to macho: "Guts, glory, RAM!" So what!

Here are two more, from New York City–area radio ads...

Yet another respect example:

- First Republic Bank. In a low-key, warm tone of voice, various narrators tell of the welcoming environment in the branches (the smell of fresh-baked cookies), and personal service (tales about handling everything in a "crisis" situation). Tagline: "At First Republic, it's a privilege to serve you." It comes across as credible.

Offering *caring help* for those dealing with serious illness.

- Memorial Sloan Kettering Cancer Center. Again in a warm, caring voice, a narrator, or the patient, relates stories about successful cancer treatments, for cases in which, at the outset, hope was not high. "Where you're treated first can make all the difference."

Use pictures and illustrations. Here's another asking-a-question example of finding the button, this one from an ad agency. Designed to appeal to men, it's a Valentine's Day ad for a jewelry store. It shows a picture of a young woman's slender neck, wearing a lovely necklace. Its words: "Would this look better on your Valentine than a box of chocolates?" Emotional appeal (to the buyer—besides humor): I'd rather that my Valentine not be snorking down that whole box.

Two more "question-form" examples of getting the emotional benefit across:

- Years ago, I was standing on the street in downtown Manhattan during a cold January rainstorm when a bus went by. The large poster on its side showed a picture of a young woman happily swimming in the waters of the Caribbean. An ad for the Club Med, it asked: "Why be cold and wet, when you can be warm and wet?" Why indeed?
- A picture of cookies, or cereal, or a pie... "Got milk?"

Other categories in which pictures can instantly create "I want that!" include: exotic or interesting places to visit, stylish clothing and accessories, luxury homes, and flashy cars.

Use videos. Having real people talk about the benefits of a product or service can dramatically increase sales—authenticity sells. This is why the often less-than-polished feel of YouTube can be effective. People don't like to feel like they're being pitched. But people *love* to buy.

Now We're Ready to Push the "Buy" Button

A (very) short course on advertising…

- People often put a high degree of faith in their own opinions. Can you help them form those opinions?

- Every effort to sell creates corresponding resistance on the part of the prospect. It's much more powerful to *draw* people toward what you offer than to push the offering at them. Imagine the prospect as a lily pad, and your offering as something that you're trying to move toward that pad. Every time you push your offering closer, the lily pad moves away. Rather, you want to get people interested in what you offer, *for their own reasons.*

- "Free" or "Two for one" cheapen what you offer. Instead, you can give the prospect a bonus or incentive they'll value.

- Be very clear about who you're talking to, what they're interested in, and might well be curious about. Because it's all about the prospect and their wants and needs. Much advertising money is wasted because of a business's selfish desires: "buy!" Instead, consider your *customers'* desires, and they'll be more likely to flock to your offering.

- Projection. Also known as "envisioning," it's the brain's favorite sport! You could call it fantasy ownership of what you offer. Use it in your ads to help people vividly imagine the emotional rewards your offering will bring them. Envisioning is a powerful motivator—a "self-persuader." And using it often costs no more than not using it. Imagine, that you're behind the wheel…

Your Ad

90% of your ad should consist of emotional appeal. And it should come first, followed by 10% logic, that the prospect's "left brain" can use to justify the purchase. The nearby after-work watering hole might use, "When you've earned the right to celebrate!"

Keep the logic line succinct and have it *justify* the emotion. Also, make it *easy to repeat.*

The Ad Itself

We're going to begin with a number of bad ads, so you can avoid the same mistakes. Most bad ads are, in essence, a gorilla pounding his chest, proclaiming, "We are great, big, important, etc. Buy our stuff." But there are other ways to be *ineffective*.

- Funny; not persuasive: Countless beer commericals.
- Annoying: We've all heard "the screaming car-dealer jerk" on the radio—until we quickly turned it off. Why does the client bother, or pay for the ad?

We'll illustrate some of the principles that go into creating good ads by tapping into the wisdom of the late Tom Collins, a founder of the ad agency Rapp Collins. For years Collins wrote a wonderful column in *Direct* magazine called "The Makeover Maven." The print columns' pages are too large to reproduce here, but *Chief Marketer* (*Direct's* successor) has graciously allowed me to post the Makeover Maven columns below on this book's website, theupsidewithinreach.com/CollinsMakeovers. Each ad is worthy of close study—the lessons are timeless, and priceless:

- Unpersuasive. Nov. '04—"Too Vague, Too Unpersuasive"
- Beautiful and unconvincing. July '06-Mandarin Oriental—"'So Where's the Copy?'"
- Incomprehensible. Aug. '06—"Open for Business? Not Quite"
- Just not clear. May 15 '05—"Omni Ad Doesn't Visualize or Address Prospects"
- Irrelevant. Sept. '06—"Too Cool"
- Mistargeted. June 2007—"Art Wins Over Copy Again"
- Buried message. Sept. 1, 2005—"New Tylenol product, all but hidden."

Here's another failing: unreadable small print. Some time ago, I saw an IBM *Info Week* ad with the text on the bottom in small white-on-yellow type. Small or unreadable type engenders suspicion, unless it's just trademark or copyright notices. Is suspicion what you want?

A Good Ad

From American Girl, it arrived as a single-sheet, double-sided, full-color flyer in *The New York Times* on an early-summer morning. It pictured an 8-year-old girl with her mother and grandmother, each nicely dressed, and the girl visibly excited. The text announced, *"American Girl events in New York this summer!"* Among the options: a visit to The New York City Ballet, a Broadway show, and others. Any girl or woman, and anyone who has raised or been a grandparent to a girl, will be moved emotionally by the ad.*

Girl: I want to do that! Can we, please?

The mother and grandmother are thinking, "What if we could give her that, and make a memory for all of us?"

The ad evokes a powerful "That's for me!" emotional response. Bright pink, it instantly captures the attention of those who'd be interested. The flyer also uses curiosity to engage, getting the readers interested in choosing which of the activity choices they want to do together.

The benefit of buying—creating a lasting memory—is important.

Many good ads:
- Use personality.
- Tell stories.
- Use pictures.
- Evoke strong emotions.

Making Your Ad Convincing...

- As mentioned earlier, invite, don't push.
- Use emotion. Stress benefits, not features, and hit on *the implications of the benefits:* The phrase, "So that..." or simply "So...", is the single best way to do this. "This cell phone has a battery that will power it for 24 hours or more, no matter what you're using your phone for, *so that* it won't go dead when you need it, and you won't have to find a place to recharge it during the day."

---

* Because American Girl, understandably, did not secure permission for the models in their ad to be used outside that context, I'm unable to show the ad itself.

- Deal with weaknesses and potential objections *up front*, i.e., in the ad. Otherwise people's natural reticence or suspicions will create reluctance to buy what you offer.

- Eliminate the prospect's risk. Offer a guarantee; the longer the better.

- Demonstrate what you offer in a way that's convenient for the prospect, like an online video.

- Be clear, and specific.

- Avoid puffery or words that don't really express anything.

- Be as complete as necessary to close the sale, but don't "keep talking past the close" by including the extraneous.

- Use an effective call to action.[76] That is, try to actually get the prospect to do what you want them to do.

- If you choose to get "professional help" (an ad agency), good luck in finding it, as most yield disappointing results. Instead, try to feel the prospect's pain, and address it in your ad.

Spreading Your (Now Powerful) Message Far and Wide— So You Boost Sales

In his earlier book, *Contagious, Why Things Catch On,*[77] Wharton professor Jonah Berger explains what causes certain products or services to be talked about more than others.

Mainly, their marketing messages use emotion, which motivate people to tell someone else about the product or service. This is best done using a story, not a testimonial (which can be viewed skeptically). Berger explains that it's harder to disagree with a story than an advertising claim, because humans don't have the cognitive resources to do so. In essence, your engaging story acts as a "bottle" containing your message.

Even better, Berger recommends trying to embed your products or services in the stories people want to tell; that is, a person can't tell the story without mentioning the product. Berger's example is the blender-maker Blendtec's "Will it blend?" video series, which demonstrates the power of their blender to shred, well, most anything.

Ways to Spread Your Message...

The table below suggests some of the ways to spread your message. Start by finding the columns headed by what you're trying to do, then look at the row headings where there's a Y (highly appropriate) or y (less so) in those columns. Also, bear in mind that the table's entries are generalities, and might not apply in every situation.

Ways to Deliver Your Message (Y=Yes, y=Yes, but less so)									
	Good For							None (0), Low, Medium, & High	
Method	Generating Leads	Building Relationships	Making the Sale	Establishing Credibility	Explaining/ Demonstrating	Reaching a Targeted Niche	Reaching a Broad Audience	Cost	Effectiveness
Direct mail-print	Y		Y			Y		H	L
Classified print ad	Y							M	L-M
Display print ad *							Y	H	L
Direct sale print ad †			Y		Y	Y	Y	H	L-M
Co-op ads	Y		Y	Y		Y	Y	L-M	varies
Print newsletter	Y	Y	Y	Y	Y	Y		M	varies
Article, whitepaper	Y			Y	Y	Y		0-VL	M-H
Talks, speeches	Y	Y	Y	Y	Y	Y	y	0-VL	M-H
PR campaign	Y			y			Y	L	VL-L

Ways to Deliver Your Message (Y=Yes, y=Yes, but less so)									
	Good For							None (0), Low, Medium, & High	
Method	Generating Leads	Building Relationships	Making the Sale	Establishing Credibility	Explaining/ Demonstrating	Reaching a Targeted Niche	Reaching a Broad Audience	Cost	Effectiveness
Emailed sales pitch (opt-in)			Y	varies	varies	Y	Y	0-VL	L
Email newsletter		Y	Y	Y	Y	Y		0-VL	varies
A blog	Y	Y	Y	Y	Y	Y		0	varies
Online pay per click	Y		Y	varies	varies	Y		M	varies
Online display ad	Y							VL	VL
Social media mention	y	y	y		y	Y	Y	0-VL	varies
Word of mouth (buzz)[78]	y		y	Y		Y	Y	0-VL	varies
Mobile ad	Y		Y	varies				L	M
TV ad	Y	Y	Y		Y		Y	VH	VL
TV Infomercial			Y		Y		Y	H	L
Videos (YouTube, etc.)	Y	y	Y	Y	Y	Y	Y	0-L	varies
Radio ad	Y	Y	Y	Y			y	M	VL

| | Ways to Deliver Your Message (Y=Yes, y=Yes, but less so) | | | | | | | | |
| | **Good For** | | | | | | | **None (0), Low, Medium, & High** | |
Method	Generating Leads	Building Relationships	Making the Sale	Establishing Credibility	Explaining/ Demonstrating	Reaching a Targeted Niche	Reaching a Broad Audience	Cost	Effectiveness
Trade shows	Y		y				y	H	L
Display (buses, airports, outdoor)	Y				y		y	M	L

* This ad form consists of an image, a graphic, and only a little type. It might contain a web address. Used for brand ads.

† These ads are type heavy. They're designed to sell what's on the page, and always include "Here's how to order!"

A Word About Brand Advertising...

These ads attempt to foster awareness of a brand: name recognition; or to burnish the brand's image. The focus is long-term improvement in the perception of the business or the offering associated with the brand. Creating an immediate sale is not the goal.

So why bother? Good question. It might have a positive effect on how people feel about, or think about, the brand. Whether it boosts sales can be hard to answer.

The clear beneficiaries of brand ads are the ad agency and the media in which they place the ads. The agencies will roll out their shiniest "baffle them with BS" metrics in an attempt to demonstrate the value brand ads can create from your precious ad budget. Whether you should bite on this apple is best decided based on the specifics of your business's situation.

Measuring Effectiveness

With many of the newer online forms of advertising, it's possible to measure your ad's effectiveness in near real time, using, for example, Google Adwords and Analytics.

You can use tools like these *to find the buy button!* That is, test your messages online, then try out the message that shows the strongest results in the other advertising media you use.

Triggering the Sale

There's a difference between hearing about, coming to want, and actually buying a product.

Unless the existing product breaks, or gets outgrown, damaged, etc., creating an immediate need—turning "I want that!" into an actual buy—requires something more: an activator. *Examples:*

- A price drop. Especially one for a limited time—a "one-day-only sale."

- Real or perceived scarcity, without an accompanying price drop: limited supply—"When they're gone, they're gone."

- Greater convenience. A store that's open for more hours, or one that's closer.

- A celebrity, an effective pitch person, or a friendly salesperson at the door (Avon), or at a party (Tupperware, Pampered Chef).

- An ad's *emotional resonance*. This can, and often does, trigger the impulse to buy, now. Can your offering's appearance, features, or performance make the prospect be *swept* away by what you offer, by using a TV or YouTube ad to demonstrate the offering in action, or by providing a sample, test drive, or free trial?

"New and improved" can sometimes work as an activator, but it's overused, and weak.

For More...

Appendix A presents a list of the best marketing books this author knows of (I've read each of them). They cover: the field of marketing in general, message making, and presenting your message, i.e., advertising.

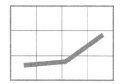

TAPPING YOUR UPSIDE:

Creating I Want That! and Triggering the Sale

In this exercise, we're going to work on increasing the sales of one of your offerings. Specifically, we'll work on how persuasively its value is communicated. You could, for purposes of this exercise, just pick an offering that's not meeting expectations, or choose one at random. However, so that the outcome of this exercise makes the biggest improvement in your results, here's a more fruitful but involved way to choose the offering to work on.

1. On a separate sheet, for each of your significant offerings:

What would be the maximum increase in sales you could hope for, if your marketing message was as persuasive and pervasive as it could be? You can also base the choice of offering on profitability instead of revenue, recognizing that profitability can rise significantly once the offering's fixed costs are covered by improved sales. Finally, you could choose based on the possible increase in business value (a weighted blend of revenue and profit improvements—we'll talk more about this in Chapter 14.)

Which offering did you choose?

_____

2. Message making:

For the offering you chose, don't put this in the hands of an ad agency, unless the individuals you work with there are among the top 1% of all advertising professionals (the "Got milk?" level). That means that they're creative, they have ears, and they routinely use them to really listen, and understand what your offering is all about, and the value it provides.

This author's experience is that most agency-created advertising isn't very effective. It's much more important that you and your team come to understand the most powerful *emotional reason* that people buy what you offer.

The do-it-yourselves approach will also make your product-or-service-design people exquisitely attuned to bringing that reason to full flower in your offering. And, it will juice the rest of your people to know what the offering is *really* about. And last, but far from least, long term, it could make your offering sell much better.

Now, to the "why buy?" The reason. List all the emotional reasons, wants and desires, why a prospect would buy the offering you selected above. What are *its emotional benefits* for that person? List them in the left column below, then rate them in terms of:

- Emotional impact (raw power to persuade)
- Believability
- Distinctiveness (with respect to the offering's competition)

Reason	Emotional Impact	Believability	Distinctiveness

Then pick a reason, or a handful, to cast into messages (next step, below) and test.

3. Phrase your reasons in the most engaging way you can:

How can you best get your emotional benefit across, i.e., how should you *say* it? Can you put it like the sergeant did? There, the emotional message was, "boost your chances of staying alive." But *the way* the sergeant put it made the soldiers "get" what was in it for each of them. It *engaged* them.

And notice that the sergeant's words weren't a claim. They were a question. One that laid out the likelihood of staying alive in clear, simple terms.

So now it's your turn to portray and/or say the emotional benefit your offering provides. Write down as many different ways as you can think of to get it across. No claims. Questions, pictures, simple hand drawings[79] and one-paragraph stories are fine. Just write/draw; don't fuss with the words, don't ponder—let it flow. And don't stop until you have at least 10 ways to say it.

If you do this in a group context, make it at least 10 ways each (no peeking). Let the results sit, over several days of showers, shaving, or putting on makeup. Jot down all of the tweaks and additional inspirations that come to you. Test a few of the best, online. Pick one. What is it?

_____

_____

_____

4. Triggers (buy activators). Do you need one? _____

What will you use:

Some type of limited-time sale? _____

Scarcity? _____

Creating buzz to seed a demand frenzy? _____

5. How will you test to choose your activator?

_____

_____

_____

6. Which media formats will you use for your messages and triggers:

   Print? _____ E-mail? _____

   Pay-per-click? _____

   Online videos/screencasts? _____

   Radio? _____ TV? _____

   Social media? _____ Something else? _____

7. It might be that your strongest message and your strongest trigger should be paired in the ads you choose to use from here on. But it's possible that they won't work that well together, so consider that, too. Obviously, you should use the strongest *combination.*

8. Having done the above, what is the expected percentage increase in revenue?

_____

9. In view of that, what do you need to change about your sales and marketing, if anything?

_____

_____

_____

_____

_____

_____

_____

UPSIDE ELEMENT ASSESSMENT: CREATING "I WANT THAT!"

Please enter your estimates for the *overall* gains and challenges you expect to derive from your enhanced advertising in the corresponding row on the book's Upside Element Assessment Sheet, just before the last page.

Chapter 6

Pricing Perspectives With Legs

Pricing: a rocket to the stars, or a flameout into the ocean. Pricing *is* a fast-acting, quick-to-implement, high-potential-upside approach to boosting results. But not in the way it's often thought of, as we'll explain after a bit of background.

Pricing's Profitability Leverage

Your business could be leaving substantial profits on the table by not charging enough. Or you might be losing sales to competitors over price. Revenue, average price multiplied by unit sales volume, has to cover both your fixed and variable (per-sale) costs. What's left is profit.

Below is a simple break-even curve for the maker of a $10 cell-phone case. Its fixed costs are $100,000 and the product's unit costs are $7.50. If the business sells 400,000 or more cases, it's profitable. The more units (phone cases) sold, the more profit—the vertical space between the dashed and the dotted lines (to the right of breakeven).

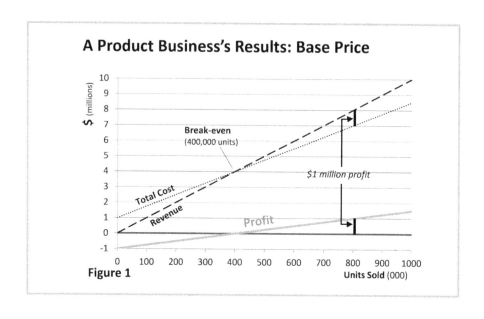

A Product Business's Results: Base Price

Figure 1

At the $10 price, it has to sell 800,000 units to make a $1 million profit (Figure 1).

At the 5% higher price (Figure 2), it can make $1 million without having to sell as many units (only about 667,000), *if* it can get enough people to buy them at the new, higher price. Overall profits could rise, if customers accept the increase and the number of units sold doesn't fall much. Or, profits could fall, if

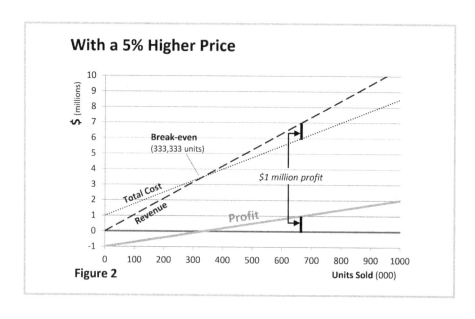

With a 5% Higher Price

Figure 2

price-sensitive customers buy a competitor's case, causing the number of units sold to drop more dramatically. Obviously, one question is how total profits compare in the two cases—will the higher price lead to sales of $1 million or more? Or not?

At the 5% lower price (Figure 3), revenue growth is shallower, so to get to that million-dollar profit, the business will have to sell not 667,000, not 800,000, but a million units. Is there enough demand, even at the lower price, to make that a reality? That is, regardless of price, do that many people *need* what the business offers? And what will happen to the business if it doesn't reach that volume?

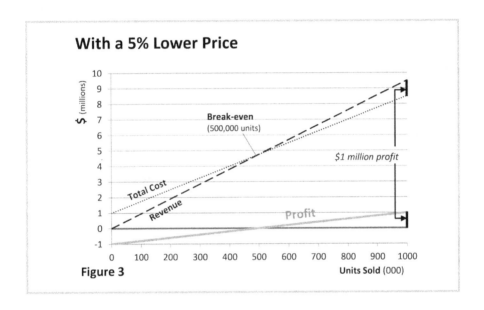

Figure 3

It's necessary to understand the size of the market: how many units of what you sell will be bought, in total, from all of the companies that sell them?

Essential, too, is knowing how sensitive your sales volume is to price. You might be able to conduct price tests in various local markets to determine this, then apply the results more widely, so you don't have to choose your prices blindfolded.

One more, huge, point—*leverage:* small price changes often create much larger changes in profits. A 1% price drop can cause a 2.5–23.7% decrease in operating profit[80], while a 1% price increase can bring an 11% increase in operating profit.[81,82]

A deeper question is *why* you would want to go with one price or the other from a customer-relationship, strategic-goal, or brand-promise perspective. That is, what are your goals for market share? For market position?

There might be a sweet spot, an ideal price, but as we'll see, pricing should not be about finding one ideal price. *Having a single-best-price is too narrow an approach to ever maximize revenue,* as made clear in Rafi Mohammed's wonderful and highly recommended book, *The Art of Pricing.*[83]

Its key concept: setting one price for a product or service, however well chosen, will *never* maximize revenue, because there are substantial numbers of prospects who want to pay less, or who can't pay enough. They won't buy at that one "ideal" price.

Interestingly, some buyers seek the prestige of paying a higher price than you'd set, just to show themselves and others that they can. They're really buying two things: your product or service and a dollop of ego gratification.

To capture ALL of the potential revenue that's out there, it's necessary to shift how you think about pricing to what Dr. Mohammed calls the *multi-price mindset.* It allows you to profit from as many customers as possible, although you won't get the same margins from each. But if overall profits come in several times higher, so what?

This works because, as Dr. Mohammed says, "Customers place different values on the same product." His insight grew out of watching an auction. Of the bidders able to afford the auctioned item, only one person won it, the person to whom its value seemed highest.

But you don't want to sell only one of your product. You want to sell it to *everyone* who values it, even though the exact value that all of those people place on the product varies.

Being adept at pricing means *creating a series of strategies* that serve the range of customers who have those different valuations for your offering: strategies that capture the available profits from them. So pricing is not about coming up with a single best price. It's about coming up with that set of strategies. Among them:

- Using a meaningful, but prudent discount to motivate more buyers to purchase a still nicely profitable offering. The unit-volume increase can more than make up for the discount.

- Offering customers low-interest financing.

- Changing the sales-channel emphasis, by analyzing the unit profitability of each channel, then figuring out how to increase the volume sold through the higher-margin channels.

In more recent (also highly recommended) work,[84] Dr. Mohammed describes an approach to crafting product offerings that he calls "Good-Better-Best." The idea is to revamp an existing, successful offering (the "better one") by removing one or more features that most would want, and offer what results at a notably lower price (the "good" offering). Some prospective (new) buyers will find that to be good enough. He also suggests adding features to the better offering to appeal to those for whom price is not their main criterion. Instead, it's how the offering performs, and how it's perceived: what he calls the "best" offering. In his article, Dr. Mohammed describes how to use what he calls "fences" to keep buyers from trading down, an important consideration in keeping revenue from tanking, rather than growing.

Pricing Approaches

Here are Dr. Mohammed's three approaches to maximizing profits through pricing.

Differential Pricing

- Selling your product to different customers at different prices. Some Caribbean resorts used local newspapers to advertise different room rates in different cities during the winter months. The colder cities, whose residents were more desperate to escape the cold, were offered higher rates.[85] Is this fair? Arguably, in the colder cities, the level of suffering from the cold was higher, making people more desperate to get some relief. That is, a trip to the resort had a higher value to those who were absolutely miserable.

- Offering senior and student discounts.

Dr. Mohammed explains seven techniques that allow you to uncover what various people are willing to pay and, based on that, to offer it to them, discreetly, so they don't feel that someone else got a better deal. Among them is the concept of hurdles. Simply, make the prospect do something, such as clipping a coupon, or registering on a website, to get a discounted price.

Versioning

Offerings:

- Different quality levels: such as Johnnie Walker scotch (red, black, gold, and blue label), American Express cards (green, gold, platinum, etc.), and hotel rooms (single, double, presidential suite).

- Charging more for greater convenience: buy online and pay a shipping charge versus trekking to the store.

Segment-Based Pricing

These approaches are intended to activate dormant prospects and customers, by making "the deal" attractive enough. The deal typically won't appeal to everyone, but some people will jump on a segment-based offering, because the value proposition has been amped up. *Examples:*

- Leasing versus owning a car. The car's value to the prospective customer is often mentally couched in terms of "the level of car" they can get for their intended monthly lease payment (and it's usually a better car, because the car can be sold by the lessor at the end of the lease). The lease customer's decision is not based on the long-run financial wisdom of buying the car and driving it into the ground. Plus, some people like to always drive a late-model car.

- Vacation time-shares. Having an ownership share in a condo in a resort location, for far less than full-time ownership would cost, has clear appeal. Too, there's the ability to swap the time slot and the location with other time-share owners.

Bundling

This approach combines several existing products and/or services into one offering, often delivering added benefits to the buyer, while the seller is spared the cost and effort of selling each offering individually.

- A prime example of this is the vacation package, in which you seem to be getting a lot (airfare, hotel, meals, and side tours) for a "such a deal" low price.

- Another bundling approach is to combine what you offer with an in-demand "hook." The poster children here are the licensed-character premiums that McDonald's offers with their Happy Meals™. In this case, the hook, an appeal to young children, often with the pitch "Collect them all!" gets the child, and the family, into the restaurant— a small price to pay for the license fee and the character that goes into the Happy Meal box. The hook's biggest effect: sales volume.

Dr. Mohammed recounts that before McDonald's 1997 Teenie-Beanie-Babies Happy Meals promotion, the chain was selling 10 million Happy Meals per week. With the promotion, they sold 100 million in 10 days (70 million per week). A nice increase if you can get it. Clearly, the hook's effectiveness will wear out over time. But, again, so what?

- Another way to increase profit is to add a service to your product, or to provide an enhanced version of your base service. Added services might include express check-in, product customization, expedited product availability, a range of extended-warranty options, or low-rate or interest-free financing.

- Finally, as made clear by television infomercials, people seem more inclined to buy something that has a number of items that, "you'll also receive, free, if you act right now," as having higher value, even though they wouldn't pay for the added items anyway. (As a species, we sure are fun to watch.)

Yield Management/Dynamic Pricing

The idea here is to continuously seek the price point that will yield maximum profit. This implies that you'll have to change prices often, but doing so could be worth the trouble.

Airlines have used this for decades, and "It's on sale!" has long been prominent in the retail landscape. Dynamic pricing's term for this in retail is *managing markdowns*.[86]

Finding a Baseline Price

OK, so you can offer multiple prices, but how do you go about establishing the price points? It's necessary to create a well-founded baseline price from which you can offer discount and premium prices. How do you find that baseline price?

The first thing you need to do is to get a solid sense of your offering's *value*. Which means its *perceived* value.

The first value question is what, specifically, is the customer buying? Two examples will help here:[87]

First Example

Let's say it's a hot day, and you're a retailer selling a bottle of cold beer. In one context, you're selling it in the lobby bar of an upscale hotel. You know you can charge, say, $6 for the beer.

In another context, you're selling the same cold bottle of beer from a snack shack on the beach. You've come to know that you can't charge more than $3 for it.

Why the difference?

The answer turns on the context of the sale: what is the customer buying? On the beach, the customer is essentially buying a cold drink, conveniently nearby.

In the upscale hotel, the customer is buying not only a beer, but the ambiance of the hotel, the chance for a perhaps-meaningful (or better) interaction with other guests, and "being seen."

The two customers are most definitely not buying the same thing: one has a drink; the other has a drink and at least the possibility of the experience he or she wants!

And our second customer is highly unlikely to pay $6 for the beer on the beach.

You sell replacement parts for industrial equipment, including parts for long-obsolete machinery, for which there's not much demand—very low product turnover. You have an offer from a metal recycler to buy them for scrap, for, well, not much. Then a large manufacturer calls in a panic because their (neglected) production line has gone down and one of those long-obsolete parts is needed, *pronto!*

What's the difference in the value perceived by the two prospective customers? One's buying scrap metal for a few dollars per pound. The other's keeping their million-dollar-a-day production line going. (Please note that I'm not advocating gouging the manufacturer; you might have a relationship to manage.)

Value, as seen by the customer, is clearly *determined by context.*

Second Example

Another situation in which context strongly affects the perception of value is how your price is seen in relation to other available prices. That is, value, what you get for what you pay, is *relative*, not absolute.

Duke University behavioral economist Dan Ariely gives the example of a television retailer who displays three flat-screen TV sets together: a relatively small one carrying the lowest price, a large-screen model for almost twice the price, and a midsize one with a price between the two.

Most people, having little basis for judging the "true" value of any of them, will pick the midprice model, as the salesperson well knows when he or she is choosing the models to display together.[88]

Faced with a high or ridiculously priced option, most people will choose the next lower-priced option. The "ridiculous" option serves as an upper limit on price, but not on value.

What about this mythical "true" value? Is there such a thing? No, but there is what they call on Wall Street, a *consensus estimate*; i.e., what most people feel a fair price would be. You do need to know this to set a baseline price.

Now, on to determining your product's value...

What, specifically, is it about its brand, design, functionality, and ease of use that makes it attractive to prospective customers? How effectively have you gotten that across to them in an emotionally engaging, "I want that!" way?

Sometimes people don't see the value until they've bought the product, or experienced the service, but can you have your ads do the best possible job of helping prospects picture or imagine the benefits?[89],[90]

Price as a Statement of Value

For most people, a cheaper product is perceived as less valuable.[91] They use price as an indicator of quality.

If something's expensive, people assume that it must be good, or great. Dr. Mohammed cites as an example the rock band The Eagles' reunion concert tour. (In their words, "We never broke up; we just took a fourteen-year vacation.")

The Eagles' manager, Irving Azoff, decided to price the concert tickets at a then-record high, making the statement that concertgoers were not going to see just any band; they were going to see one of the greatest rock bands of all time![92] This amounted to asserting that the concert would be worth the price, *using the price to do so.*

Another example is what I'll call, Ariely's "aspirin." Dr. Ariely cites a study showing that a significantly higher percentage of people reported that they felt better when they took a high-priced medicine than did those who took a considerably less expensive one. But the two medicines were identical; their only difference was their price.[93]

We know that people who are able to, will pay high-end prices for what they consider worth it. But the high-end price has to be justified.[94]

This leads naturally to the concept of *value engineering*: what features does it make sense to put into an offering, in view of the resulting cost?

A variant is price-led costing: "What can we make so we can sell it at X price?"[95]

Obviously, perceived value depends on:

- Your, and your competitors', prices.
- The availability of substitutes for your product.
- Your offering's characteristics compared to the competition's (relative perceived value).
- Your target prospect groups' income levels—limits on their ability, or willingness, to pay.
- Changes in market environment. These are things that are mostly, or completely, outside of your control, but they affect your offering's value, such as:
  - Your product, say, an expensive dress, suddenly becomes a fashion hit, or passé…
  - For urban car owners: the arrival of parking meters or the advent of alternate-side-of-the-street parking rules affect the desirability of owning a car in these environments—a new hassle related to owning a car that previously didn't exist.

Then there are the product characteristics that determine value:

- Brand
- Convenience
- Quality
- Features
- Service
- Style/Design

From this, you ought to be able to gauge at least a relative value for what you offer compared to the competition. That will help in coming to a judgment about your baseline pricing.

Setting That Baseline Price

It's necessary to start with a well-founded perspective on your pricing environment.

There are situations in which your power to raise prices is nonexistent—the competition, a powerful buyer, or a substitute for what you offer, has seen to that. And you can't cut prices any further without your offer becoming unprofitable. Thus, your current price *is* your baseline price. It's time for efficiency, to get all possible costs out of what you offer (next chapter).

But in other cases, as they say, don't negotiate against yourself by assuming that people won't pay. Instead, test.[96]

Part of that testing should include understanding *what* those who bought *value* about what you offer. You can then use the aggregate results to review your offering's features so that, long term, you're only offering the aspects that have value, and can eliminate those that don't, increasing margins or lowering price to increase sales.

If there's a Happyland in pricing, it's in pricing luxury brands. Luxury pricing seems to defy common sense, but it's actually very logical. The buyer needs to feel, and show others, that they are special. The more they pay, the more special they are. Great for the seller, but the offering has to indeed be of the highest quality, with a brand cachet to match.[97]

In, say, a luxury retail store, where everything is priced to the max, people will often buy a small, still pricey item, just to be able to tell people that they bought it there.[98]

Some claim that one way to prosper is to sell a better version of something popular and to charge significantly more for it. You should test this if you believe it might apply.

In most cases, finding the right baseline price is an art. An art bedeviled by human psychology, our famed irrationality, cutthroat price competition, the availability of complex price-optimization software, and the need to collect a lot of outcomes data. That said, the most profitable outcomes are brought about primarily by price testing.[99] Some say this is unwise, as the customers who paid the higher test price will discover that others paid less. But there are firms such as Zilliant, a price-consulting firm featured in Mr. Fishman's article just referenced, that have made a sustainable business out of this.

And of course, even when you find your base price point, or something close, it can change frequently based on the economy (as some high-end consumer-package-goods companies found during the financial crisis); and competitors' changes in either their prices, their offerings' designs, features, and trendiness, or their value propositions.

Raising Prices

When you're considering raising prices, give a good bit of thought to how you're going to justify the increase. If the cost of what's sold has risen, people will often understand that, and accept the increase. *Example:* a fuel surcharge added to the price of an airline ticket.

If you can't justify a price increase to your customers' satisfaction, think twice about doing so, because it could well lower sales volume, and perhaps more seriously, tarnish the brand: "You're ripping us off!" (even if you're not).

When you do raise prices, offer customers coupons or special offers to accommodate those who would find the increased price hard to deal with. Without the coupon or offer, the higher price could cause defection or simply foregoing the next purchase. Those who need the discount will take the trouble to use the coupon or other incentive. Other wisdom about increasing prices:

- Don't cut the size or quantity of what you're selling and maintain the same price. People *will* notice, and it will not go down well for the brand.
- If there's a choice between raising the price of a discretionary or essential product, maintain the essential product's price.

For more on increasing prices, please see this *Wall Street Journal* article.[100]

Pricing Mistakes

Some pricing mistakes seem innocent enough on the surface, like, "Everyone prices it that way." It's a mistake, because you could well be leaving profit on the table. The *Wall Street Journal* recounts six other pricing mistakes.[101]

- Sneaky pricing, such as a surprise fee, creates distrust and harms the brand.[102]

- Targeted pricing, or using a low price as an incentive for others' customers to switch to what your business offers, comes with tripwires. If your current customers find out that they're no longer getting your best prices, some will get mad and go elsewhere (defeating the whole purpose of growing your customer base). And it's hard to keep them from finding out.
Better: offer your existing customers some (real) benefit as well, like a discount card.[103]

- Haggling, for some people, is too much of a hassle, and they'll avoid it. For such target customers, everyday low pricing makes sense.

Plugging Price-Related Profit Drains...

Staying profitable is hard. But some aspects of the challenge are in your court...

- Atop the list, providing unnecessary discounts, or running unprofitable promotions. Knowing prospects' price sensitivities can prevent both.

- In trying to keep prices where you need them to be, there are situations in which bundling, combining products, or combining a product with a service can better maintain profitability. Obviously, this works best when the prices of the individual elements in the combination are not easy to ferret out. Another caution is that the combination's value proposition needs to remain comparable to that of its individual elements, or it won't be attractive to buyers. In other words, don't throw useless junk in there.

- Price transparency, a new situation. Recent years have brought mobile-phone-enabled showrooming: customers checking out products in your store, then buying them online from someone else for less.[104,105] That evolved into competitors tempting your customers, on their phones, right in your store! Some businesses have tried to counter all this with offerings that are unavailable elsewhere, but generally, it's been a struggle.

If showrooming is seriously affecting your business, perhaps it's time to reconsider whether your core customers should include price shoppers. If you do decide to deal with them, here's how Best Buy did so. First, they guaranteed that they'd match Amazon's prices. They also rented space within their stores to the major electronics makers, so each could display all of their products together in a dedicated setting. This created a new revenue stream for Best Buy. Finally, Best Buy offered free, in-home consultations with its technical-support (Geek Squad) staff on prospective purchases.[106,107]

- There's software that can help with dynamic pricing, but it should be used in situations where it makes sense. Because your current price points could be close enough to ideal that further futzing with them is not the highest and best use of your people's limited bandwidth. The software typically takes considerable effort to implement initially.[108] Some of this optimization software enables price testing, so you can see what will happen with a price change before you roll it out on a large scale.[109]

In retail, you can couple the software with technologies like RF tagging, to actually know, in real time, how your offerings are selling.[110]

Special Pricing Situations

Pricing Services

You can't own a service, but you can *experience it*. That experience forms the foundation of the value the recipient expects they'll receive. From the customer's perspective, using a service means incurring two types of costs: monetary, and what we'll call hassle. Hassle is what the customer has to go through to use the service. A poster child for hassle might be an airline passenger, someone trying to use "customer service," or even more famously, "tech support!"

Fostering repeated use of a service means delivering sufficient benefit that the customer will feel that, in view of both monetary and hassle costs, their experience was worth it, ideally, well worth it.

Complexity in pricing—the wording of guarantees, and confusing, or missing-in-action terms and conditions, and in disclaimers—does not boost sales. Rather, it increases hassle and engenders suspicion and distrust.

To price a service, it's helpful to have a clear and accurate picture of the cost of delivering it, and its value. Activity-based costing (see Chapter 7) is a good way to get your arms around, and likely reduce, costs.

Undifferentiated service offerings can be assessed only on the basis of price, so a good next step would be to find something that will distinguish your service, and price it in line with the increased value.

Ways to price services include:

- Satisfaction-based pricing. The price you pay is related to how satisfied you are: a service guarantee, such as, "a hot pizza, at your door within 30 minutes, or it's free." (Better: find a promise that doesn't license young male pizza-delivery dudes to floor it.) Customers value this pricing approach because it reduces their uncertainty. And it can make your business more valuable long term, because it provides an incentive to deliver well. Businesses that aren't sure they can deliver shouldn't do this until they are.

- Competitive flat-rate pricing is another way to minimize customers' perceived risk.

- Relationship pricing. Good examples of this are long-term contracts, coupled with joint efforts at cost reduction, and sharing the resulting savings. A less attractive approach is the volume-purchase agreement, where the more the customer buys, the less they pay per unit.

- Efficiency-based pricing. If your business has the lowest cost structure in a category, you can use low prices to compete, at least until another business with a still-lower cost structure comes along. *Point:* a cost advantage is prone to evaporating.

Retail

Retail is a specialized form of service that usually involves the sale of physical goods—as would a supermarket, hardware store, or restaurant—but can involve the sale of a service, such as airline tickets from a travel agent. The perceived value of the retailer's offerings is dependent on four things: the experience provided, the retailer's brand and its promise, the quality of what's offered, and the price charged. Together, they provide a lot of variables to work with in establishing prices.

Manufacturers

Manufacturers that need to protect profit margins in the face of rising raw-material costs, coupled with an inability to raise prices, can sometimes use surcharges to compensate, such as a temporary fuel surcharge, that's clear and well explained.[111]

Online Pricing

There's an interesting article about pricing for online sales in a recent issue of the *Marketing Sherpa* email newsletter.[112] It discusses:

- When is it best to present the price: on the first (landing) page, when someone has clicked through to your offering, or when they visit a follow-on page to learn more? It can make a sizable difference.
- When is it appropriate to build shipping costs into the price, and what does that accomplish?
- For an online service, for what types of customers is an annual fee, versus a (somewhat higher overall) monthly fee, most appealing?
- When should you try to match competitors' online prices, versus beating them?
- What is the best way to pre-announce price increases so as to drive sales now?

Price Wars

This often ruinous topic, in which one or more competitors try to drive others out of business by cutting prices to the extent that some of them no longer remain profitable, is too specialized to treat here, but this reference[113] is a good place to get smarter about it.

Creating a Pricing Mindset—
Throughout the Business

With a sense of value and pricing strategies in hand, there's another, crucial, pricing issue that has to be addressed. In a typical company, a lot of people touch the price that's eventually paid: people in product management, marketing (promotions), distribution (allocating product), finance (discounted financing), sales, and senior management. Vital questions:

- Do they all understand what a sound final price means to the business, and the parts they play in maintaining it?

- Do they all have the information and the incentives to do what's necessary? For example, does the sales force know the unit profit of each item they sell? And is their compensation plan based on gross profit or just revenue?

- Does everyone in the business have the tools needed to bring about the profit result the business needs or wants?

Getting everyone on the same page requires creating what Dr. Mohammed calls "a culture of pricing." It means that everyone needs to buy into, and to play their part in, keeping prices where they're intended to be. More on this can be found in his *Art of Pricing* book.

A Formal Pricing Methodology

One approach to holding the line on price, in a division of a large company, is Six Sigma pricing. The idea is to have an agreed-upon, and followed, process that produces an invoiced price for a customer, one that's bought into at all levels of the business, from the salespeople to senior management. This means the sales force isn't out there selling at, well, cost, and getting compensated on a percentage of revenue—while the company goes broke.

The Six Sigma process puts an end to excessive, out-of-control discounting. In their article describing its use,[114] Manmohan Sodhi, a professor at London's City University, and Navdeep Sodhi, a pricing strategist at the materials company Kennametal, Inc., report that annual revenue grew by $5.8 million in the 6 months after the process was implemented. (The base level of sales was not provided.)

A Great Question

Given all this, how can you go about maintaining customers in the face of lower-priced competition, with deeper pockets?

- One good way is to *change the value proposition,* on a personal basis, by just showing a little respect or appreciation for the customer, or an unexpected personal favor, such as an introduction to a potentially valuable person or resource. If the contact with the customer is in person, showing genuine appreciation for their business, or just a sincere respect for them, will go a long way. But it can't just be lip service.

- If the communication with the customer is electronic or by phone, you have the same bonding opportunity as you might have in person, though it will take more effort to create the intended outcome, either in the creation of the electronic messages you use, or the hiring, training, and winning ways of those staffing your call centers.

- Offer an occasional discount or freebie.

- Just helping customers realize that you "have their back" (if you really do).

TAPPING YOUR UPSIDE:

*Pricing Perspectives
With Legs*

1. **What can you gain from working on pricing? Pick one of your offerings to analyze here.**

   _____

   The next steps will help you find your opportunities...

   a. From the *Tapping Your Upside* exercise you did for Chapter 3, what were the most cost-effective ways to enhance your offering's value proposition?

   _____

   _____

   _____

   b. Given the value-proposition improvements, by what percentage should your baseline price change, if at all?

   _____

2. **How does the resulting baseline price compare to that of your competitors?**

   _____

   _____

   _____

3. What "value message" is conveyed by your pricing?

_____

_____

4. Are you clear on your *pricing power*?

_____

_____

5. Have you identified any pricing mistakes? What are they?

_____

_____

_____

6. What, specifically, are you going to do about them?

_____

_____

_____

7. Have you been able to find any pricing-related profit drains? What are they?

_____

_____

_____

_____

8. Exactly how are you going to plug them?

_____

_____

_____

_____

9. Which of these pricing strategies make sense for your business?

a. Offering different versions of your product or service at different price points?

_____

b. Should you put more attention on catering to customer segments?

_____

c. What about bundles? Do any of those you can come up with make sense?

_____

d. If any do, could any of them be rolled out with strong hooks, à la Happy Meals?

_____

e. Would dynamic pricing fit what you offer?

_____

f. Would it be worth the trouble?

_____

10. On a 1–10 scale, how evolved is your business's culture of pricing?

_____

11. What, if anything, do you need to do about it?

_____

12. Is it worth moving all the way to Six Sigma pricing?

_____

_____

_____

13. What are you doing to enhance customer loyalty and goodwill (and gain a little flexibility in your pricing)?

_____

_____

UPSIDE ELEMENT ASSESSMENT: PRICING

Please enter your estimates for the *overall* gains and challenges you expect to derive from your improved pricing in the corresponding row on the book's Upside Element Assessment Sheet, just before the last page.

Chapter 7

Deftly Managing Costs

Compared to growing revenue, cost cutting is not overly hard, and has limits in terms of profitability you can achieve.

Since it's often the case that considerable cost cutting has already been done, the low-hanging and "short stepladder" fruit might already be harvested.

Here we'll briefly treat some of the most effective ways to cut costs.

If you're the executive running the business, you can likely delegate the work of cost cutting more easily than addressing some of the other upside opportunities, like brand positioning and value-proposition development. A CFO or skilled controller should be able to handle the needed analysis.

The first thing you're after is a sense of whether further effort to trim costs is worthwhile, given your other options. This chapter's *Tapping Your Upside* exercises will help you find that answer.

The art in cost cutting lies in choosing *which* cuts to make. Here we've loosely categorized them by bottom-line impact.

Dramatic Cost Impact

These three topics can dramatically affect profitability.

"Pulling Its Weight" Assessment

The basic idea is to cut marginal offerings and redeploy the capital and resources freed up. Here you identify the offerings that are not pulling their weight from the perspective of return on capital employed, and sell, fix, or eliminate them. Marginal offerings often result from innovations that turn out to be less than blockbusters, from those whose time has passed, or from a company you acquired for its blockbuster unit that came along with an also-ran unit or two. But you'll need to consider whether discontinuing an offering will have a negative impact on your brand, as we discussed in Chapter 4.

Activity-based costing (later in this chapter) can help with the pruning.

Managing Risk: Really

The risk we're referring to here is the unlikely but high-cost-impact variety. A bazillion-dollar fine, a product recall, a class-action employment or liability lawsuit, or an unaddressed safety hazard can wipe out the benefits of many years of judicious cost management and investment in your business's brand. Think of risk management not as a cost but as an investment worth making—in saving what could be a whole lot of money, and preserving your business's value long term.

To begin, make sure that all of your business's risks are at least identified, and develop a plan to mitigate the "shots below the waterline." Yes, this might add to costs now, but failure to manage risk prudently, and thus contain the cost of unlikely-but-very-expensive events, has made many executives "former."

Leverage Technology (as much as you can)

Astute application of technology can sometimes dramatically reduce costs. It can also make possible things that simply couldn't be done before.

- Two notable examples from the petroleum-exploration industry:
  - An innovative Shell/Noble drill ship can operate with 40% fewer crew members than usual, and drill deeper, much more precisely, more safely, and with a lower environmental impact. This is thanks to a combination of GPS, sensors, and computer-controlled thruster propellers on the ship's bottom.[115]

- Halliburton's suite of innovations, including the ability to tap hard-to-reach oil reservoirs *from the side,* generated new revenue and cut their customers' cost of reaching these deposits. Technologies like this provide a competitive cost advantage that can win business, driving revenue.[116]

- Automating things, like design, production, marketing, front- and back-office operations, distribution, support, and service, can reduce costs dramatically. Automation helps control people costs and can make life easier, *if* it is well designed, and it works. Same for web services, using self-identifying data to more easily enable autonomous electronic interactions between companies, across divisions, and with customers' orders.

  - Another (niche) example of automation is Radio Frequency Identification (RFID) tagging. These "smart tags" attach to items, or collections of items. They provide information about the items to scanners that need not be close by. The tags can contain sensors to detect contaminants, excessive temperature or moisture, and spoilage, and can log such readings. They have a wide and growing range of uses, including managing inventory better, decreasing shrinkage, lowering handling costs, and improving safety and security, e.g., in containerized shipping.

- Other automation options include:

  - Highly automated warehouses, factories, and supply- and/or demand-chain monitoring.

  - Effective information and business-intelligence systems.

The basic question with automation options is the level of investment needed, the payback time, and the reliability of the cost and duration estimates used in its justification.

Moderate Cost Impact

Zero-Based Budgeting

The idea behind zero-based budgeting is that every element of the budget is built anew, scrutinized, and justified yet again, in each budgeting cycle.

This technique has a fearsome reputation among employees and suppliers, who often suffer, but it can have value when employed judiciously, while taking a balanced view of that other major contributor to overall business value: growing revenues. As discussed in the Introduction, Kraft Heinz has been using zero-based budgeting since the two companies merged in July 2015; however, having cut considerable costs, as of this writing, the company is still growth challenged, and is running out of costs to cut as a way to grow shareholder value.[117]

The first and last references in this citation[118] will give you a sense of whether zero-based budgeting would be appropriate for your situation, though the technique's star has again dimmed because of its use by Kraft Heinz.

Activity-Based Costing (ABC)

The essence of activity-based costing is pinning all costs, including fixed costs, or "overhead," on the product or service that causes the cost to be incurred. Doing so lets you understand the true profitability, or lack thereof, of your products and services, so you can do something about it. An activity that soaks up a lot of, say, a talented manager's time, or a lot of "fixed" resources—floor space, machine usage, or capital—will then bear its appropriate share of those costs.

In addition to operations like manufacturing and distribution, activity-based costing can be used to understand which customers (or consumer segments) are actually profitable to sell to, and which suppliers provide the lowest lifecycle cost.

Regarding customers, you first need to assess the profitability of each business customer or segment, including marketing, sales, and post-sale support costs. You can then work to improve profitability for those not meeting your objectives. For example, you can charge for each support incident rather than including a guesstimate in the purchase price. You also might eventually have to "fire", or stop selling to, customers who cost you more than they're worth.

With suppliers, you can pass more business through fewer suppliers in exchange for lower unit prices, and work with those remaining to jointly lower their costs and yours, through improved processes, and tighter communication and cooperation—a long-term, sustainable approach.

The mechanics of activity-based costing are conceptually simple. It's a two-step process: you first assign all costs to activities, then associate those activities with the products, services, customers, or consumer segments and/or suppliers that cause them. (Arguments will arise in making those associations, but they're good discussions to have.)

The activity-based costing approach clearly makes sense for analyzing the profitability of products, services, and suppliers. It can, as well, make sense for customers or consumer segments where the prices you charge them, or the cost of serving them, differs significantly. Doing so gives you their true cost, and a basis for keep-or-cut decisions.

You can find much more in the references at this chapter's end. Of particular value are: Kaplan and Cooper (in depth) and Cokins et al. (a fast, accessible, read).[119]

Streamline Processes

This is about finding less costly ways to deliver services; to develop, manufacture, distribute, and support products; and to administer your organization. Unless your organization has already done considerable process streamlining, doing so could prove fruitful.

Sleek processes cut across organizational silos, and can deliver both lower overall costs and better performance, from a customer's perspective. Common processes include:

- Customer acquisition
- Supply chain (in some cases, this is broken down further)
- Demand chain
- Product development and support
- Attracting, hiring, and keeping talented people
- Financial reporting
- Order to cash

Process streamlining is, however, neither easy nor quick.[120] The deciding factor in whether to seriously consider a process-streamlining initiative could be pain, not cost. It could be that one of your operations is so screwed up that it's exasperating to everyone involved, causing customers to complain, or leave (decreasing revenue), or just fomenting expensive quality problems. (Johnson & Johnson's 2010–2013 quality problems spring to mind here.) Related to process streamlining are *lean* and *quality* discussed next.

Lean

Lean[121] is a technique born in the manufacturing sector that promotes the use of streamlined, efficient processes to boost productivity and cut work-in-process inventory. *Essence:* eliminate any activity that the customer is not willing to pay for—everything else is considered to be some form of waste: examples of which are unnecessary delays, poor organization of work, management chaos (and often, politics), and less-than-ideal process design. Lean's methods can also be used to streamline services: maintaining call centers, processing mortgage applications, paying invoices, etc.

Quality Products and Services

Quality can cut manufacturing, service, and warranty costs—dramatically in many cases. Quality improvements can minimize or eliminate the costs of rework/repair and reduce the chances of post-sale customer dissatisfaction. Six Sigma is often considered the ultimate metric for quality, but the key is to adopt a level of quality that's *appropriate*. Six Sigma might be overkill—it's mainly suited to larger companies, as it comes with a fair amount of "black-belt" consulting and training, and other forms of overhead.

Buy Well

Somewhat less sustainable, and less fun, is to create and cultivate multiple suppliers for major items you buy; form tight, clear specs for these items; and have suppliers bid, online or off.

Another less sustainable approach is to order high-volume components and materials online through a much broader range of suppliers or approved vendors—an auction. Price transparency can make this a powerful way to cut costs, but it can also leave your best vendors feeling like they're not valued partners, so they might decide to bolt. As the old saw goes, "business goes where it's welcomed, and stays where it's appreciated." An approach that's fair to both parties works best.

Of course, with any of the above supplier approaches, you have to measure their performance, and make changes, if need be.

Make Advertising Investments Effective

Simple pay-per-click internet advertising keyword tests can reveal what people want: what they're searching for. You can use appeals to those wants in your ads, increasing their effectiveness, and lowering the advertising cost-per-sale.

Supply and Demand Chains[122]

The opportunities here are to move the source of materials closer to where they will be used or sold, or practice just-in-time delivery through better communications with suppliers. This reduces the interest-cost of materials that are just moving around, and not yet creating any value while they do so (see *Lean,* above). Long term, the impact of that moving around is usually an increase in the end product's cost, regardless of who has to originally absorb the cost of the materials that are just sitting in transit.

There are also significant risk-management aspects to a business's choice of suppliers:

- Avoiding the impact of a supply-chain breakdown, such as the computer industry experienced due to the flooding in Thailand in 2011, and the 2020 Covid-19 outbreak in China.
- The brand hit from a supplier's front-page labor-conditions report, or a hazardous factory fire.

On the demand-chain side of things, it's also necessary to rightsource, i.e., to put your supplier(s) in the best possible locations—ones that allow you to quickly and economically adapt to serve your markets.

A great example of this is managing "fashion risk," which happens when what your market wants is no longer what you offer, and you have to scramble to get what your market does want available for sale. In such a situation, where your suppliers and manufacturers are situated geographically can matter, a lot. Eight weeks of lost sales because your now-in-fashion finished goods are "on the water" from Asia can also damage your brand's "hipness," if that applies. And of course, having to air-freight them will hit gross margins.

People

Do you have the right number of people to do the work your business has? Obviously, this can drive costs down, or up. Cutting headcount is, at this point, an almost knee-jerk reaction to an actual or anticipated results shortfall. Or it's sometimes done to force further automation.

But cutting headcount has obvious downsides:

- A fearful, unmotivated, resentful, and even vengeful workforce, some of whom interact with customers, make their feelings about your business known to them, and generally don't represent your business in a good light.

- The best people leave when they hear that cuts are coming, and you're left with those whom others won't hire.

- Quality issues and follow-ups that now "fall through the cracks" because everyone has too much to do, can aggravate customers, cause their defection, and ding your reputation.

> **Point:** cutting headcount by x% might not be the smartest thing you can do.

Outsource

Find companies that can perform noncore tasks for less. This can add to the time and effort demands on management, so it needs to be applied either broadly, with just one or a handful of providers, or in high-cost, noncore areas where the savings are clear.

R&D Joint Ventures

This arrangement can spread the cost of product development across several firms. But there are issues around ownership of the intellectual property developed, and, possibly, antitrust concerns.

Customer Self-Service (online)

Let customers order, obtain needed documents, or request service, largely without involving a person such as a call-center operator.

Manufacturing

Use *design for manufacturing* (eliminating potential sources of defects, and cutting the time and cost to assemble a product). It will lower the cost of making and maintaining what you offer. An example would be casting or 3D printing as one, what were heretofore separate metal parts.

Dynamic Performance Measures

In continuous-process manufacturing: refining, food production, and others, optimizing the economics of operating individual processing units in a production facility involves measuring salient operating parameters (process flows, fluid levels, temperatures, and pressures) and automatically, or with an operator's help, continuously tuning the process. Measuring and continuously adjusting the parameters that control a process can both maximize the volume produced (for the same fixed cost), and maximize yield (saleable product), reducing unit cost.

Modest Cost Impact

Inventory

This involves the management of various types of inventory: materials, work-in-process, finished goods.

De-gunk the Capital Budget

The small-ticket requests that go into a capital budget can frequently be trimmed (eliminated, shared, or reduced). In his *HBR* article, Copeland provides a process for getting the unnecessary spending out of the budget, with the result showing up on the bottom line.[123]

Find and Fix the Profit Drains

You know what some of these are: the ones that always seem like they're not worth the trouble. They're a symbol of what you'll put up with, and of how serious you are about cost control. Examples: overly fancy office space, products or services that are not earning their cost of capital, manufacturing waste, underperforming staff, less-than-convincing advertising, poor ad placement.

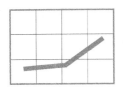

TAPPING YOUR UPSIDE:
Deftly Managing Costs

1. **You must have done some cost streamlining at some point, and have likely done it recently. Look through the headings above to see if there are relevant areas you've not yet touched, to come up with a short list of costs you could still cut.**

   What's your sense of the percentage by which you can realistically cut overall costs from here? (_____ %)

   At your current sales volume, by how much would that percentage cut boost profits? (_____ %)

   If your resulting profit gain is not dramatic, you have a choice:

   • Hold off on cost cutting until you have a clear sense of the results potential of the other things you can do, as we'll work through in Chapter 14.

   • Have someone, not you, work on cost cutting now, while you're assessing the upside elements that could prove even more worthwhile. That way, you won't be leaving results on the table. (Whomever you put on the job, have them avoid the counterproductive: "counting paperclips," or creating ill will.)

2. **In the following chart, rank the *relevant* cost-cutting opportunities listed in this chapter by *net* savings, then list the management and staff-time investment they'll consume below, using high, medium, or low (H-M-L) ratings, or a 1–10 numeric scale. Then pick those you'll pursue.**

No.	Opportunity	Cost Savings	Cost to Implement	Net Savings	Staff Time	Mgmt. Time	Pursue?
1							
2							
2							
3							
4							
5							
6							
7							
8							
9							
10							

3. Once you've picked the opportunities you'll pursue (we suggest four or less), capture how you'll "make it so," below.

Opportunity No.	Who will do this?	Who will lead/ coordinate it?	When will it be done?

UPSIDE ELEMENT ASSESSMENT: DEFTLY MANAGING COSTS

Please enter your estimates for the overall gains and challenges you expect to derive from your improved cost management in the corresponding row on the book's Upside Element Assessment Sheet, just before the last page.

This is the last chapter covering what you can do somewhat quickly and easily to boost results. In the next five chapters, we'll explore things that can have a truly dramatic impact on your results, but that usually take a good bit more doing.

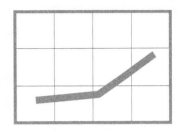

Part 3

The Initiatives That Take More Doing

We'll now treat the big upside elements: capturing opportunities, finding hungry markets, market strategy and business design, product-and-service design, innovation, and management practices. Each can have a dramatic positive impact on your results, but they're major initiatives—consuming management time, considerable money, and thought.

Here be fortunes: Facebook,
Netflix, Amazon.
Here be fortunes; or not...
"Think we should bet the company
on creating our new mobile app!"

Chapter 8

Detecting and Seizing Opportunities

If you don't actively look for opportunities that will dramatically grow revenue or significantly lower costs, your business could grow relatively weaker over time. And being *unable* to pursue opportunities because you lack the resources will have the same effect.

Here, and in the coming chapters, we'll look at the most common types of opportunities: Markets (Chapter 9), Business Design (Chapter 10), Product-and-Service Design (Chapter 11), Innovation (Chapter 12), and Leveraging Your Assets (part of Chapter 13).

Let's start with...

Finding Opportunities

Recent progress has added powerful new approaches to the classic ways to find opportunities. We'll cover both here; the time-honored ways are still useful. They're ordered by my rough sense of how much they can help you prosper, but don't take the order too seriously.

1. A Needed Task (A Job to Be Done)

As covered in Chapter 3 (Value Propositions), Christensen et al.'s *Competing Against Luck*[124] takes *finding worthwhile opportunities,* things that people need to accomplish, into a straightforward, learnable process. Those tasks are real and important, but the ways they now have to accomplish them are either not very satisfactory, or simply don't exist. *Examples:*

The *Job* to Be Done (the Customer Need)		The Solution(s)
Existing	Rapid review and approval of contracts.	The fax machine; express-delivery services, e.g., FedEx; emailed PDFs.
	Inexpensive accommodations away from home.	Services such as Airbnb.
	A low or no-cost way to communicate with others, worldwide.	Services like WhatsApp.
	A way to show off what my children do, to those far away.	Social media, e.g., Facebook.
	More accessible transportation options.	Lyft, Uber.
Huge, Unaddressed Opportunities	Truly effective ways to combat climate change.	
	Pure drinking water, everywhere.	
	Feeding the growing population.	
	More widely accessible, affordable-or-free education.	
	Universal online web access.	

2. What's a Real Hassle?

In his book *Demand*,[125] Adrian Slywotzky, suggests using what he calls *hassle maps*. There's a way of finding opportunities in the frustrations and shortcomings that people encounter in using products and services. (Peter Drucker's *Disconnects* category, below, is related.) *Examples*:

- Renting movies. Time was when you had to go to a video-rental store, see what they had in stock that you wanted to watch, get it home and try to watch it as you'd planned, then return it to the video store on time to avoid paying a late fee. Hassles: going to the store—twice; the movie you wanted was not in stock; late fees. Solution: Netflix. Hassles? None of the above. The major video-rental company, Blockbuster, soon became toast.

- Many modern offices are overly air-conditioned during warm weather. The Japanese clothing company Fast Retailing, with its Uniqlo brand, was able to capitalize on this with its HeatTech lightweight (and warm) underwear.

3. What Technology Just Enabled

What will technology let you do now, that you couldn't do before?

Examples: Mobile apps and social-media platforms now allow customers to find and interact with your business. And a few years ago, the web, and online advertising, newly allowed a local specialty store to reach a global market.

4. A Blue-Ocean-Strategy Approach

The 36 spaces in the Blue-Ocean-Shift[126] authors' Buyer Utility Map (https://www.blueoceanstrategy.com/tools/buyer-utility-map/) can also be used to find the market spaces in which greater value can be provided. If the attribute in one of those spaces is indeed important to the buyer, and there's a realistic way for your business to create a marked increase in the preference that space represents, it could be an opportunity.

For example, if you can make your offering dramatically easier to use, or change it so it would rarely break, while competing products often do, those might be good reasons to pursue the opportunity.

5. What's Missing?

Richard White's classic, *The Entrepreneur's Manual,* has a wonderful chapter on surfacing worthwhile market gaps.[127] He suggests first establishing criteria for evaluating the opportunities (size, profit opportunity, longevity of the opportunity), then choosing a demographic to focus on (working adults), a period of time in their days (after work), and all of the problems that could come about in that period, then focusing on those that can be profitably solved. White reports that this method tends to yield a lot of opportunities, which must then be pared down to one or two, which is hard.

The next seven ways to find opportunities are from Peter Drucker's book *Innovation and Entrepreneurship,*[128] with my take on their order of importance now, and Drucker's original ranking noted.

6. What's Changing? (Drucker's #4)

Change often begets opportunity. Opportunities can result from the evolution of industries, regulatory changes, shifting governmental priorities, and, of course, technological progress. *Examples:*

- Combatting climate change, and changing economics, have moved the energy industry to use cleaner sources of power, leading to increased demand for products that can generate electricity from wind, the sun, wave motion, the Earth's heat, and other sources.
- Another is increased demand for hybrid or all-electric automobiles.

7. Disconnects (Drucker's #2)

These are differences between the way things are and the way things could be. Great sources of these are customers' complaints and unmet needs—yours and theirs. *Example:* a poorly performing vendor leads to a company's request for other firms to replace it.

8. Unexpected Successes, Failures, and Events (Drucker's #1)

A good example of an unexpected success is Facebook, originally conceived as a way to look at pictures of people on one college campus. The degree to which

Facebook caught on was unexpected. To their credit, its founders took the hint and drove the company to what it's become today: a vehicle for personal PR (thanks to Ken McCarthy of The System for this insight).

Finding opportunity in an unexpected failure brings to mind Post-It® Notes. Its adhesive wasn't sticky enough for its originally intended application, but 3M had the wisdom and open-mindedness to look for other uses. But having a solution does not always mean that there's a worthwhile problem to solve.

9. Demographic/Psychographic Changes (Drucker's #5)

Examples: a shift in the age mix of a region's population, due to the overall population graying or higher birth rates; a shift in a neighborhood's ethnic makeup, which might be apparent from an influx of new restaurants, hair salons, and clothing stores; or event-driven migration, which can change the demographics of an area quite quickly.

Another would be an election outcome such as Brexit, and its impact on the availability and cost of housing in Dublin, Ireland, because of London-based financial institutions moving their operations there.

10. Process Needs (Drucker's #3)

Example: Manufacturing plants need to avoid costly downtime; avoiding it has long been a major focus. The recent emergence of networked sensors and the Internet of Things are being harnessed for preventive machine maintenance, driving the adoption of these technologies, and creating opportunities for those who can design and secure them.

11. Perception, Meaning, and Mood (Societal Changes) (Drucker's #6)

How people feel about things, and what they want, changes over time.

Examples: The contemporary feeling that having to be connected to one's workplace all the time (if only electronically), has led people to seek respite off the grid. Some lodging providers have made that a draw for their properties.

Another is that in light of the perception that a solid background in the Science, Technology, Engineering, and Mathematics (STEM) disciplines can bring about a well-compensated future, many parents encourage their children to pursue these studies.

12. Knowledge (Drucker's #7)

Realizing the potential of a knowledge-based opportunity can take decades. And it's more timing-dependent than other types of opportunities, in that the market has to be *ready* to adopt offerings based on the new knowledge. Pursuing it requires analysis of the needs, and importantly, the *readiness* of the market.

Example: Artificial intelligence, the development of which poked along until the techniques of machine learning began to be applied in the 1990s. Once machine learning had evolved sufficiently, it resulted in market opportunities for software that could, acceptably in most cases, recognize speech, filter spam, and pilot vehicles.

If a knowledge-based opportunity appears ripe to enter the mainstream, it could be worth pursuing, but that depends on being ready and able to do so. In some cases, a company that is not ready, but that has the money, can just buy a firm founded by those who've worked to create the knowledge, giving its founders a big payday.

There might, however, be faster-acting sources of opportunity you could pursue.

Drucker also suggested that managers keep both a problems page and an opportunities page, and spend equal time on each.

What Else Should You Pay Attention To?

As Christensen, Drucker, Slywotzky, and White have all pointed out, you can often find opportunity in the *problems and frustrations* of your customers and prospects, or that you or your people experience, and *pay attention to the opportunities that are presenting themselves.* Simply asking, "What is painful about activity X?" can bring them to light.

About Your Opportunity Detector

- Do you have an effective "sensor network" for finding opportunities? Can you describe it, and how it works?

- Is looking for, and assessing, opportunities someone's *job?* You might need outside resources and contacts to strengthen this capability. But *you absolutely have to have lookouts,* just like when you were a kid, and concerned that "enemies" would attack the "fort" you just created. Except that now, lookouts might keep your business booming.

Being Ready

Defining What You Will and Won't Pursue

Where are your points of leverage?

- A corporate asset. *Example:* IBM's salesforce (the asset) can add newly acquired software to the lineup of products they already sell.

- Relationships with customers. If they love you, they'll be inclined to help you, by agreeing to give you feedback on or endorse your offerings, serve on a customer panel, or recommend you to potential customers.

- Your brand(s) and reputation. If there's damage here, realizing opportunities will be harder. Is your business's accumulated goodwill sufficient to aid in your repair efforts?

- Technology. What does it let you do today, that you couldn't yesterday?

Ability to Pursue

You have to:

- Be able to take advantage of opportunities when they come along, because you have the financial wherewithal, resources, etc.

- Have processes in place for *assessing* opportunities and prospective acquisitions, and for *integrating* the latter.

- Have the guts and organizational alignment needed to pursue them.

Assessing

Market testing is a complex area, and beyond the scope of this book. But the first question should always be: is a prospective opportunity real?

If so, for an opportunity to be worth your time and trouble, it should be able to dramatically boost your top and bottom lines. How far will it move the needle? Beyond that, you need a realistic sense of:

- Whether your business has the knowledge, skills, resources, willingness, and overall bandwidth to realize the opportunity.

- Your chances of seizing the opportunity before others do. To what degree does that matter?

- The odds that the opportunity will turn out to be a shot below the waterline for your business's financial health or its brand.

And once you've assessed all that, if you've got more than one opportunity still standing, you need to look at how they stack up to one another, and how many you can pursue.

You also need to carefully consider whether the opportunity is compatible with the other three characteristics of a success-bound business design, as described in Mark Johnson's book, *Seizing the White Space*,[129] and summarized in Chapter 10 (Crafting a Powerful Business Design), page 207.

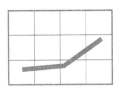

TAPPING YOUR UPSIDE:
Opportunities

1. Finding Opportunities...

Cause of Opportunity	Comment	What We Can Do
1. A job to be done	What job do your customers hire your product or service to do for them?	
	Are there aspects of that job where the solution you offer does not get an A, in terms of the experience it delivers?	
	What are they?	
	What can you do about them?	
	What other jobs are you aware of that people need done, that are not being handled to their satisfaction?	
2. Hassles	What drives people nuts? Or frustrates them? Can you do something about these?	

Cause of Opportunity	Comment	What We Can Do
3. What technology recently enabled	Will a new technology, or a novel combination of technologies, let you do something to boost results that you couldn't do before?	
4. Blue-Ocean-Shift's Buyer-Utility-Map approach	Can you find an uncontested and fruitful opportunity using this approach?	
5. What's missing?	Can using Richard White's gaps approach provide a worthwhile opportunity?	
6. Unexpected changes in an industry/market	What opportunities will trade wars, political movements, regulatory changes, shifting economics, and technological progress present?	
7. Disconnects	What should have happened and didn't? Why? Is that a clue about a new opportunity?	
8. Unexpected successes, failures, or events	Which businesses are succeeding, dramatically, that you wouldn't expect to? How about those that looked like slam dunks, but tanked. What happened that no one saw coming? Can you forge opportunities from any of this?	

Cause of Opportunity	Comment	What We Can Do
9. Demographic/ psychographic changes	Increases in an area's population, its attributes and cultural leanings, its average age or its education level create demand. Are such changes likely to spawn new businesses or boost your results? Which ones?	
10. Process needs	Are there opportunities to streamline or make more effective any processes your business now employs, such as order to cash? sales leads passed from marketing to sales? or customer acquisition? What are they?	
11. Perception, meaning, and mood: societal changes	As society comes under more climate stress, becomes more tribal, or more concerned with income inequality, are there things your business can do to make things better in some way, and benefit from doing so?	
12. Knowledge	Is there a now-ready-for-prime-time discovery out there that would enhance your value proposition? What would it need to be? Is it within your reach via an acquisition or a license?	

2. **Focusing:** So that you're ready to capture opportunities when you find them, or, on those all-too-rare occasions when they find you, make a list of the types of opportunities you will and won't pursue.

Pursue:

Category	What the opportunity is	Upside (H-M-L)	Why?

Ignore:

Category	What it is	Why we should ignore it

3. **Being Prepared: What do you need to do to get your business's ability to pursue promising opportunities where it needs to be, in terms of:**

Being able to take advantage of opportunities when they come along, because there's the financial wherewithal, resources, and management bandwidth?

_____

_____

_____

Processes for integrating acquisitions?

_____

_____

The organizational guts (commitment) and the team alignment needed to pursue them?

_____

_____

People, who have the time to devote; the analysis, financial, and negotiation skills; and the judgment needed?

_____

_____

Resources: industry contacts? expertise?

_____

_____

4. **Leverage: What are the most powerful results engines your business can leverage?**

Existing asset(s)—which ones? _____

_____

Relationships with customers—which ones? _____

_____

Your brand(s)—which ones? _____

_____

Your reputation—which aspects? _____

_____

Technology—what, specifically, can you leverage? _____

_____

5. **Paying attention: How, specifically, will your business go about finding opportunities?**

What does your "opportunity-sensor network" consist of? _____

_____

What, or whom, should you add to it? _____

_____

Whose job is looking for, and assessing, opportunities? _____

_____

Is theirs a full-time responsibility, or something done "when they can get

to it?" _____

_____

Can outside resources like MBA interns help in this effort? _____

_____

How else will you discover opportunities? _____

_____

What do you do to really *understand* the problems and frustrations of your customers?

_____

And your prospects (others' customers)? _____

_____

What do you do with the insights you gather? Is there a defined flow toward deciding what to do about them?

_____

6. **Assessing: What is your process for evaluating potential opportunities?**

Getting the upside assessment right? _____

_____

Ensuring that the opportunity is realistic, in terms of its potential financial rewards and its feasibility?

_____

7. **Being careful: Doing a risk assesment.**

Risk	Severity (H-M-L)	How to mitigate?

Risk	Severity (H-M-L)	How to mitigate?

How will you mitigate the risk of a "bet the business" situation?

_____

_____

_____

On net, is the opportunity worth pursuing? _____

_____

_____

8. **Approach: Once you've found an opportunity you want to pursue, how, specifically, will you go about it?**

_____

_____

_____

_____

Is there a way to inexpensively, and at low risk, pursue the opportunity by making a pivotal hire, or engaging someone with critical knowledge as a consultant?

_____

_____

UPSIDE ELEMENT ASSESSMENT: DETECTING AND SEIZING OPPORTUNITIES

Please enter your estimates for the *overall* gains and challenges you expect to derive from your newfound opportunity in the corresponding row on the book's Upside Element Assessment Sheet, just before the last page.

"Sales covers a lot of sins."
So does being in a growing,
hungry market, *especially*
if you're there early.

Chapter 9

Finding and Serving Growing, Hungry, Markets

The merits of many of the opportunity sources in the last chapter depend on the characteristics of their associated *markets*. For each market: how big is it? how fast is it growing? can we serve it? how *hungry* is it for what we might offer?

Becoming (and remaining) a great business often requires pursuing growing, hungry markets that the business is well suited to serve.

A market is a group of people with a common want or unmet need.

They could, but need not, be in a particular geographical area. A great business is hard to build atop just any old market, though. It's much more lucrative to find, and serve, a *hungry market*—a group of people who want something, badly, and will pay decently for it.

A hungry market is exemplified by the difference between most golfers and most tennis players. Tennis players will buy racquets, balls, and clothes. But golfers will buy *anything they can* in the hope of improving their game. For example, there's a company that sells specially formulated *vitamins for golfers* on the internet. Golfers are a hungry market. Other known hungry markets:

- Parents, who want the best for their children, particularly in areas like education, sports, music, and the performing and fine arts.
- Parents who want to make their kids' lives a rich experience, the poster child for which is American Girl.[130]
- Those trying to attract, woo, or impress others.
- Lifelong learners.
- Video gamers.
- Avid mystery readers.
- Quilters.
- Stock-car racing fans.

As you can see, we're looking for *passion and drive* in our prospective customers—it creates hungry. No passion or drive? Well, I can probably live without what you offer.

A First Step

If you're in business now, you're serving one or more markets. Here we'll explore whether that market can provide your business with a prosperous future, and how to hunt for others. It's also important that you are now, or become, clear on *what you want* in the way of a market to serve:

- How hungry does it have to be? That is, *how intense* is the need? What will they forego for it? Erasmus: "When I have a little money, I buy books, and if any is left, I buy food …"
- Is the market big enough?
- Is it growing? How fast?
- Is serving the geographic area realistic?
- Do you now have, or can you create and sell, what the market seems to want, profitably?

- Is your business potentially its best provider, or at least a credible one?

- Is there a way to keep the competition at bay?

What Creates Hungry Markets?

Powerful Wants

We listed several above.

No Good Solutions, aka Market Gaps

Some hungry markets are *underserved*. Here we'll find capabilities and experiences that a lot of people really want, but they're not satisfied with what's now being offered. A good example would be "a comfortable bed that won't hurt my back,"* at a reasonable price. Even a good new mattress seems to be fine for a month or two. But then…

Here, creating a product that delivers is hard (or it would have been solved already), the product investment is significant, and distribution could be a challenge. But the market is indeed hungry, and the "you solved my aching back" payoff could be huge.

Another example … mobile phone service in the U.S. It mostly works, and it seems to work better on the networks offered by the major carriers. But the way they charge for their offerings, and the terms they offer, lead many customers to view the carriers as, variously, blood-sucking parasites, or worse. And that's without considering their experiences with technical support or customer service: often, rage.

As an alternative, one carrier, T-Mobile, has decided to position itself as *for* its customers, as described in Chapter 2. Its pricing and policies are much more customer friendly. As of this writing, its technology and coverage are perceived to be slightly below that of the other majors, but it gained 3.6 million customers in 2017.[131]

The consumer is left to trade off technology that works more often, coupled with higher prices and a lot more aggravation, versus lower prices, better treatment as a customer, but more dropped, or poor-quality calls.

---

* A phrase from the Mary Chapin Carpenter song, "Passionate Kisses."

In other words, the mobile-phone-service market is underserved (and hungry), but the barrier to entry is high.

Here's one where it's much lower: workwear for women—overalls and protective clothing designed specifically for women. These days, women are working in many fields historically staffed by men: construction, the shop floor, farming/ranching, etc. But most of the readily available clothes for these roles are designed to fit men's bodies. Recognizing the gap, not only in fit, but in the availability of colors and patterns that would appeal to women, several startups—Rosie's Workwear, Gamine Company, and Red Ants Pants among them, most of them now profitable—have entered this formerly underserved, but less than huge market.[132]

This type of market gap is often called *white space*. You'll find much more about it in Mark Johnson's fine book *Seizing the White Space*.[133] This example could also be thought of as a job to be done, "dress me for work," as described in Christensen's *Competing Against Luck*.[134]

Lastly, in the early twentieth century, those who needed to get a document to someone else, within a tight timeframe, had few, or no ways to do so, depending on the availability of a messenger service in their locales. Then came the FAX machine, and later, FedEx and email. Each provided a solution, and in doing so created huge markets (and businesses).

Markets and Strategy

What is called business strategy really boils down to *two choices about markets,* as we'll see.

Strategy is *the idea:* the concept of the business.

The strategy is made real by its corresponding business design (or model), covered in the next chapter. But first we need to get the strategy straight.

The Two Choices About Markets—Your Strategy

1. *What* market should we serve? (For now, focus on just one.)

2. What *position* should we try to establish in that market?

Choosing a Market

The market you'll serve is the first strategy choice. For those in business now, the question is: *How good is the market we're in?* Should we consider other options? Is there a "better" one? So choosing a market can involve both finding and assessing.

Tools for Finding Markets

The best exposition of Market Gap Analysis this author is aware of is Chapter 4 of Richard White's *The Entrepreneur's Manual*.[135] Market opportunities just pop out, using his method.

W. Chan Kim and Renée Mauborgne's *Blue Ocean Shift*[136] also provides market-finding tools, notably Buyer Utility Maps (page 147 in their book), briefly described in this book's Chapter 3 (Value Propositions).

Kim and Mauborgne also suggest considering the needs of noncustomers: What keeps them from *participating* in the market?

One prominent reason is know-how. Solution: "We'll teach you to dance, ice skate, etc. (and you'll want to keep coming back), to have fun, socialize, and get better at it." Works for both parties.

Other "market-finding guidance." Blue Ocean Shift also provides six ways to systematically reconstruct market boundaries: adopting ideas from other industries, redefining the group of buyers the business serves, drawing ideas from complementary offerings, etc. It's possible, though not a sure thing, that pursuing the process the book's authors provide will turn up a hungry market.

Another way to find a market is to recognize that there is not now *a way* to do something. Not everyone carries cash these days, but sometimes you need to pay a friend for something in cash. Thus, a business opportunity: provide a mobile app to facilitate person-to-person money transfers, and take a small fee for doing so. (Or you could use PayPal, Venmo, or another payment app if you're both signed up for it.)

More generally, uncovering the hidden pain points that people have, as laid out in the previous chapter and in Chapter 3, can result in a hungry market.

Assessing Markets

How Hungry Is the Market?

Does most of what is offered to this market, yours if you have one and others', pass its "Gotta have it!" test?

How Fast Is the Hungry Market Growing?

Getting into a market just before it blossoms has made many executives appear to be business geniuses, when in truth they were simply prescient, not that that's easy. When a market you serve blossoms, so will your business. Too, the investment made when a market is small will compound nicely as that market grows. But pursuing even a hungry market that's not growing robustly might not be your very best option.

This is why beachhead opportunities in emerging economies, and the ability to offer breakthrough innovations, are considered so valuable—the market grows, and the business that addresses the market grows with it.

How Real Is the Market?

In contrast with a decade or two ago, much more is possible in terms of testing. Ads on the internet are an inexpensive way to assess interest, and to test many market niches. You can see if there's interest in what you might offer through on-line ads: pay-per-click, or on targeted-niche websites. To do so, you can offer information related to the problem or particular interest that your potential offering would address. If you get a decent response, you might be able to move on to testing possible price points, depending on the offering.

A Short Story About the Reality of Markets—The Diving Pool

This vignette is also courtesy of Ken McCarthy, creator of The System Seminar. It captures, memorably, the key lessons about making sure that markets are real.

In the first scenario, a high-diver leaps into a pool—and is fatally injured—because there was only an inch of water in the pool, and the diver didn't look before leaping.

In the second scenario, a high-diver leaps into the pool and suffers a concussion and several broken bones because the pool was covered with thin plywood sheets, and the diver didn't look before leaping.

In the final scenario, the high-diver leaps into warm, blue-green water and emerges to wild applause.

The pool represents a market to which a business might offer a product or service.

In the first scenario, disaster ensued because very few in the market really wanted what was offered—there was little demand.

In the second, the initiative failed because the market was not economical to reach, i.e., selling into it was too expensive or it was too hard to find buyers.

And in the final scenario, that market really, really wanted what was being offered (and the marketer or executive was then lauded as a genius).

It's easy to be seen as a genius when you're standing on a rock that's rising out of the water. The genius, however, lies in picking that rock, before it starts rising rapidly. (Or in some cases, to have the rare ability and the resources to *make* it rise, like lots of *truly effective* advertising.)

How Lucrative Is the Market?

Obviously, each sale (or the net result from a "shopping basket" at checkout), should be sufficiently profitable. When designing a business (including the industry it will be part of), or considering potential acquisitions or divestitures, it's critical to bear in mind Michael Porter's timeless work in identifying the five forces (profit reducers) that shape the attractiveness of various industries and competition within them:[137]

1. **Competition:** How will your offering(s) fare against those of present and foreseeable competitors? Will what you offer be compared with others strictly on price? In that case, how does your cost structure compare with the competition's? That is, will they, by cutting prices, be able to drive you out of business? Or, does what you offer have some *defensible uniqueness* that's desirable in the eyes of a sufficiently large segment of the market, and that will make your offerings less sensitive to competitors' price changes? Is there some relatively persistent "unfair

advantage" enjoyed by a current player? A recent example of this would be Amazon initially not having to charge sales taxes in the U.S., while local retailers were required to do so.

2. **Barriers to entry (also known as "economic moats"):** How easy is it for new competitors to just "jump in," or are there real reasons that prevent them from doing so? To start a staffing company, all someone needs is a telephone, people skills, and some judgment. (Doing it well requires considerably more.) On the other hand, becoming a major retailer requires substantial capital, logistics and distribution, product-selection expertise, etc. Another frequent wide-moat example: proprietary pharmaceuticals.

3. **Substitutes:** Do I really need an accountant, or would a good personal-finance/tax-preparation software package or web-based service suffice? Should I buy a car, use a ride-sharing service like Zipcar, Lyft, or rent a car, on occasion? Is there now, or will there be soon, some far less costly "good enough" substitute for what you're planning to offer?

4. **Powerful buyers:** Are there one or more large buyers of what you'd offer that can push the prices of your offerings down to the point where it doesn't make business sense to sell to them? Are there other buyers that you could build a business selling to? Porter gives the example of Paccar, a truck builder, that doesn't sell to the large fleet operators who buy on price. Rather, it sells customized truck cabs to independent owner-operators, who can order their vehicles just the way they like them: comfortable sleeping cabins and driver's seats, interior noise reduction, infotainment systems, and eye-catching color schemes. These features bring their owners bragging rights at the truck stop, and they can be more comfortable in their long-haul, multiday runs. For that, the owners are willing to pay a premium.

5. **Powerful suppliers:** These will raise the cost of what you sell. Examples include labor unions, and Apple's one-time exclusive deal to sell its iPhone through AT&T in the U.S. when it first came out, with Apple taking a very high percentage of the iPhone's sales, because it granted AT&T exclusivity.

Can You Actually Serve the Market?

Serving a hungry market is about having something that it wants, badly, and having the ability to reach the market at a reasonable cost.

The final question is whether your business can provide what the market wants, as few others can. Part of this is that you might well need a physical presence in a geographic area. It also requires the ability to create and support what you'd offer, and to do so better than your potential or established competitors. Be brutally realistic here: dig into details, ask what-if's, find ways to work around what surfaces, if possible, or pivot to consider another market.

What Position Should We Try to Establish in That Market?

There is also a tool for *uncovering* a market position. It's laid out in W. Chan Kim and Renée Mauborgne's master work, *Blue Ocean Strategy,*[138] another recommended purchase.

The tool, the Strategy Canvas, is a line chart. The characteristics important to those in the market are listed along the bottom. Then, each potential

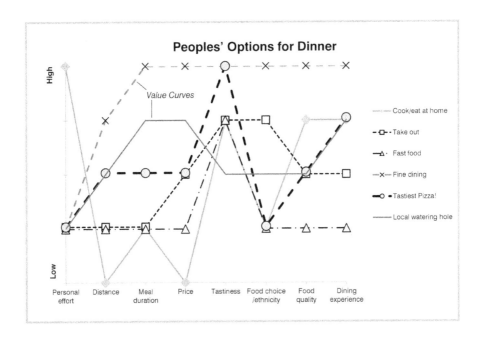

provider to that market is ranked on a scale with respect to each of those items. This is more easily seen than explained. What follows is a Strategy Canvas for meeting a universal need, dinner, put together by the owner of an imaginary restaurant, Tastiest Pizza.

Each zig-zag line on the canvas is called a *value curve*. Careful study of the canvas for a market sector can indicate an opportunity. As shown, the owner of Tastiest Pizza is trying to match the attraction of a fine-dining restaurant, simply based on his pizza's *taste* (the dashed line).

The canvas makes the market's player's positions clear, and shows how they differ. It does not indicate whether any of the positionings are *viable, or good.* That requires real-life testing.

For much more on market positioning, you can consult Al Ries and Jack Trout's classic, *Positioning*,[139] Denny Hatch's article cited earlier on how American Girl surrounded its market,[130] and Andy Cunningham's recent *get to Aha!* on becoming clear on your business's essence, its DNA, before trying to position it.[140]

Summary

In looking for a market, try to detect a rock that's about to start rising out of the water and go stand on it. Make early detection an important role of your look-outs, as described in the opportunity-detection section of the previous chapter.

In the next chapter, we'll treat turning the market strategy (the *idea* of the business, that we just developed) into a real entity (the business design), and the design choices involved.

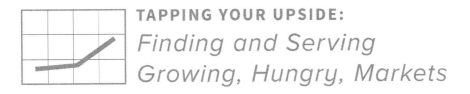

TAPPING YOUR UPSIDE:

Finding and Serving Growing, Hungry, Markets

1. **Is the market your business is now serving, worth serving in the future?**

   _____

2. **What other markets could your business serve?**

   _____

   _____

3. **In addition to the markets listed on page 178, what other hungry markets can you think of? For each one...**

   Why is it hungry? _____

   Is the reason one that's likely to *persist,* or is it a fad or fashion?

   _____

4. **The candidate market's other characteristics:**

   Size? _____

   Spending power? _____

   Growth rate? _____

   Receptivity to a business like the one you're considering? _____

5. **Where are the market's prospects, physically, and can you adequately serve them?**

_____

_____

6. **What will you offer the market?**

_____

_____

Is it something that no other business can offer? _____

_____

If not, does your offering have:

A defensible uniqueness? _____

   It is: _____

A preferable value-proposition? _____

   It is: _____

Do you have more than one potential offering? _____

For each offering, you'll need to answer the questions above.

7. **Which hungry markets will you test?**

_____

8. How will you go about it?

_____

Is there a way to do this quickly, such as gauging the response to an online offer?

_____

What results will a test have to produce, to convince you to pursue the market?

_____

9. What market(s), if any, have you ultimately decided to pursue?

_____

UPSIDE ELEMENT ASSESSMENT: HUNGRY MARKETS

Please enter your estimates for the *overall* gains and challenges you expect to derive from your hungry market in the corresponding row on the book's Upside Element Assessment Sheet, just before the last page.

Chapter 10

Crafting a Powerful Business Design

The *job* of every executive responsible for a P&L is to *be* in a great business.

Please take a little quiet time to really think about that. Warren Buffett understands it, and buys such businesses. Not everyone gets it, or acts as though they do.

A great business is one that is growing handily, making a considerable profit after all of its costs (including capital) are taken into account, and its results are highly likely to endure.

A business's *design*, often termed a business model, determines *how* the business makes money, and how it keeps on doing so. It's been said that the degree to which a business succeeds or fails is determined *before it ever opens, because of its design*[141] (regardless of whether that design comes from a corporate plan, is discovered using the tools of Blue Ocean Strategy|Shift, is inspired, as was American Girl, or is a lucky accident, like Facebook.)

Companies with successful business designs include: Facebook (the network effect: the more people who are on it, the more people who want to be on it), Microsoft (a platform others build atop, with heyday gross margins of 85%), and Google (sky's-the-limit revenue-growth potential from search ads). Granted, neither Microsoft's nor Google's founders might have clearly known when they started them that their businesses would become what they have. Nontech examples include Visa, MasterCard, Fastenal, and Monster Beverage (each of these was highly ranked, over multiple years, in *Chief Executive* magazine's Wealth Creation Index).[142]

Here it's also critical to take to heart one of Buffett's famous quotes: "With few exceptions, when a manager with a reputation for brilliance tackles a business with a reputation for poor fundamental economics, it is the reputation of the business that remains intact." That is, none of us has superpowers. Really! *Wisely choosing* a strategy and a business design beats both talent and brainpower. To overcome a lackluster business design, we have to either evolve that design or change the business we're in.

We're going to use the term business *design* here, rather than business model, which seems to connote something static, like a model ship. Rather, the word *design*, in its verb sense, is used to indicate that those who run the business should be *actively* designing it. As in the natural world, the design of a business needs to continuously adapt to its changing environment, often more rapidly than living things can.

Why bother about business design? It's an extremely powerful way to create a highly valuable business, which often comes about because of the design's superior wealth-creation ability. A great business design (and the strategy it's based on) tends to make more money over the long term than its competitors, because it has *lasting* competitive advantages.

Prominent among those advantages is usually the unique value proposition the business offers to customers; witness: Southwest Airlines, Amazon, IBM, Costco, Facebook, Google, and American Girl.

Costco is a good example of why its customer-value proposition is preferred: remarkably low prices in return for an annual membership fee, the quality of what it offers, and a no-questions-asked return policy.

Another reason for enduring preference is a distinctive, defensible *combination* of characteristics, such as Amazon's finely honed customer experience (with product reviews), deep knowledge about its customers, delivery infrastructure, and brand, not to mention its Amazon Prime incentive program.

The final example is a company that has shaped its business around the needs of its customers, Fastenal. Fastenal distributes fasteners and other maintenance, repair, and operations (MRO) items, primarily in the United States. Fasteners, its core offering, are essential to its customers' ability to keep production going—they're very costly to be without. And because fastener cost is inconsequential to its customers, Fastenal can price what it offers to earn decent margins.

The company's competitive advantages include an exceptionally broad and locally available inventory, and an internal (and economical) logistics capability that gets needed parts to its stores daily by 8 AM. Fastenal locates its stores in less-populated areas that will likely support only one store of its type. But it's likely that the local store has what customers need, even if they're in the boondocks.

What Is a Business Design?

The term *business model* is used to mean different things, as described by *Harvard Business Review*'s Andrea Ovans.[143] For some, it's the assumptions about the business; for others, its competitive strategy. We'll focus here on the upside-related aspects of a business's design—its wealth-creation ability: a powerful value proposition, and a sustainable competitive advantage, in contrast with Alex Osterwalder's Business Model Canvas, which focuses on all of the elements of the business, including its operational aspects.[144] Another business-design resource is the paper by Lucier et al.[145]

An Ideal Business Design

Simply, you're after a design in which what you offer fulfills a significant, enduring need for its large market, and is defensible against competition and substitutes. "Ha," you say! And in the main, you're right. But there are examples: like ride-sharing services and Airbnb (network effect and value propositions), and Fastenal's design, just discussed. Less ideal, but still powerful, is Nike's business design, which is based on continuous product improvement and effective marketing.

These are powerful *results engines.* If you create or find one, then your job becomes *fueling it for all it's worth!* Sadly, such situations are not common, or we'd all be rich.

What's in a Business Design?

A complete business design should consist of:

1. The market(s) it will address: their sizes and growth rates, based on its strategy, as detailed in Chapter 9.

2. Its value proposition, and the proposition's attractiveness, relative to those of existing and prospective competitors now in, or entering, those markets (also in Chapter 9). This is a big factor in your results engine's power.

3. Realistic assumptions about the profitability of each sale, sales volumes, fixed and variable costs, an assessment of the business's ability to create wealth under those assumptions, and how that ability compares with management's other options.

4. A way to *attain* and *sustain* (in light of competition and alternatives) the business's wealth-creation ability, its *resilience*.

5. *How* the business will go about delivering that value proposition to those markets.

- Necessary and critical: relationships, resources, and resource intensity, such as capital, materials, and skilled people. Will the business guzzle any resources in short supply, limiting the business design's results potential?

- Essential processes.

- How it will keep up with demand.

The Financial Characteristics of a Business Design

We'll start this chapter with the basics, to get everyone on the same page, and to provide a shared terminology for the material here. We are decidedly *not* out to insult anyone's intelligence or finance/business knowledge. That said, long observation has demonstrated that businesses are most often upended by the basics.

Businesses sell goods and services. What customers pay for these is called *revenue*. Businesses also have costs: of creating, distributing and marketing what they offer for sale; the materials involved, the labor force and management that produces what's sold, warehousing, shipping, advertising, sales compensation, and others (variable costs), and of simply existing: corporate management, equipment, buildings and their upkeep, and internal services like IT, finance, HR, and legal (more or less "fixed" costs).

In this simple model, profit is what you have left after deducting the total of your fixed and variable costs from revenue. The goal is to have a business that operates to the right of the breakeven point on what we'll call "the Mother of All Business Graphs": a MOABG. MOABG 1, below, shows a business with $100,000 in fixed costs, a product that sells for $1 on average, and costs the business an average of 75 cents ($ 0.75) to make, distribute and sell.

MOABG 1: Base Business Design

Operating to the right of breakeven means that the business is profitable. But there's more to be gleaned from the graph and the numbers, which are all in thousands. The greater the difference between revenue and variable costs, the more quickly you can cover your fixed costs as revenue grows.

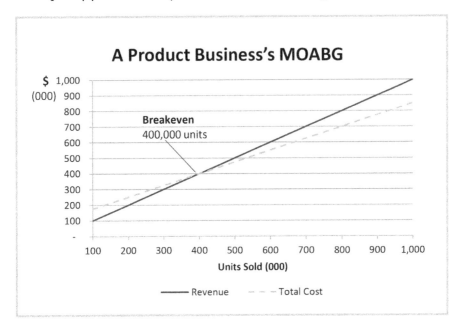

(For the related figures, see endnote 146.)

MOABG 2: Cutting Variable Costs Lets You Make Money with Fewer Sales

With a 10-cent-per-unit drop in variable costs, you can become profitable selling 29% fewer items, 285,713 versus 400,000. At the 400,000 sales volume mark, you would have made $40,000 rather than nothing. And at the million-unit mark, you'd have made $250,000 rather than $150,000.

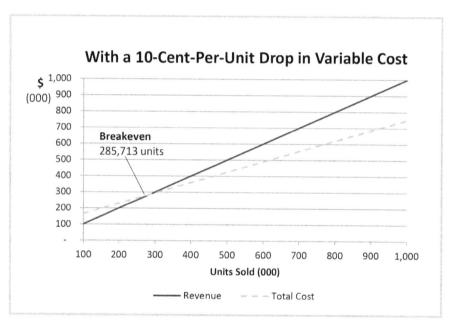

(For the related figures, see endnote 147.)

MOABG 3: Cutting Fixed Costs Also Lets You Make Money with Fewer Sales

Obviously, profitability also comes more quickly when the fixed costs are lower. And with today's ability to create "asset-light" (low-fixed-cost) businesses, and the low variable costs of some lines of business, it's sometimes possible to have a business with both.

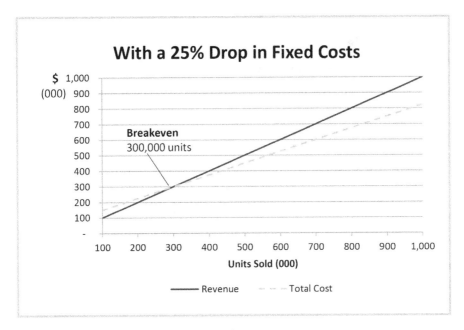

With a 25% Drop in Fixed Costs

Breakeven
300,000 units

Units Sold (000)

——— Revenue   - - - Total Cost

(For the related figures, see endnote 148.)

MOABG 4: Cutting Both Types of Costs Lets You Make Money with Even Fewer Sales

Now, what can be done about revenue (average price times unit sales volume)? A wonderful lesson is provided by Ram Charan and Noel Tichy in their book, *Every Business Is a Growth Business*. Charan tells of a market in Nicaragua in which the vendors were charged usurious interest rates (34.5%, on an annual basis) for the money they needed to buy the goods they sold. And it turned out that each sale netted about 5% more than the goods' costs. How could they possibly be making any money?

The vendors knew that they had to sell *a lot of* goods to make it. In business lingo, this is called turning over your inventory quickly: *high asset turns.* Charan and Tichy have a more descriptive word for this—*velocity*—sales divided by total assets. Colloquially, this is known as "making it up on volume."

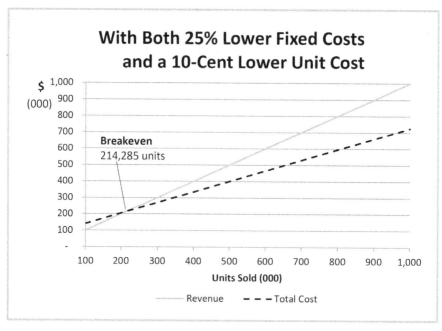

With Both 25% Lower Fixed Costs and a 10-Cent Lower Unit Cost

Breakeven
214,285 units

(For the related figures, see endnote 149.)

Velocity is also a key element of the health of a business: return on investment, or ROI (profit margin times velocity). ROI shows how good your business is at turning effort and stuff into money. ROI also determines how willing others will be to invest in your business or loan it money. For more on velocity and ROI, please see Charan and Tichy's excellent book.[150]

We'll discuss the effect of price on velocity and revenue in more detail in Chapter 14.

Beyond the basics, you want strong ultimate potential: the ability to go global, the likelihood that you'll dominate your industry (because of some real reason, not simply a will to win), an *enduring* value proposition, tolerable risk, etc. The power of the business design is rooted in the market-assessment findings of the previous chapter, and:

- Its financial characteristics:
  - For each item you sell, how much money will you make (revenue, less the item-specific costs of the sale)?

- How significant are the business's fixed costs, and its fixed future commitments?
- How many sales can you reasonably expect to make in a given period?
- Are there realistic ways to keep the competition at bay?
- How scalable is the business?
- How intense are the business's needs for cash, scarce resources, talent, and other elements?

An up-and-running business *might* be able to quickly change profitability, the first item above, through pricing, depending on the competition and the customers' alternatives. It can't change the others on a dime, yet it can evolve. And it can take the above factors into account as it does.

But let's press on with the basics a bit longer.

Ingredients of a good business design include:

Its "Weight"

As we saw with MOABG 3, the sooner you can blow past your fixed costs, the better.

Management consultant Dan Wertenberg tells the story of how, early in his career, he worked for the Ford Motor Company, under Robert McNamara. There, he said, he worked with some of the most brilliant people he'd ever encountered. Yet Ford was always riding the roller coaster of results, many of them steep, money-losing drops. And of course, it was sometimes necessary to make additional and sizable fixed-cost investments.

Later, he worked in the gambling industry, where he met some of the biggest, well, jerks, in his life. And yet, the gambling industry consistently seemed to make a lot of money.

Why? Between its infrastructure's high fixed costs and those of its workforce, Ford had to get sales volumes far to the right on its MOABG. Not so in the gambling industry.

Fixed costs are an element of what is sometimes called the *weight* of a business. The term generally refers to whether the business can make good money with few assets: Google and social-media networks are considered asset-light—relatively few assets are required. On the other hand, U.S. Steel is asset-intensive.

It's easier to make money in an asset-light business (lower fixed costs), but once an asset-intensive business blows past its fixed costs, its profits rise more dramatically with sales volume growth.

Profitability

We covered the main determinant of profitability, Porter's 5 Forces, in Chapter 9. But there's more that drives profit, the combination of sales volume and price that's called revenue.

Revenue

It's been said that the best things a business can sell are expensive, consumable, and addictive. Illegal drugs aside, the expensive aspect is represented by luxury goods of all stripes, high fashion, wines and spirits, etc. What if you were able to create more purchases through:

- More widespread product availability: a Starbucks on every corner.
- A more addictive product formulation: Gotta have my weekly visit to Tastiest Pizza, my exercise class, daily visits to my favorite news sources and social-media sites. For the media, curiosity has been a time-honored way to drive this—the serials of the early 20th century. The taste of certain foods can do it, as can pursuit of an athletic goal, such as getting into top shape for the next big race.
- Environment creation: an "I love this place" atmosphere at my neighborhood breakfast place or bar, through décor, a theme that customers can identify with, its friendly (or attractive) wait staff, entertainment, and so on.
- New uses: Arm & Hammer Baking Soda, as a room deodorizer, and tooth whitener.
- Purchase rewards (Staples) and other so-called loyalty programs.

Fixed Costs/Up-Front Investment

Some businesses no longer require the level of initial investment they once did because of rented IT infrastructure, open-source software, application-creation tools, and 3-D printing. But if you're going to be making tractors or cosmetics, that won't be an enormous help.

What can you outsource, license, rent, barter, or create a partnership arrangement for, to keep your up-front or fixed costs to a sensible minimum? Cloud-based computing can dramatically cut the cost of a business's information technology. For a startup, that can markedly reduce the need for capital, allowing the founders to keep the business completely under their control longer, perhaps forever.

> ### Creating the **Habit** of Buying What You Offer— So Sales Recur
>
> Initially, people will choose a product or service based on what it provides them. But particularly for frequent purchases such as groceries, as time goes on, and as long as a product or service continues to meet their needs, people will continue to buy it, forming a habit. They're no longer making a conscious choice; they're making the easy (or automatic) choice: something they don't have to think about—which would be more work. Easy is good.
>
> You'll find more on this in the customer-themed article collection in the January-February 2017 issue of the *Harvard Business Review*. The main article suggests that rather than trying to create loyal customers, a business should try to get customers in the *habit* of buying what they offer—see "Customer Loyalty Is Overrated: Focus on Habit Instead. A Theory of Cumulative Advantage," by former P&G CEO A.G. Lafley and University of Toronto Rotman School of Management dean Roger L. Martin, 45–54.
>
> For habit-based offerings, the authors recommend innovating carefully, and staying consistent with the brand, to preserve the

habit, and using simple language to describe the changes. Doing these will help to prevent the customer from having to make a new conscious choice.

Another article in this issue notes that habits are still susceptible to disruption, e.g. Dollar Shave Club. See Rita Gunther McGrath, "Old Habits Die Hard, But They Do Die," 54–57.

This author's take is that although creating habitual purchases works, it does not necessarily create any feelings about the company behind the product or service (zeal), so that when a competing alternative comes along, the customer could be more susceptible to adopting it.

A zeal-creating approach to habit formation also appears in this article collection: "How Lego does this: A Conversation with Jørgen Vig Knudstorp, CEO and President of The Lego Group," by David Champion, 58.

A Business's Full Potential and Porter's Five Forces

Here are some of the things that determine the potential of a business:

The characteristics of the industry you're in, or are thinking about entering. Here Harvard Business School professor Michael Porter's Five Forces (presented in the Hungry Markets chapter) and later work[151] is the gold standard. The *HBR* paper just cited shows profitability for selected industries from 1992 to 2006. At the high end, returns on invested capital for soft drinks, prepackaged software, and pharmaceuticals were north of 30%. At the bottom of the ranking, airlines' returns were 6%. But industry analysis, while generally insightful, assumes that the competitive forces of an industry will persist, and can't readily be disrupted. As we've long seen, that's clearly not the case in the technology sector.

Too, basing decisions mainly on industry analysis ignores the possibility that a bright entrepreneur—perhaps you—will find a profitable niche in an unattractive sector, as Paccar did (see the Porter article just cited, or Chapter 9).

Also included on page 1 of Porter's article are ways to reshape your industry's five profitability-determining forces in your favor.

A winner-take-most business: Can the business harness network effects like Facebook, Google, YouTube, Zagat, and now Netflix have done? The more people who use your online offering, the more valuable it becomes: the obvious destination, to the exclusion of the also-rans.

Inherent advantages in its value chain: A good poster child for this, in its 1997 heyday, was Dell. Its value proposition: "My computer is exactly what I want." With just-in-time parts inventory (their component costs were dropping 32% per year, giving them a 6.1% cost advantage), no finished-goods inventory, direct-to-consumer (with the 5.9% cost advantage that allows). Total cost advantage: 12%.[152]

Addressable markets that are large, hungry, and growing: As detailed in the previous chapter.

Scalability: With a scalable business, there's ample ability to deliver what's offered in high volume. Each sale will be more profitable than the last, because the dramatic increase in revenue less variable costs makes fixed costs of less consequence. Companies like Microsoft, Netflix, and Airbnb are good examples of what having a scalable business design can create.

Resource intensity: To what degree do the elements below weigh on costs, particularly variable costs? Can the limits of any of them can be exhausted, restricting the business's ability to grow, or profit? As an example, automakers are resource intensive. They need a lot of:

- Materials
- Capital
- People
- Skills
- Expertise

Offerings: As we said earlier, the best offerings are high-margin, consumable, addictive, and legal. The closer the business's offerings are to that characterization, the higher its potential becomes.

The longevity of its offerings: How quickly will what the business offers be made obsolete or, have to be updated or upgraded? In some businesses, what's offered needn't, even shouldn't, change. Examples: Coke, and brand-name candy bars. At the other end of the spectrum, we have technology products, which require major ongoing development expenses (and support); and fashion. In either of these, missing the next thing can bring on a crisis of cash flow.

How risky is the business:
- Critical dependencies: Does it require staying on Walmart's vendor list? A steady supply of borrowed funds? Raw materials from politically volatile/dangerous regions? Uncertain regulatory approvals? Peace with labor unions that's been hard to come by?
- Is there significant litigation risk?
- What could be the impact of: compliance violations, security/privacy breaches, patent-violation exposure, etc.?

Another important dimension of business design is harnessing its synergistic strengths. An example is 3M, which manufactures products for industry, safety and graphics, electronics, energy, health care, and consumers. 3M does this using:

- Its well-earned reputation—its products will perform to expectations.
- Its R&D—3M's world-class, centralized R&D has garnered more than 100,000 patents, many of which can be utilized in more than one of the above businesses.
- Its astute judgments about *where to play* (what businesses to be in). For example, it makes consumables such as industrial sanding disks, and components that are embedded in other manufacturers' products. Each of these drives *recurring* revenue.[153]

A business's wealth-creation potential (the economic value it can create, as defined in Chapter 14) is also determined by these characteristics and capabilities:

- Pace: Its ability to hit market windows.
- Agility: Its ability to pivot when things don't go as planned.
- Robustness: How reliant the business is on others for what it needs to:
  - Create what it sells.
  - Finance it.
  - Reach customers.
- Leverageable assets—*Examples*
  - IBM's buying small software companies whose products they can integrate into IBM's own product line, then sell worldwide through their much larger sales force (the leverageable asset).
  - Similarly, Disney's purchase of Lucasfilm's Star Wars franchise leveraged Disney's more powerful distribution capabilities.
  - A product, as distinct from a service that's primarily delivered by people who you need to pay, like Intuit's TurboTax.
  - Intellectual property (IP): Qualcomm's mobile-phone-chip patent portfolio.
  - Know-how and processes: Memorial Sloan Kettering Cancer Center.
  - Reputation, trusted brands: T. Rowe Price.
  - Customer relationships: REI.
  - Unusually skillful or talented people: IDEO.
  - Corporate culture: Patagonia.
  - A trove of valuable information: Bloomberg.
  - Product performance; learning from problem reports: Microsoft.
  - Fixed-asset utilization: Fastenal.

Business Design Examples

- *Good:* Lightweight—Priceline (an asset-light business design), Facebook (network effect), Apple (the iTunes, now Apple Music, ecosystem), Microsoft (Windows), C.H. Robinson Worldwide (a third-party-logistics company with an asset-light business design, a proprietary technology advantage, no dominant customers, and strong customer relationships).

- *Mediocre:* Industry rollups (these are acquisitions of multiple companies in the same industry, often with the intent of reducing some fixed costs by sharing finance, HR, and legal support staff, and perhaps more fully utilizing major production assets). They can be good, but not great, financially. They come with integration risks like terminally incompatible cultures and headaches such as integrating technology systems.

- *Bad:* Airlines (asset-intensive, high costs, substantial competition), Micron Technology (a semiconductor manufacturer with a competitively challenged, low-margin, asset-intensive business design), Archer Daniels Midland (a food-processing company with little power over pricing or the cost of its ingredients).

Finding a Good Business Design By Looking a Lot, and Wisely

There's an interesting approach to finding suitable opportunities from what are called search funds. Such a fund would hire top MBA graduates to comb through small ($10–$30 million in revenue) acquisition opportunities, for one to two years. When they find one to recommend, the fund's investors could choose to acquire the business, join the board, and counsel the MBA grads, who would then run the business. If things worked out, everyone would benefit. 'Course, they don't always. But on average, the Center for Entrepreneurial Studies at Stanford reported average annual gains for the search funds' original investors of over 30% (a skewed result because of a few big successes).

The biggest search-fund success story was the purchase of a roadside-assistance company called Road Rescue for $8 million in 1995. Post-acquisition, the company grew 50–100% in the next four years. Then "the big idea" struck the entrepreneurs—evolving into the cell-phone insurance business. After making three major acquisitions, by 2009, Asurion, as it's now known, had grown into a $2.5 billion company with 10,000 employees.[154] (Note that a big part of that success was riding the explosive growth of the cell-phone market during that time—see previous chapter.)

But even aside from, er, stepping in it, in its first four years, the investment worked out very well, demonstrating the power of wisely choosing a business to be in, based on its design.

Another approach along these lines is to watch where venture-capital investment is flowing, although caution is certainly needed here, because of these investors' famous herd mentality.

Evolving a Business Design

A good example of evolving a business design is Milliken, described in more detail in Chapter 12 (Innovation). Briefly, they went from challenged, as a U.S.-based textile manufacturer facing extreme offshore price competition, to an innovation-based maker of specialty chemicals, high-performance materials, and floor coverings—because they had to, and were open to doing so.

Milliken's transformation was not easy. They needed: the vision, the *intent* to evolve to what they became, the expertise (some of which they presumably had), the financial resources and reputational foundation, and the ability to stay on their evolution path.

Pursuing a New Business

It might seem that the new business you've identified, rather than the one you're now in, offers a greener pasture. Now comes the trick, "validating the greenness," while doing the best you can running the business you've got. Why validate? That should be clear, from the diving-pool story in Chapter 9 (Markets).

As Innosight founder Mark Johnson and his co-authors point out[155,156] knowing you have a customer-value proposition that will work is only part of what's needed. There are three more elements that have to pass muster.

- Profit: Will you be able to make money in the new business: pricing and sales volume (revenue), and cost structure (variable and fixed costs), which, when combined, determine the new venture's break-even sales volume, and wealth-creation potential?

- Resources: Whether you have the key resources the business needs to succeed, like software-development talent, industry knowledge and relationships, manufacturing capability, and others.

- Processes: Having the processes needed to scale up the business to meet your expected sales volume.

Finally, if all of the above indicate full speed ahead, how should you go about keeping both the new and the old plates spinning? At root, this is an organization-design question, for which the best answer seems to be to put a dedicated manager (or team) on getting the new business up and running. If you try to do so with people who are responsible for parts of the existing business, the new one will be unlikely to get off the ground, because of the existing business's demands. Those demands will prove to be an ongoing, often terminal, distraction from the new business.

In the next chapter, we'll take a look at what product/service design can do for your results, but for now, dive into the questions below.

TAPPING YOUR UPSIDE:

Crafting a Powerful
Business Design

1. **Given what we've covered here, do you need to change anything about the business you're in, or the one you're planning?**

   _____

   _____

   _____

2. **What, specifically, are those things?**

   (Summarize them in the Initiative column below, then prioritize them based on their results impact, the likelihood that you can pull them off, their cost, the effort required, and risk they bring. Initially, it might be easier to just use High, Medium, and Low ratings for the four rightmost columns below. When done, check the Do? column for those you want to move further with.)

Do?	Initiative	Results Impact		Chance of Success	Cost	Effort	Risk
		Revenue	Profit				

3. How, specifically, will you go about doing the things you chose
   to pursue?

_____

_____

_____

_____

With your promising business-design changes identified, you could
choose to pursue them now, or wait until you've worked through
deciding among all of the results-boosting initiatives you've identified,
as you'll do in Chapter 14, Insight-Based Management.

UPSIDE ELEMENT ASSESSMENT: CRAFTING A POWERFUL BUSINESS DESIGN

Please enter your estimates for the *overall* gains and challenges you expect to
derive from your evolved business design in the corresponding row on the
book's Upside Element Assessment Sheet, just before the last page.

"If you wanna be warm, it wins far and away;
it's like walkin' around in your bed all day."
—*The Roches, "My Winter Coat."*
Words and music by Margaret A. Roche. *

Chapter 11

Product and Service Design to Die For

Yes, there's an actual song about product design. Inspired by an actual product! That inspiration sprang from the emotion the product created in the buyer, in this case, even after years of use. In other words, great design creates *emotion,* which is almost always the reason for a purchase.

Why Design Is Important in Boosting Results

Outstanding design has lifted many a business from near-failure to prosperity, most notably Apple. Design has also created quick prosperity for new businesses—Under Armour, for example, with its moisture-wicking athletic clothing, and Uniqlo, with its lightweight, stay-warm underwear.

Here are a few products—you can call them "hit records"—that design-focused companies have created, bringing them prosperity:

Apple: The original iMac.[157] Exciting (great colors), cute, and friendly looking (adoptable), nonthreatening to operate. In short, COOL! Pictures and more on https://en.wikipedia.org/wiki/IMac_G3.

---

* From their "Can We Go Home Now?" album.

OXO: Their first product: a fruit and vegetable peeler with a thick handle. "My aching hands can grip this."

HumanScale Office Chairs: HumanScale offers several self-adaptive chairs that just move with you, adapting to your changing positions, without your having to do anything, or break your concentration. In other words, you don't have to manually adjust any of its seating controls when you change positions.[158] As the web-usability guru Steve Krug so well put it in his book's title, "Don't Make Me Think."[159]

The PowerSquid: Someone finally thought about the ever-maddening power strip, in which you can only use every other outlet because large transformer bricks cover part of the adjacent outlet, or at least prevent putting two such bricks into adjacent outlets. That someone is Chris Hawker of Trident Design, who came up with the PowerSquid.[160] Its design allows up to six plug-in power transformers, regardless of their size, to be plugged into its outlets. Also, the wall plug is thin and rotates 360 degrees, so it can be plugged from above, below, or the side, minimizing the need to move furniture. Another thoughtful touch: several of the outlets glow, so you can find them in the dark under a desk or workbench.

Point: The PowerSquid provides substantially *greater utility* than conventional rectangular power strips. And speaking of utility…

Apple's iPhone: The pathbreaking smartphone, now with Siri, replaced: the classic clamshell cell phone, the portable music player, the personal organizer, the voice recorder, most video and still cameras, the GPS, maps, the calculator, the magnifying glass (camera), and the travel alarm—all in one device. It was beautiful, intuitive, and worth its high price. Apple prospered.[161]

The Gillette Mach 3 Razor: A dramatic improvement in shaving comfort and effectiveness, and the product of considerable effort, investment, and product-development secrecy.[162]

Calloway Golf's Big Bertha Driver: This golf club was a hit for one simple reason—performance. Its design (a larger club head) enabled golfers to hit the ball farther, playing right into most golfers' most ardent desire: to improve their game.

Uniqlo (a brand of Japan's Fast Retailing): I can only speak for this very popular clothing retailer's New York area stores, but my experience with their well-designed checkout process, which keeps the line moving at the busiest of times, and their attentive, "I'll take you there," salespeople, clearly attests that someone has thought about the experience they offer.

A Word About Design and Innovation

Either of these can dramatically increase sales, and each can yield proprietary assets:

- Design deals with both how things work, and their look and feel. While often thought of as product design, its principles apply to the delivery of services: a dining experience, picking up breakfast before work, air travel (ugh!), or a resort stay. And designing the process by which the product or service *is introduced* makes its acceptance more likely.[163,164]

- Innovation is about creating something that's never existed, or improving on it. This often has to do with addressing an unmet need, or one for which the existing solution still has issues or annoyances. We'll treat innovation in depth in the next chapter.

The point here is that both design and innovation offer a substantial upside, and that you can, and should, pursue both—the combined result can be an even bigger hit. And both spring from the same gold taproot: *Improving people's lives.*

Design Thinking

Being good at design and at creating *relevant* innovations requires "the empathy muscle." Its essence: go interact directly with the people for whom you're designing something, whether they're local, or halfway around the world. Absorb their challenges at a visceral level, so that you're emotionally motivated, and have the depth of understanding to appropriately, not cluelessly, address them. Empathy is taught at Stanford University's D. (Design) school,[165] founded by David Kelley (who also created the renowned design firm IDEO). Its goal is to give students "the tools to change lives."

Interestingly, IBM, under its recent CEO, Virginia Rometty, adopted design thinking as a key to its future, seeing it as a path out of the challenging market transition it faces. IBM needs to grow revenue from its new initiatives faster than sales of existing offerings decline. To help pull that off, IBM looked to have 1,100 designers, a hefty increase, working with product teams and customers, and in its design studios by the end of 2015. One of its new initiatives is Smarter Cities, encompassing, well, everything about a city: public safety, schools, infrastructure, social programs, management, and city planning. The problems that come up in helping cities deal with these areas require substantial design talent.[166]

Here's a classic example of design thinking (though it wasn't called that at the time): *Life Savers*. They were born as candy with a strong value proposition—the first cure for, well, the "hog breath" that sometimes afflicts us all, and one that wouldn't melt in the summer heat. Two other elements helped: the candy's nautical design, mimicking the design of life preservers, and the play on words, as in, this breath mint could rescue my first conversation with someone I find attractive. It was perfect for its intended use.[167]

Achieving Prosperity Is a Whole Lot Easier If You're Good at Creating "Hit Records"

By products and services that you can call "hit records" we mean something that's so overwhelmingly attractive that it dramatically outsells competing alternatives.

You can, and should, be "on purpose" about creating these—like Ikea, or the automakers. To do so, you need a hit-record-creation *team.* Surprisingly, quite a few businesses don't have one—they've never even thought about it. Yikes!

The team need not be as large as described below, but it needs to have people able to provide:

- The prescience, wisdom, and discipline to choose a problem well worth solving—one that a lot of people will pay a premium for, or at least a fair price.
- Vision, of the solution they could create.
- A better-than-average sense of whether it would sell.
- The design skills to form the concepts they come up with into something attractive, be it a product, a service, or an experience.
- A strong, sage, gatekeeper, with the power to reject mediocre design. Another term for this role would be "Design Tyrant," like the role Steve Jobs played at Apple. In the words of his successor, Tim Cook, "There's always a large junk part of the market. We're not in the business of making junk."[168]
- The technical skills to make the product or service work as well as, or better than, buyers expect.
- In the case of a physical product, expertise in *the materials* that go into it: fabrics for clothing, glass for mobile phones, woods for fine furniture, metals for construction, ingredients for food, etc.
- It might also need to include those adept at design for manufacturing, and at component sourcing.

Also, the team:

- Should *not* have other responsibilities, or your hit record might never get made, because of, for example, the incessant demands of operating responsibilities.
- Needs the strong interest and support of the CEO, and frequent interaction with them. In some companies, such as Electrolux, with

its passion to distinguish its offerings using design, the Chief Design Officer reports directly to the CEO.[169]

- Needs to test the daylights out of their creation, with real-live users, and to wisely decide which elements of their feedback to incorporate.

Lastly, once the creation is approved for production, or introduction (for a service), the *instructions for its use* should receive rigorous scrutiny from real users, and correction. This is, at times, overlooked, to the company's detriment. *Example:* Dyson is famous for its product design. Yet its "graphics-only" instructions for removing, cleaning, and reinstalling its vacuum cleaner's roller brush were both incomprehensible and incomplete, producing an emotion stronger than frustration and closer to rage.

Hit Record Characteristics

Regarding the hit record itself, there are a few essential underpinnings…

The design process needs to be firmly rooted in the prospect's wants and emotional needs. The resulting design must create *feelings.* As did the winter-coat song that opened this chapter.

Its closing lines:

> *"I know you're not supposed to be so fond of a thing,*
> *but today this is my heartfelt inspiration to sing.*
> *I hope you don't think I'm merely trying to be clever.*
> *I wish this coat would last forever."*

The songwriter wanted her coat to last forever because it was *appropriate* for her needs.

You'll know you've achieved this when the customer blurts out, "It's perfect!" followed instantly by "That's for me! I'll take it." To do that, you *really* have to know the customer. And make what you offer perfectly suit what he or she wants. Those words, perfectly suits, are also taken from *My Winter Coat:* "The cuffs are purple which perfectly suits the pair I already had of boots."

What you offer should *perfectly suit* a large group of potential buyers.

And providing customization as a way for people to express themselves creates "even more perfect" perfection.

Note, too, that nothing about your product can appear complicated to its user. Confusion begets frustration. That's not the emotion you're after—confused people don't buy. As Stefano Marzano, the Senior Managing Director of the design department at Philips, N.V., in the Netherlands, so well put it, "Good ideas are sometimes very simple, and very successful."

What Does a Hit Product or Service Look Like?

An example: a garden cart. Here's the author's.

Looks well worn. And it is. It's carried a lot of logs, before and after they were cut to fit our wood stove; held a set of paint cans as we painted the house; and mulch and rocks; and has overflowed with weeds, for over 17 years.

Let's start with what a suburban homeowner shopping for such a cart would want.

For one thing, it probably does *not* include having to balance it, because it only has one wheel in the front, and two handles attached to supports. Such a design tips over easily, and everything falls out. Plus, when the cart's loaded, you have to be strong enough to balance it. In some cases that easy-tipping characteristic is wanted: delivering wet concrete exactly where it's needed being one example. But that ability, and the easily tipped product characteristic, doesn't perfectly suit most homeowners. So what would?

The cart would need to be:

- Lightweight.
- Easy to move.

- Not easily tipped.

- Able to carry a lot.

- Not get stuck in holes or mud.

- Made of carefully chosen
  and well-tested materials, so
  it won't break. (The author's
  cart survived the tossing of
  unduly heavy tree sections
  onto its flat bottom. It cracked, but only at the point of impact. Kudos
  to the materials engineer!)

- Not prone to "rusting to death."

- Good-looking.

- A snap to assemble (or come preassembled).

- Inexpensive.

The Ames garden cart pictured earlier perfectly suits, because a visionary marketing team worked with talented industrial designers to bring it about. *This. Is. a. Big. Deal!*

Some of the most effective ways to create something that perfectly suits follow.

- One is to create something that will make the buyer *feel important.*
  That is, you went to the trouble of creating something that would do so,
  and fussed over it until it was just right. Luxury goods are often in this
  category: fancy men's watches, high-end cars, fine-dining restaurants,
  upscale hotels and resorts, a few airlines, haute couture, etc.

- But luxury goods are not the only ones you can do this with. Getting
  the buyer to feel important just takes showing that you thought long
  and hard about your offering's design, and their experience with it.
  That is, the buyer mattered to you. *Examples:*

  - Oxo hand tools.

  - Apple's iPad.

- The neighborhood restaurant, where the wait staff, hired on the basis of their people skills, knows your name, and likes you.

- Subaru— They've thought deeply and empathically about their cars' designs.

- A related example is a set of collectibles that motivates the buyer to "collect the complete set" and makes them feel important when they've done so.

- There are also offerings that make the buyer feel more capable, or attractive:
  - "Cool" clothing.
  - Beauty products that actually work.
  - Phone apps like Waze (turn-by-turn driving directions), and language translators.
  - Nail guns.

- Or those that have desirable features or functions.
  - Wind-proof jackets.
  - All-wheel drive.
  - The warm winter hat that won't create "hat hair" (the static that makes a mess of your hairdo).

Other dimensions of what a buyer would find attractive:

- Demonstrated caring about the buyer's *total* experience, as evidenced by everything about the product or service: its capabilities, its appearance, its ability to fulfill its purpose reliably and without hassle, its durability, its usability, its learning curve, the instructional and reference materials intended to provide same, its guarantees and return policies (L.L. Bean, for example), and the attitudes and manners of the people who provide and service the offering.

  This applies to products intended to be hits at *all* price points. Giving buyers a sense that they're important is even more compelling in nonluxury goods and services, because those buyers are seldom made to feel special.

- Reassurance, in the form of knowledgeable, accurate, friendly, respectful, and rock-solid-consistent customer support. Examples do not abound here, but there are some: my web-hosting provider, *hostmysite.com,* being one.

- Empowerment

  - Packaging: sand, as mentioned in Chapter 3 (Value Propositions). Giving customers the freedom to not have to wait around for the delivery of the decorative sand they ordered, and the peace of mind that it will be the right color and texture, and that it will be placed on the desired spot on their property, so they won't have to move it around again.

  - "Hipness": (buying the new, new thing will show people I'm with it.)

- The *feeling* (status, fun, excitement, etc.) your offering provides.

  - Prestige automobiles—those able to deliver an "I can really control this baby" driving experience, a luxury ride, or simply make an impression.

  - Performance: muscle cars.

  - Sound quality in speakers.

Finally, notice how an exceptional product or service design is synergistic: a great design can also enhance your value-proposition and brand-promise upside elements.

But design needs to be *in service of* your customer experience. A cautionary tale…

Design Arrogance

Recently, I needed two new sets of bluetooth headphones: one for exercise, one to silence my neighbors' din.

I've long been extremely satisfied with Panasonic's audio products, so I bought the new exercise headphones from them.

They arrived in an appropriately descriptive, and recyclable cardboard box containing the headphones, a charging cable, and a large, two-sided sheet of instructions in English, French, and Spanish, dealing with the headphones' use, safety and mandated regulatory information, and warranties. Setup was fast and easy. All was well. Not so with the other set.

Long ago, I owned a pair of Bose noise-canceling headphones. They worked well, but after many years, they went to headphone heaven. So I ordered new ones, directly from Bose, as I wanted Bose to get as much from the purchase as possible. They're considerably improved, even though the last pair was pretty good.

But there were several, intentional, aspects of their "out-of-the-box experience" that just enraged me.

Also, it's worth noting that these headphones list for $350—not cheap.

The Bose headphones arrived in a pretentious, rigid, and unrecyclable cardboard-and-felt box. Opening the box entailed pulling on a hard-to-see black zipper-like thing. Like, why?

Inside was a *Start here* booklet, and a thank-you card. *Start here*:

- Directed me to download Bose's phone app.
- Contained one drawing on how to pair the headphones with the phone (which I had no interest in doing).
- Provided safety, regulatory, and legal information in seemingly all of Earth's languages. (The warranty information was provided via a web link.)

The thank-you card directed me to Bose's community support page for all of its products. Did you notice any mention of instructions in the above list? More on that in a moment.

Then there was the carrying case. In a nonobvious (black-on-black), unlabeled panel inside the case, with the tab to open it squashed, invisibly, against the rest of the black interior, were the charging cable and an adapter for wired use.

I could have complained that they were missing, because there was no included list of what was supposed to be in the box.

Still trying to find the instructions, I chanced to look on the back cover of *Start here,* which provided a link to the headphone model's very own web page.

There, I could download both the instruction manual and the warranty. The manual's pages measured 4.25" wide by 5.5 " high (four pages on one 8 ½ x 11" sheet). If you had sufficient technical savvy, and equipment, you could print the manual, four pages per letter-size sheet and, perhaps even, front and back.

The first nine pages of the manual were regulatory, safety, and legal stuff. The manual's table of contents was on page 10, what's in the box on page 13, and charging the headphones appeared on page 35, after sections on pairing with Amazon's Alexa and Google Assistant. Cue the eye roll!

Inexplicably, the manual was written as though it came with the headphones. It says, and I quote, "Keep these instructions."

So this is what frictionless looks like?

Interesting, too, is why someone thought that a premium product should be more painful to set up than a mainstream product. Given its price, shouldn't Bose have provided Panasonic-like set of instructions in the box? It's just a few sheets of paper, for cryin' out loud, but perhaps not fancy enough.

End of rant, but not end of lesson. **Don't do this.**

Have your customer-experience designer (you have one, right?) review the planned out-of-the-box experience early on, and give them veto power.

And designers: there's no need to be arrogant, and no benefit from it. As it's currently taught, the first principle of good design is *empathy*. It seems that it's gone missing at Bose.

Instead, ask, "Why should something about our customer experience antagonize?" If you find something that would, drop it (and perhaps its promoter).

In the next chapter (Innovation), we'll explore how creating new solutions to worthy problems can lift your results. But first, please work through the exercises below.

> **Note:** In earlier chapters, there was only one theme in the *Tapping Your Upside* exercises. Here, there are three: unrivaled product design, fabulous customer experiences, and creating or strengthening your hit-record machine. Please do them all.

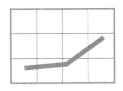

TAPPING YOUR UPSIDE:
Product Design

1. What are the moments in the lives of those who'd buy your products, in which the design of those products matters in a meaningful way: decision to purchase (looks good, will do the job)? the purchase itself (low friction)? setup (a snap)? product performance versus expectations (delivers, keeps working)? others?

_____

_____

_____

2. In the context of each of those moments, where are you now in leveraging product design to boost sales, on a 1 (poor) to 10 scale?

Decision to purchase	1 2 3 4 5 6 7 8 9 10
The purchase itself	1 2 3 4 5 6 7 8 9 10
Setup	1 2 3 4 5 6 7 8 9 10
Product performance versus expectations	1 2 3 4 5 6 7 8 9 10
Other(s)	1 2 3 4 5 6 7 8 9 10

3. And for each, why or why not? (This might seem a silly question— the intent is to bring those reasons to mind again.)

Decision to purchase? _____

The purchase itself? _____

Setup? _____

Product performance versus expectations? _____

Other(s)? _____

4. **Which reason(s) are you not satisfied with?**

_____

_____

_____

5. **In what three ways could you do something more in terms of leveraging product design to produce higher sales from those moments you mentioned above, like the product's looks, convenience, intuitiveness, tactile impression, taste (food, drink), safety, and reliability?**

_____

_____

_____

6. **How will you do that in terms of:**

a. Design team (including external resources)? _____

_____

b. Organizational changes? _____

_____

_____

c. Funding? _____

_____

_____

UPSIDE ASSESSMENT:
PRODUCT AND SERVICE DESIGN

Please complete the Product-Design-to-Die-For row in the Upside Element Assessment Sheet, just before the last page.

TAPPING YOUR UPSIDE:
Customer Experience

7. List the moments in which your customer experiences: what you provide, from the customer's initial exposure to your marketing material or sales efforts, through purchase, setup, ordinary use, something going awry, and, if relevant, disposal.

_____

_____

_____

8. For each, write down: What's expected? What can go wrong? What would be a big win in terms of goodwill (repeat purchases and recommendations)?

_____

_____

_____

9. Decide what you *could* do about each of the above.

_____

_____

_____

_____

10. **How will you do them in terms of:**

a. Design team (including external resources)? _____

_____

b. Organizational changes? _____

_____

_____

c. Funding? _____

_____

_____

11. **How will you counter design arrogance?**

_____

_____

_____

UPSIDE ASSESSMENT: CUSTOMER EXPERIENCE

Please enter the above into the Fabulous-Customer-Experiences row in the Upside Element Assessment Sheet, just before the last page.

TAPPING YOUR UPSIDE:
Hit Records

12. What does your company's process of trying to create hit records look like now?

_____

_____

_____

13. What more could you do?

_____

_____

_____

14. What, if anything, is preventing you from doing it?

_____

_____

_____

15. **Which of those limitations can be creatively overcome?**

_____

_____

_____

16. **How will you do more in terms of:**

a. Design team (including external resources)? _____

_____

b. Organizational changes? _____

_____

_____

c. Funding? _____

_____

_____

UPSIDE ASSESSMENT: HIT RECORDS

Please enter your estimates for the gains and challenges you expect to derive from the hit records you envision in the Create/Strengthen "Hit-Record" Machine row on the book's Upside Element Assessment Sheet, just before the last page.

Chapter 12

Innovation: The Why and How of Solving Worthy Problems

What We Mean by Innovation, Here

Innovation for its own sake is not this book's focus. Because this book is about how to create a more valuable business, we're interested in *upside-directed innovation*.

We have already discussed many of the ways in which Peter Drucker once suggested that an innovative approach be applied:[170]

- A winning customer experience (as discussed in Chapter 2).

- A more powerful value proposition. Relevant here is the work of Kim and Maugborgne on Value Innovation (Chapter 3).[171,172]

- Fresh, high-impact ways to *communicate* your value proposition (Chapter 5).

- An amped-up brand promise that you can deliver on (Chapter 4).

- Creative pricing (Chapter 6).

- New cost-saving ideas (Chapter 7).

- Adopting a higher-yielding business design (Chapter 10).

- Innovative product-and-service designs (Chapter 11).

- More effective management practices (coming, in Chapter 13).

In this chapter, we'll focus on new or improved *solutions* to problems whose market potentials justify the cost and effort required ... and which are one of the more difficult ways to fruitfully innovate. But, ah, the rewards for those who succeed!

Some of those solutions: the wheel, the printing press, the automobile, the airplane, telecommunications, electronics, software, biomedical devices, nano-materials, and others. Here are two examples of innovative solutions, more limited in scope...

Philips's Smart LEDs: LEDs paired with light sensors—a better lighting solution.[173] Its features:

- *Safety:* Illumination, right where it's needed, just as much as needed, when.

- *Efficiency:* Uses a small fraction of the energy of a conventional lightbulb, reducing carbon emissions in the same degree.

- *Durability:* The lighting element(s) will last 20 years, important in applications in which changing the lightbulb is difficult, dangerous, or expensive.

- *Efficacy:* The color (the mix of light frequencies) in a smart LED is adjustable. That characteristic, applied appropriately, has been shown to increase the yields of crops grown indoors, by using the light frequencies the plants prefer, and to speed recovery times in human patients. There's also evidence that this ability can:

  - Create environments in which people's concentration, alertness, or ability to relax are enhanced.

  - Create an environment that people just prefer.

- *Utility:* Smart LEDs can be controlled by a cell-phone app, inviting all manner of new uses.

Braskem of Brazil's raw-materials innovation:

- Making plastic bags and packaging from sugar cane rather than oil.[174]
  Not as fancy as Philips's LEDs, but perhaps more environmentally
  impactful.

Why Seek New or Improved Solutions?

You Can Create Preference, and Prosperity

An innovative solution can make prospects prefer what you offer. The resulting
increased revenue, profit, and business value can make the solution's creation
worthwhile indeed. Consider how Philips's Smart LEDs, and Braskem's packaging, have created prosperity for their creators, as have a host of others, as Sir
Harold Evans, longtime editor of London's *The Sunday Times,* reports in *They
Made America.*[175]

If the innovation is defensible, that prosperity could last a long time—because
it's the edge that no one else has. *Example:* Coca-Cola's innovation, for its proprietary soft-drink formulation, was bottling it.

You'll Have Other Sources of Revenue
When a Disrupter Strikes

Disrupters, whose offerings can threaten your value proposition, can come from
anywhere: literally. *Examples:* Western Union ignored the telephone. Both Digital
and Wang ignored the PC, and wound up extinct.

Disrupters can also threaten your brand. As recounted in Chapter 4, while
competitors thought Big Ass Fans' brand a bit crass, it totally overshadowed
their much more technical, OK, boring characterizations of their products.

Disrupters can seriously mess with your business design: "mini" steel mills,
online retailers, app-based booking services such as Airbnb.

Sometimes, the disrupter sneaks into a market "on little cat feet." But it need
not, because most businesses ignore disrupters until it's too late. Microsoft initially
ignored Netscape, but to his credit, Bill Gates eventually saw and reacted force-
fully to the threat from Netscape's at-the-time-superior web browser. And Gillette
ignored the Dollar Shave Club until it started to eat into their market share.

Disrupting Yourself Beats Being Toast

It's dangerous not to innovate against yourself.[176] Someday, probably soon, someone will create a solution that prospects view as better than the one you now offer. That someone could be you. Then prospects would continue to buy from you.

Is that reason enough?

Are You Willing to Risk Not Innovating?

If so, you'd be like Sycamore Networks, whose failure to adapt its product line to the changing technologies used by its customers was among the reasons that its market cap fell from $45 billion in 2000 to $64 million, and liquidation, in 2013.[177]

And what if you don't innovate *enough?* Witness Kodak, late to digital photography because of their lucrative film business. Competitors' continuously improved phone cameras, and the wide availability of photo-manipulation software, just outran Kodak's offerings, and its brand became more associated with the past.

So, is having a future a good reason to innovate?

Innovation-Based Turnarounds

Milliken

Consider the upside found by Milliken, a former textile maker in South Carolina. As John Bussey's 2012 *Wall Street Journal* article describes, U.S. textile makers were being made extinct by overseas competitors.[178] Milliken started innovating because they had to. Or else. And they wanted to. So they did.

They diversified out of traditional textiles, focusing on niche products that leveraged their knowledge of both textiles and specialty chemicals. They now make:

- The fabric in duct tape.
- The additives that make food containers clear, and children's art markers washable.

- The products that make mattresses fire-resistant, countertops antimicrobial, windmills lighter, and combat gear protective.

They have thousands of patents and a research-focused culture; with a relatively high concentration of PhDs. Researchers get a portion of their work time to "follow their curiosity to a marketable end." And Milliken brings in outside experts to "stir the pot," ultimately finding enough niche markets to form a thriving business.

Milliken continues to innovate, tapping a thorough understanding of customers' needs and their deep, collective knowledge of physics and chemistry. For example, they've created ways to stabilize deteriorating infrastructure, and protect it going forward.[179]

Without their innovation focus, Milliken, like its textile-making brethren, would have been gone.

And without a sufficiently *intense* focus on innovation, Milliken would have gone into chronic decline, like Kodak. The message: "When the horse you're riding is wheezing, *get off!*"

And use the money that's still coming in to mount another horse, or horses.

P&G

Under A.G. Lafley, from 2002 to 2004, new products such as Mr. Clean Auto Dry, Crest Whitestrips™, and others added $2 billion to its sales. Both Auto Dry and Whitestrips were new solutions to people's problems: having to towel-dry the just-washed car to avoid water spots, and less-than-pearly-white teeth.[180]

Characteristics of an Innovative Solution

What characteristics should such a solution have?

According to Peter Drucker, an innovation has to be simple, do only one thing—or it will confuse—and be a big enough idea that it will become the new standard.[181] In the case of PCs and cell phones, that "do only one thing" aspect is debatable, but Drucker's suggestions of simple, and a big idea, make sense.

Simplicity brought a radical innovation—to shrimp farming. Shrimp are farmed in tubs of water laid side by side. Producing shrimp at commercial scale requires a large indoor facility, to accommodate the shallow tubs in which the shrimp are grown. The low yield per square foot makes domestic shrimp farming uncompetitive with imported shrimp. The solution was to stack the tubs atop one another. But water is heavy, so to maintain safe floor loads (and to protect the lower layers from those above), the water levels in each tub in the stack couldn't be too high, an engineering problem that was solved.[182] Shrimp yields per square meter increased more than 10 times compared to current shrimp-farming methods. The idea has now been commercialized by Royal Caridea. There's more on their well-thought-out design approach on royal-caridea.com.

As Harold Evans observed, an innovation does not require inventing anything. It can be done simply by *combining* things that already exist. Examples include Instant Pot, a combination pressure cooker and rice cooker; new recipes; and, well, yo-yos and pogo sticks.

How to Innovate

Introducing new solutions into developing or high-growth markets is often both promising and risky. And almost always, your solution has to be cost-appropriate for the market.

In most markets, your solution should be clearly better than what's now offered in terms of capabilities and looks, or it should come at a substantially lower price point.

Where to Find the Sparks

Your initial efforts should be on finding problems worth solving, then assessing which ones you can realistically address. Consider, in examining possible solutions, what the evolution of technology and other forms of progress, like crowdfunding, will now enable.

But crucially, have the discipline to keep the finding of a worthy problem the first thing, because creating a solution in search of a problem usually leads to frustration and red ink.

One of the best ways to do this is really paying attention to the problems you, your customers, or those close to you encounter (their jobs to be done, as explained in Chapter 3). You already have a relationship with these people. And hopefully, there's some trust, so they're more likely to open up to you about their problems and concerns. Charan and Lafley call this co-producing innovation. *Example:* Some of Procter & Gamble's people actually lived with customers using early versions of their products (with permission), to get a visceral sense of their frustrations and satisfactions.

Sometimes a problem or frustration that you personally experience will lead to an innovative solution. One example comes from a bright teenager who had a problem—getting rid of her frequent hiccups. After trying 100 folk remedies, she found something that worked, and that could be sold in the form of a lollypop: Hiccupops.[183]

Once your people *completely understand* the problem, or the job to be done, solutions can pop out of their heads. *Example:* hammering a nail. As many have experienced, hammering a nail often ends up with you hammering your fingers. The inventors of the Safety Nailer, Drew and Cory Zirkle and Dan and Kristen Eifes, understood, completely, what was needed. Ta-da!

The Safety Nailer's main feature is, of course, its finger protection. Inside is a magnetic holder, to keep the nail vertical, which also helps prevent it from bending. "The strike plate gives you a bigger (and eye-catching) target to aim for. Miss the nail? No worries. The durable holder is made from impact-resistant ABS plastic that can handle a hammer."

Finally, "the strap-on design fits on left- or right-handed folks and is small enough that it won't get in your way of what you're working on. Store it on your hammer between jobs."[184]

The Safety Nailer's inventors understood that hammers can hurt, and that nails need to be at right angles to the hammer's head. They had to devise a way to prevent finger damage, knew the protective element must be rugged, and that such an element could easily be lost or misplaced.

In other cases, forging a solution takes long, dedicated head-scratching. For example, Marc Koska spent 14 years devising and bringing to market a single-use syringe, to prevent the spread of infections like HIV. When someone tries to reuse it, it breaks.[185]

Large companies often have trouble doing things like this, because the communication channel between the detection of a customer need and the person who needs to green-light the creation of a solution can be distorted by the agendas of those along the channel. That can be solved by creating clear, direct channels. In other words, the head of the business could meet, say, monthly, without the sales management team, with a different member of the sales force to learn what problems and issues customers are having, and what seem to be new trends in the market. Then there are the possibly long and uncertain development time scales involved.

Note, too, that listening to customers doesn't always work, because many people can't envision things like air travel, cell phones, or automobiles, years before they come to be. It's hard for most of our species to see the truly big breakthroughs long before they become real.

A second approach to finding worthy problems to solve is to look carefully at the wide world's needs. If you don't know your intended target audience very well, coming up with new solutions for them can be aided by ethnographic research.[186] This can help you really understand a culture, be it an ethnic group, those in a profession or skilled trade, or an industry.

A third approach, seemingly a favorite of large companies, is to look at demographic or psychographic trends, and to try to capitalize on them. For example, there's considerable effort to create products: for a graying populace, such as GPS-equipped sneakers for people with dementia (other such examples can be found here[187]), or for millennials, who always want to be connected.

Will It Sell?

Before you create it, try your damnedest to see whether your new solution will sell. The author was once a member of a 500—yes, 500-person project team. Its mission was to develop a data-communication network that could be programmed by its users. As the network neared commercial introduction, after more than four years of development, a senior executive asked the sales force to "find three customers" for the service. It turned out that they couldn't, and the project was soon canceled. What a waste of R&D funds.

The question the executive posed could have just as easily been asked back when the project was in the early-concept stage. The answers would not have been definitive, but the absence of enthusiastic early adopters would at least have given rise to a market-risk question or two.

What is likely to become a successful innovation is notoriously hard to predict.[188] We can do two things about that:

Start With Many, Test, Assess, and Winnow

Launch as many promising innovation efforts as your budget will allow, track them closely for marketability (including hitting market windows), feasibility, resource requirements, and projected ROI, and prune bravely as soon as a go/no-go decision can be made.

Buy Your Way Into Something Successful, and Make It Bigger

Acquire a business that has the innovative offering or technology you want, or license it, rather than trying to invent everything in-house. Pharmaceutical companies do this often—they'll take an exclusive license for a startup's promising drug while it's still in clinical trials. Or a tech company will acquire a firm with software, expertise, or a capability they need. Sometimes companies with products that are proven sellers can make even more money, by leveraging greater distribution capability or a larger sales force. But, with acquisitions, take care to consider whether you'll get full value for your investment, in view of the prospective culture fit with the business you're acquiring and, if relevant, the incentive stock and change-of-control provisions in its executives' contracts. You don't want to be left with "just a handful of feathers."

Examples of successful acquisitions include Disney's purchases of Pixar and Lucasfilm (*Star Wars*), and Walmart's buying the online retailer Jet.com.

A Useful Thought Experiment

With either approach, it might prove helpful to try the approach of *analyzing failure beforehand*. With this approach, called a *premortem*, the goal is to find flaws in the solution's concept, and to encourage people with concerns about the innovation to express them before the solution gets too far along.[189] It's also a way of improving the innovations you're already working on before they're introduced.

To do this, ask, hypothetically, what went wrong with the innovation? The team's job is to generate reasons for its supposed demise. That can take some of the wind out of the "full speed ahead" approach often employed, and lead to a better-thought-out offering.

Your Timing

Another aspect of market-testing your solution is to consider whether the time is right. The need for your solution has to be there. Otherwise, you'll be "pushing a rope." Solutions tend to appear at a particular time, because the need for them arises at that time.

Example: There was no need for a wheel until our species needed to move something heavy over land. People's problem-solving gene often takes it from there.[190]

And your timing has to be roughly right, not too early or a "me-too" effort, trailing behind products that have already met the need. The classic too-early example is AT&T's Picturephone video calling service, introduced in 1970, and dead by late in that decade.

Creating Your Own New Solutions

You can "do it yourself" if you have the right people, with the needed level of inspiration. A good guide to doing this is by Tom Kelley, general manager of the well-regarded design firm IDEO's, *The Art of Innovation*.[191] IDEO's innovation wellspring is their culture, but they do have a process, which is to first really understand the situation (problem, client, available technology, and the constraints on a solution), observe the experience of people using current solutions, visualize new approaches, and quickly prototype them.

Depending on the situation, you could also hire an outside firm.

Or harness the wide world's creativity. To get help in solving difficult problems, there are innovation networks like Innocentive. There, you can put out a problem that your innovation requires you to solve, along with an amount that you're prepared to pay for a solution.

Making Innovation an Organizational Strength

To remain relevant, have an innovation effort in which your business's future competes with its present, to replace it! That is, have an active, funded effort to improve what you currently offer, or to make what you offer now obsolete over time.[192]

Creating an innovative business starts at the top. The leader has to make it clear that long-term prosperity is an imperative, and that successful, continuous innovation is one of the major ways of getting there—if not the all-important one.

In speeches, reward systems, and in shaping the business's culture, the primacy of innovation has to be kept front and center. Then a few other things are necessary...

After saying that "We want innovation," the next sentence should be, "We want ideas, and here's how we'll collect them and evaluate them." This is the notion of idea management and leads to the broader approach, systematic innovation, both of which are detailed in Robert Tucker's, *Driving Growth Through Innovation*.[193]

In their book, *Corporate Creativity,* Alan Robinson and Sam Stern recommend encouraging self-initiated (unofficial) activity.[194]

Drucker[195] recommends that executives keep two lists, one of problems (which most do), and one of *opportunities.*

Then it's about using the available R&D funds effectively. As Michael Shrage of MIT's Sloan School has pointed out, "If it were really true that people who spent the most on R&D were the most successful, we wouldn't be subsidizing General Motors."[196]

At minimum, R&D spending should be aligned with market opportunities and the *ability* to deliver innovation's fruits to the market. For all but a well-heeled handful, innovation is *applied, not pure,* research.

For more on innovating in a large organization, A.G. Lafley and Ram Charan's *Game Changer*[197] is an excellent resource.

The Crucial Role of Culture

A predominant culture that's unwilling to change, or that lacks the vision to see how they might create a brighter future, can, and has, doomed many a leader's innovation efforts. But guess whose role it is to manage and shape the culture? The leader can create reward systems, bring in (and transition out) people, and foster an atmosphere that will create positive change.

Good: An innovative culture is one in which people in the company, like the sales force, are empowered to decide what to do about the opportunities the company has, using a process honed over time and proven to yield useful ideas.[198] A good example of this is W.L. Gore. Its products include the water-resistant fabric Gore-Tex™; its Windstopper™ membrane, and fibers and materials are used in a host of industries, from electronics to medical devices and pharmaceuticals.

Bad: "We are what we do, now," companies think, because our imperative is to continue making the kind of money we do now. We shouldn't get distracted by what now seems like small potatoes. Perhaps that's the reason Hasbro didn't create the online game Farmville and one of the major supermarket chains didn't launch Whole Foods.[199]

Innovation Killers

Why, despite the best of intentions, do so many innovation initiatives (and the innovations themselves) fail to live up to expectations?

For one, successful innovation is hard.

Also, according to Christensen,[200] some of the blame rests on financial analyses that beget wrong answers:

- A discounted-cash-flow analysis can wrongly assume that if the innovation investment is not made, the business's current level of returns will continue forever. In view of all of the progress we see being made today, though, that assumption could well prove unrealistic.

- The production machinery figuring into an incumbent's fixed costs is often somewhat dated. It will likely already have been paid for and depreciated. But the incumbents will try to leverage their existing production assets to produce new offerings. Legacy assets are not always efficient, however. New entrants, on the other hand, have to pay for everything that comes under fixed costs, but what they get for it might well be more efficient, leading to lower average costs in the long run, beating the incumbents'. Or the new entrant might outsource production entirely. Either might bring a cost advantage.

Christensen provides, as an example, rolled sheet steel—Nucor (the new entrant) versus U.S. Steel (the incumbent). Over time, Nucor's more modern production process gave it a lower cost to produce sheet steel. U.S. Steel, on the other hand, showed a more attractive *marginal* cost to produce the same sheet steel by leveraging its existing plant, rather than building a new one. In the end, Nucor's lower cost-to-produce won out in the market. And the reason: for Nucor, driving its costs below U.S. Steel's was do-or-die, while U.S. Steel, saddled with its existing plant, couldn't respond.

Finally, the ever-present Wall Street earnings-per-share focus inhibits forward-looking (innovation) investments that dilute those earnings in the short run.

A Better Way to Advance Innovations

In common use, stage-gate planning is: deciding whether the innovation's numbers pass muster before deciding whether to let it progress to the next stage of development. Often, the business case's underlying assumptions can be tweaked to provide an answer desired by the innovation's promoters.

An alternative, discovery-driven planning, presents the numbers, along with *the assumptions* that must be proven true, for those numbers to come about. Having the assumptions laid bare for all to assess can lead to wiser choices and prevent embarrassing disasters.

Summary

Conceiving and delivering a new solution to the market can change everything for the better, but it's certainly no slam dunk. For most businesses, stasis leads to eventual, sometimes rapid, failure. At minimum, leaders need to consider innovating in one or more of the ways listed at this chapter's outset, including new or improved solutions.

The next chapter will focus on the management aspects of tapping your upside, but please work through the following exercise before proceeding.

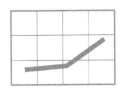

TAPPING YOUR UPSIDE:

Innovation

1. Of the types of innovation listed in the beginning of the chapter, which ones: hold high results-improvement *potential*? seem *feasible*? are likely to *energize* your organization so it delivers them? (In each row, place an H in each column that you believe merits a high score, then seriously consider pursuing rows with 3 H's.)

	Chapter	Rate each item <u>H</u>igh, <u>M</u>edium, or <u>L</u>ow		
		Potential	Feasibility	Energize
A winning customer experience	2			
A more powerful value proposition	3			
Fresh, high-impact ways to *communicate* it	5			
An amped-up brand promise	4			
Creative pricing	6			
New cost-saving ideas	7			
A higher-yield business design	10			
Innovative product-or-service designs	11			
Improved solutions	12			

If one or more of your improved solutions made it onto your "pursue" list, continue with the questions that follow. Otherwise, keep your eyes and ears, and those of your people, peeled for worthwhile ideas, and as they come, run them through the quick assessment above.

2. **For *each* of your improved solutions, what's:**

The problem you'll solve? _____

The size of the opportunity? _____

The upside? Gains in:

Revenue _____

Profit _____

Market share _____

Strategic position (chance to dominate) _____

_____

_____

ROI? _____

3. **Why is your business uniquely qualified to bring the solution into reality?**

_____

_____

_____

_____

_____

4. Will the solution be consistent with your brand promise?

_____

_____

5. And with how you want your business to be viewed long-term?

_____

_____

_____

6. What's your solution's market window?

_____

_____

_____

7. And your likely time to market?

_____

_____

8. What are the technological challenges in creating the solution?

_____

_____

_____

_____

9. How hard will it be to reach your intended customers?

_____

_____

10. How expensive will reaching them be?

_____

_____

11. Rate your ability to operate in the market (presence).

_____

_____

12. How will you support your solution in the field?

_____

_____

13. Are there likely to be any intellectual-property issues?

_____

_____

14. What political, legal, or regulatory situations pose risks to the success of your solution?

_____

_____

15. What's your ability and willingness to provide the funding, and other needed resources?

_____

_____

16. On net, what's the risk/reward of this solution?

_____

_____

17. Will you pursue this option?

_____

_____

18. What has to be resolved before you can decide?

_____

_____

UPSIDE ELEMENT ASSESSMENT: INNOVATION

Please enter your estimates for the *overall* gains and challenges you expect to derive from your innovation initiative(s) in the corresponding row(s) on the Upside Element Assessment Sheet, just before the last page.

Chapter 13

Management Practices for Delivering the Upside

Realizing the potential of the upside elements we've covered thus far won't happen without effective action on your part. This chapter's seven management practices are essential to both tapping your business's upside and sustaining its prosperity: effectively leading; making sage decisions; managing risk; leveraging assets; optimizing your portfolios of offerings, brands, and businesses; plugging revenue leaks; and crafting business processes that let you focus on the upside—not the alligators.

In other words, without crackerjack management practices, your upside initiatives are less likely to bring abundant rewards. Your practices can and should serve as a springboard.

Leading

Leading is about getting the parts of the business to move easily, in the way you want them to, toward the goals that need to be achieved. Here's leadership's master key...

> *Leadership is a permission thing—people give you their permission to lead them.*

To *earn* that, you have to:

- Care. Be genuinely interested in them. You could, for example, treat them as though they were "someone's precious child," in the words of Bob Chapman, CEO of the $3 billion manufacturing company Barry-Wehmiller.[201] He advocates a management philosophy he calls "Truly Human Leadership." Which works.

- Extend yourself for them whenever possible. *Example:* I'd just started a consulting role at a major company in New York City, and needed to get a photo ID, which I'd have to do in another building. My client manager walked me to the other building, in the teeth of an indescribably windy March day, took me to the floor and the office, and just waited patiently while I got the picture taken and the ID processed. We then walked back. He had me, from then on.

- Respect them, listen to what they think, and when you can't do what they suggest, explain why.

- Trust them to do their jobs, rather than micromanaging. (If you find yourself doing that, it's usually a signal that something has to change, or that someone needs to be "changed out.")

- Become ultra-clear about where you want to take the business. That has to be somewhere worthwhile, well-defined, and, ideally, inspiring. It also needs to be lasting, e.g., "We will deliver the best product for the money, so that our customers can <do whatever it enables them to do>, now, and as long as they need us to do so." Finally, the goal should not be a revenue number, or a place on a list like the Inc. 5000 or the Fortune 100. It should be something enduring and worthwhile.

  Management consultant Gerry Faust asks business audiences, "How many of you are following someone who's lost?" Which begets knowing nods and nervous smiles. So, if you don't know where the business should go, say so, and craft a way to find out that people can get involved with and fired up about.

- In the memorable words of David Novak, former CEO of Yum Brands, "Take 'em with you!" That is, inspire them, show that you're *for them* (as explained in Chapter 2), by enriching their careers and their lives as much as possible. You and your people—all of them—need to be on an exciting journey, *together!* A visual telling of this is Simon Sinek's little book *Together Is Better.*

- Be competent—work at really *understanding the essence* of your business, and your industry.
- Be straight with your people.
- Do what you say you'll do, or don't say it. And if doing it becomes impossible, say so and why.
- Be, really be, someone who can be trusted. Act accordingly.
- And, easy to say, don't come off as a jerk, someone with issues, or worse.
- Last, but by no means least, say *Thank you!*

Without your people's permission to lead, you'll have to resort to coercion, fear, or accept that you'll be pushing that rope, i.e., ineffective.

Aligning

Having gotten people to want to follow the business's flag, next up is *creating alignment* around the crucial things your business needs to do. All of the critical roles should have someone capable and well-suited in them. The goals for each role should be clearly *orchestrated* so that the net result is that the business actually accomplishes what it needs to do, without a big kerfuffle, and without your "madly waving the baton at the podium."

Simon Sinek's *Start With Why* (highly recommended) presents a powerful way to achieve alignment: the Golden Circle.[202] He suggests that, as the book's title implies, the business first articulate its clear, engaging purpose—its *why* (the small core of the Golden Circle). Surrounding why is *how,* the ways in which the business will fulfill that purpose. In the outer ring lies *what* the business will do. Everything about the business flows outward from its why. More on Sinek's site: https://simonsinek.com/.

Sinek cites as an example Southwest Airlines. Its *why* is to enable people to travel inexpensively and enjoyably in the United States. Its *how* is its business design: direct flights, no frills, and out-of-the-ordinary hiring practices. From its *how* springs its *whats,* specifically the customer-facing and operational processes that Southwest will employ to provide its service. Having its operations rooted in its business design, and that design rooted in its purpose, provides great power. The *why* inspires and creates loyalty, while the aligned *how* and *what* together convey that its stated purpose is for real.[203]

Sustaining the Alignment

Sinek shows that the power in this model can survive over management transitions, as long as the *why* remains clear and unchanged. But when *why* goes fuzzy, as he puts it, the power in the model leaks out and decline sets in.[204]

Mr. Sinek cites a few examples of where *why* went fuzzy, and several where it didn't. One to add to those whose *why* continues to shine through is the ice-cream company Ben & Jerry's. From its hippie beginnings, its brand has had a strong social-activist component. Now, Unilever, which bought the company years ago, has continued that activism, even through transitions in the Unilever executives who have recently run the business.[205] Obviously, Unilever gets it.

Note: We've only touched on the highlights of Mr. Sinek's book here, but anyone leading a business, or managing a brand, should read the whole thing. You'll gain a powerful perspective that will show up in both your financial results and your business's longevity.

Creating a Culture

Let's think of a business as a living organism for a moment, say, as a person. Where would, or should, it be on the ambition scale?

Laid back   **Real go-getter**

This is about the business's *intent*. Intent springs from the leader's biochemistry. You can see that in the list of its poster children, and not all of it is positive—more on that in a moment...

Amazon: Jeff Bezos	Lenovo: Yang Yuanqing
Apple: Steve Jobs	Microsoft: Bill Gates
Comcast: Brian Roberts	Oracle: Larry Ellison
Intel: Andy Grove	Yum Brands: David Novak

Intent is infused into a business from the top down. If the leader lacks a strong intention to succeed, it could be that the business will, too. And the observation that everyone's not on the list of "intent poster children" shows that some leaders have a more pronounced "intent drive" than others.

Not that that's bad. Some of those poster children were, or are, notoriously difficult to work for, encouraging the best people to go elsewhere, or to never want to work there in the first place.

So, if you're the leader and your biochemistry doesn't match the poster children's, what can you do to provide the oomph your business needs, while living in your own skin? That is, how can you *infuse* intent? There are several ways:

- *Relevance* is one way to get your people fired up about what they're doing. "We need to markedly improve our website's customer experience, *so that* prospects can easily get information on what brought them, and they don't head off to a competitor." See Sinek's *Start With Why* for more.

- An inspiring or worthwhile goal, as perfectly captured in the words of a greeting card: "Dreams come a size too big, so we can grow into them." (Verrier)

  The dream fueling that inspiration might spring from:

  - How *cool* what they're doing seems to be.
  - Its societal value: its *contribution*.
  - The *thrill* of competition.
  - What their work *enables* the customer to do.
  - Bringing something *new* into the world.
  - Its resonance with their values, or with, perhaps, their unconscious needs to show the world *who they are*.

  And dream-fueled inspiration *is sustainable*.

The business's culture *is* its personality. By inspiring, communicating the essence of the mission and vision you set, hiring, and yes, firing, you *create* that personality. But formed it will be, whether you actively sculpt or not. The culture's form can reflect your choice; you might not like the result of just letting the culture happen.

Crafting a culture can be huge. Here's a recent example of what crafting (in this case, altering) a culture can bring, and how it was done.

Between his appointment as CEO in February 2014 and mid-2017, Satya Nadella added more than $250 billion to Microsoft's market value.[206] How?

Under the previous CEO, the company had what Nadella called "fixed mindsets": our technology platforms, like Windows and Office, are the best, and we must control where they're used.[207]

Microsoft Office for the Mac was not an emphasis, for example. Did that mindset have any value to the customer? Did it help Microsoft stay relevant and lead to increased sales?

Nadella shifted the cultural emphasis to *staying relevant,* because being open to customers' needs can enlarge the markets you serve.[208]

"We needed a culture that allowed us to constantly refresh and renew," Nadella said.[209] To do so, "We have to meet the unmet, unarticulated needs of the customers. That's the source of innovation."[210]

How you get to those unarticulated needs is by empathic listening: taking the time to understand, down to your toes, what customers need. What they're trying to tell you that perhaps they can't even articulate. (Hint: find the job they need done, à la Christensen et al.)

It's also about *wanting* to craft solutions that will empower the customer: letting them do things they couldn't before, or do them a lot more easily. (*Note:* this wanting often creates zealous customers, because they feel respected, and sense that the company feels they're important.)

Finally, it's about being open to collaboration with other companies, if appropriate, in crafting solutions for customers.

In Nadella's words, "The CEO is the curator of an organization's culture." And, "We are one company, one Microsoft—not a confederation of fiefdoms. Innovation and competition don't respect our silos, so we have to learn to transcend those barriers."[211]

Making Sage Decisions

Wisdom, from a fortune cookie:

> *Good judgment comes from experience.*
> *Experience comes from bad judgment.*

Deciding wisely is an executive's most crucial skill. It's what you get paid the big bucks to do, because there are consequences, both good and bad. *Examples:*

Good (Wise, Prescient)

- IBM's move into services in the early '90s under CEO Lou Gerstner, which saved the company.

- The New York Times Company's decision, in the face of a marked decline in print-advertising revenue beginning in 2000 and through the time of this writing, to invest significantly in providing quality journalism and in expanding its online distribution worldwide.

- Walmart's 1987 decision to create its own satellite network for managing its rapidly expanding operations, and, more critically, giving management the information needed to both insightfully manage a rapidly expanding enterprise with a complex supply chain, and to scale it.[212,213]

- In 1914, Henry Ford offered his workers the then-very-attractive wage of $5 per day, so turnover would be cut dramatically, and—his master stroke—they'd be able to *buy* the cars they were building. Ford was *creating a market* for his cars![214]

Lucky

PanAm's decision, in 1936, to fly commercial passengers to Hong Kong, in Sikorsky S-42 flying boats, for what now seem extraordinary fares: round trip from San Francisco for $14,000 in 2018 dollars. But it cut a six-week (by sea) trip to six days (five hops). It turned out to be a viable business, as was the transatlantic service it launched in 1939. Fortunately, rising demand justified the investment.[215]

Bad

I'm Better, Smarter, etc.

Eddie Lampert's 2004 decision to acquire the struggling retailer Sears and merge it with Kmart, which he'd bought out of bankruptcy in 2003, leading eventually to the demise of both. Putting two challenged businesses together, each competing with larger rivals (Kmart with Walmart and Sears with Home Depot and Lowe's), seemed to emerge from a sense of "I'm smart. I started a hedge fund at age 25. I'll make this work."

I Can't Get My Head Around It

Some, OK, many, decisions seem bone-headed because of an all-too-common human affliction. As mentioned earlier, we see signs of this affliction prominently posted along curvy highways. It's called "Limited Sight Distance": many people's inability to grasp the potential of something new. Two prominent examples are the leaders of the one-time minicomputer/word processor makers Digital and Wang.

Personal, or Power-Related

John Scully's firing of Steve Jobs at Apple.

Big (Bet the Company) Decisions

In the examples below, the companies did not have their backs to the wall. Rather, the decisions they made to pursue opportunities required guts. Insight helped with the successful ones.

Successful

- The IBM System/360. Until the mid-sixties, IBM offered two incompatible lines of mainframe computers. IBM CEO Thomas J. Watson, Jr. made the $5 billion decision to scuttle both and to create one line, the 360, to serve all of the needs of its customers, with an architecture that could be upgraded while software compatibility was maintained. That ability endures today in IBM's mainframe line. It was a Herculean effort, that had to succeed, or else. And succeed it did, because of the new product line's stronger value proposition.[216,217,218]

- Intel's transition from a (commodity) memory-chip supplier to a proprietary CPU supplier for PCs, under Andy Grove and Gordon Moore.[219]

- In 1955, a $5 million toy company had the opportunity to sink 10% of its revenue, the company's net worth, into an unproven advertising channel, television. 10% of sales. For a tiny company. On a then-unproven medium. Yikes!

  But the CEO, Ruth Handler, took the opportunity to advertise hats with mouse ears on The Mickey Mouse Club. And her company, Mattel, took off, with sales almost tripling in the next three years! (This was pre-Barbie.) Handler's decision was both gutsy and sage, because the percentage of homes with television sets was rising rapidly, and the company could advertise their toys directly to kids, rather than to their parents. Though the investment was a stretch, the payoff didn't seem far-fetched.[220]

Not Successful

- Time Warner's agreement to be bought by AOL, which nearly killed both companies and caused massive losses for shareholders. Why? The CEO, Gerry Levin, was smitten with the promised value of a tech/media combination. An overdose of Kool-Aid™, perhaps.[221]

- Under antitrust pressure from the U.S. Justice Department, in 1984, AT&T decided to split itself up, keeping Bell Labs, its manufacturing unit, Western Electric, and its long-distance business, while spinning off its seven regional, regulated local-phone-service companies, making them independent. The decision exposed its long-distance service, with its monopoly-era, gold-plated cost structure, to much-stronger-than-anticipated price competition, sorely limiting how it could respond. It grew weak, while the local companies, without much competition, grew strong. One of them eventually rescued AT&T and took its name. Why? AT&T's CEO, Charlie Brown:

- Did not seem to have a gut-level sense of the ferocity of the price competition that would come in long distance, and that the company was saddled with an uncompetitive cost structure.

- Seemed to not fully grasp the essence of the local and long-distance telecommunications markets (price protected, and not, respectively).

- Was not alone in being swept up in the high-tech business's glamor and growth possibilities, which did not materialize as expected.

In sum, the decision resulted from not thinking the situation through, and emotional distortion.[222]

So how can you and your team make more good, or great decisions?

Decision Styles

Blinkers Versus Thinkers

The two most common decision-making styles are the instant decision, often seemingly employed by former U.S. President George W. Bush, and the more fact-gathering, deliberative approach of former President Barack Obama.

Malcolm Gladwell superbly described the instant decision in his book *Blink*.[223] A blink is a gut-level decision, made at the unconscious level. You believe that you know what the right decision is—you just *feel* it. You just don't know, consciously, how you know. A blink decision is often rooted in an emotion, such as deciding you want to marry someone you just saw walking down the street. True story: a middle-aged man walks up to a woman in an airport and says, "You look like my first wife." And she says, "Oh, how many wives have you had?" He says, "None." They're now married!

Instant Decisions

There are situations in which making a blink decision is good, and when doing so is dangerous...

In their book *Decisive*, Chip and Dan Heath maintain that, "Intuition is only accurate in domains where it has been carefully trained."[224] These are situations in which the decision maker is indeed trained—by lots of repetition and quick feedback on the outcome—for example, playing chess. Duke University professor Rick Larrick calls them video-game worlds: you play, succeed or not (die), then you come back to life, play again, and get more feedback.

Going with your gut is more likely to be right in such situations. It was, too, in this real-life one: A fire company entered a burning house, hoses full-on. But the fire wasn't responding to the dousing as the company's experienced commander expected. Sensing that something was wrong, he ordered everyone out of the house, *now!* Moments later, the floor of the room they'd been in collapsed.

When later asked how he knew to get out, the commander just said that he had a bad feeling. Actually, that feeling (or unconscious knowing) sprang from his many years of firefighting. He just couldn't articulate how he arrived at his decision.[225]

The less experience you've had in the area in which you're making a decision, the more that blink decisions can prove wrong. In George W. Bush's case, the repetition element was absent, and the feedback too slow in coming, in deciding whether to go to war in Iraq.

Instant decisions are rarely the type that business leaders need to make. At best, "feelings" about what to decide should be treated as a data point, and only one of a broader set of decision inputs. Deliberative decisions involve data-gathering and analysis. But more is needed. Consistently good decisions tend to stem from a decision-making *process*.

Deciding Processes

The first thing is to decide whether a decision is necessary. Will the various options create roughly similar results?

Next, is the outcome of major consequence? And is the decision reversible? If it's major, and irreversible, the decision process merits significant attention.

That effort should begin with *really* understanding the situation, and what's to be decided.

Here, you're looking for what I call simplicity on the far side of complexity. Admittedly, this can take time, which you might not have. And taking that time might leave your business poorer, because the opportunity could have passed. But here's the concept…

You're walking down a path. Your decision seems simple at the start—it might well be simplistic. As you chew on it, confusion sets in, and the decision seems more complicated. Keep walking; the psychic discomfort of the confusion will propel you. Exploring the confusion will help you come to understand more about the decision's facets and consequences.

If you focus intently and long enough (a big *if*), a much simpler view of the decision might emerge—its *essence*. Now, you understand. It seems that Charlie Brown at AT&T didn't do this.

Helpful in this effort, as Ram Charan recommends in this article and book,[226] is Amazon's practice of creating a six-page narrative. Doing so, in well-structured prose, can be agonizing, but it forces you to clearly think through the decision and its implications.

I've not been able to find an available example of Amazon's six-page narratives, so I created an outline you might use as a starting point; see box, below.

What Should Be in a Decision Narrative

Clearly describe the context for the decision: how did the need to make this decision come about—what led up to it? Include the decision's importance.

What, specifically, needs to be decided? Framed succinctly—what's the decision's essence?

List the alternatives. For each, what are:

• The potential rewards (the upside)—revenue, profit, and profit-margin gains?

• The foreseeable outcome(s), along with the consequences and desirability of each?

• The costs: in capital, expense, management time, and use of scarce resources?

• On a 1–10 scale (10 being high), rate the decision's: riskiness, feasibility, impacts on those affected (who would benefit? who would not? what would each then do?, and how likely is that?), and the ability to back out of this alternative, once implemented (considering the associated cost, brand, and customer-experience impact, if doing so is even possible).

- Other pros and cons?

For making considered decisions, there are two frameworks worth using. The first, WRAP, applies to more types of decisions, while the second, MAP, is useful in getting certain types of high-consequence decisions right.

WRAP

In their highly recommended book *Decisive,*[227] Chip and Dan Heath describe a process for making good decisions, framed by the acronym WRAP:

> **W**iden Your Options
> **R**eality-Test Your Assumptions
> **A**ttain Distance Before Deciding
> **P**repare to Be Wrong

If you're paid for making good decisions, reading their book is necessary, as are a few others they reference, such as Daniel Kahneman's *Thinking Fast and Slow,*[228] that provide a more fundamental view into the psychology of decision making, and our blind spots and biases.

In more detail, the steps in WRAP are to:

Widen your options, creating more choices around your decision.

- Go outside your work environment and look at what others have done when faced with a similar decision. What did they decide? How did their decisions work out? Would they make the same choices again?
- Vanishing options: Imagine that there's a mean genie who takes away the option you thought you had, forcing you to create an alternative.

- Look at the problem using a wide-angle lens, to capture *all* of its facets, and suggest more options. Alternatives will help you avoid "Whether or not" or "Yes/No" decisions.
- Having created several options, you can initially assess them in parallel, and even choose to seriously consider doing more than one.

Reality-test your assumptions.

- Gather evidence and data. Then ask, "What would have to be true for the choice we're considering to be the very best one?" This author feels that another step is often needed here: *Really* understand the situation. This is not a casual, unconsidered acceptance that an assumption is correct.
- Next, invite disagreement. What would be the consequences of doing the opposite of your preferred choice?
- Try to do what the Heaths call "ooching."[229] Treat the decision you're wrestling with as a small experiment, rather than a big commitment. See what happens, *then* commit. Because, as they say, we're all terrible at predicting. But why predict, when we can *know? Examples:*
  - Proof-of-concept test a new technology in a new application.
  - Test-market a successful product in one geography, rather than doing a full-scale rollout.

Attain distance before deciding.

- Try to eliminate the powerful and distorting influence of emotion in the moment of deciding.*Example:* car dealers and TV pitches prey on your emotions, to get you to "buy, now."

  These are often not the best decisions you can make. Errr, anyone want to buy a slightly used treadmill?
- Mentally test how you'll feel about the decision in 10 minutes, in 10 months, and in 10 years.[230] The three perspectives tend to reduce the emotional intensity you might feel.
- As humans, we're wired to value avoiding loss more than achieving gain. Fear wins.

- "The first 10 callers will receive..."
- "When they're gone, they're gone..."

But it warps our judgment. An antidote is to detach—take a reporter's perspective, rather than yours, the participant's. What insights into the decision does that bring?

- Make sure your decision is true to your business's core values. As an example, Google once famously said that it was guided by the words, "Don't be evil." Then it decided to spy on its customers, skewering their trust. Sometimes an agonizing decision is an indication of a conflict with your core values.

Prepare to be wrong.

- Consider whether the decision could become a shot below the waterline, and sink the business. Lee Iacocca, former CEO of Chrysler, was said to ask, "If we're wrong about this, what's our plan for backing out?"

- Boost your chances of being right. OK, we as humans are almost always overconfident about whether we're right, and about how long something will take. But, we know that. And we can, and do, correct for it, using safety factors, padded schedules, etc.

  What can you do with some of the elements that flow from your decision to ensure that it doesn't turn into a bad one? A good example is to add a bit of what's called over-engineering to a product to make it fail-safe. Also, as mentioned, reality-test, early.

- Consider convening a premortem: a meeting of those tasked with the decision, to surface and analyze why the decision was the wrong one, before it turns out to be.

- The Heaths also advise that we should prepare to be *right,* using a planning step they call a *pre-parade.* What if the decision is right on, and leads to blockbuster success? How will you handle it? Will you be able to get enough components for your hit product to meet overwhelming demand? (Advance planning beats scrambling.)

- Here's one last element, source unknown. Decide, but don't act on it immediately. Then pay close attention to *how it feels*. If you're having pangs of regret, maybe the decision wasn't right and your subconscious is trying to tell you so. Take that as an input, then finalize or revise the decision, *then* act.

Taken together, WRAP's decision steps form a process, which should be designed so that it's perceived as fair, with everyone's views considered. Then it's used, refined over time, and becomes the trusted way to make important decisions.

The management consultant Gerry Faust tells a story about his son working with him in his firm, which had a decision-making process in place. When the son had a good idea, they'd run with it. When the son had an idea that Gerry thought was the dumbest he'd ever heard (to that point), he'd say, "Let's use the process." And of course, the son quickly got the sense that Dad wasn't bowled over by the idea.

But it likely helped to raise the percentage of good decisions.

In his afterword to *Blink*,[231] Gladwell reports that relying on analysis can work well in relatively simple situations, but when the decision involves many factors, human psychology among them, a blink choice might turn out best. But again, blink choices are far more likely to be right in situations in which the decider has deep experience, the subconscious being better at integrating lots of diverse information.

There are times in which, as mentioned above, it's best to combine the deliberative and blink approaches, using what they're each best at: analyze, so all of the options are clear and weighed, and pay at least some attention to those "I have a feeling about this" moments.

MAP (Mediating Assessments Protocol)

MAP is a new approach to making considered decisions in common, high-stakes, business situations, created by Nobel laureate Daniel Kahneman (*Thinking Fast and Slow*), and others.[232]

It's for making consequential decisions in which *multiple* people's assessments play a role: key hires, acquisitions, venturing into a new market, which opportunities to pursue, what products to develop, which new locations to serve...

MAP is designed as a way to get our foibles, biases, and groupthink out of the deciding process, to the extent possible.

Approach

Start by identifying who needs to be in the group of those doing the research, the interviewing, the recommending, and the deciding. Acquaint them with the MAP method, if need be.

Define the set of evaluation criteria, and the numeric scales on which those people will assess each of them. Also identify any make/break criteria.

Have each person, *individually,* use research or interviews to come up with their set of fact-based numerical ratings on each criterion. It's important to have the assessments done independently by individuals, not groups, to avoid the influence of strong personalities or those in higher positions. (This is why MAP's creators call these *mediating assessments.*)

If there are deal breakers, stop.

Otherwise, once all of the assessments are complete, assemble the group, and hash out a recommendation. Include among the options, doing nothing. Provide all of the material collected to those who'll decide what to do.

Then, and as with WRAP, allow your gut to weigh in, give it a few days if you can, then decide.

If the decision to be made is likely to recur, e.g., another key hire or acquisition, preserve the results of the current investigation so you can refer to it next time.

Managing Risk

To state the blindingly obvious, there are a host of things that can sink a business, or drain its value in short order, as we've seen in the coronavirus pandemic. That particular risk seemed far-fetched. Until it wasn't. Before the lockdown, it seemed more of a public-health concern than a business risk. The lockdown forced many businesses to try to pivot into another way: to carry on their existing business (sit-down restaurants offering takeout /delivery), to focus on a different customer (farmers selling at farmer's markets instead of to restaurants), or to cast about for an entirely new way to make money, and fast. Here are three ways to protect against risks we've seen in more ordinary times:

Value-proposition or technology disruptions: Detect them early, so you can respond in time, before the disrupters sink your business. To do so, you need a Chief Lookout (or a small team)—with ready, direct access to your business's leaders, experience in your industry, and the technologies related to your business; an open, perceptive mind; persuasion skills; and, of course, credibility. Plus, a keen sense of what could upend your apple cart.

Once the lookout(s) surface a credible disruption, it's the leader's and the top team's *obligation* to respond. Or else.

Have a risk-management program: We'll describe this at an appropriate scale for a small- or mid-sized business. A large public company will need something like a full-blown Enterprise Risk Management system, about which there are a number of books and resources.

Someone we'll call the Chief Risk Officer should have the job of formulating and maintaining a list of the things that could markedly reduce your business's value, cost it a lot of money, or sink it—a list of significant risks. Then that person needs to work with the top team on plans to mitigate those risks. As a recent *Wall Street Journal* article suggested, for a public company, it might be helpful for this person to report directly to the full board.[233]

Vital, too, is a candid assessment of your business's risk-management culture. How seriously are the potential risks taken? What about "Black-Swan" (highly unlikely) events that often carry catastrophic consequences? How often are the list of risks and the risk-management plan reviewed? At what level of the business? What is *done* in response?

Create a process for avoiding "the acquisition from hell": This is an area in which a lot of value can be lost; the combined businesses never realize their expected potential.

Sometimes the acquired company detonates, creating a threatening hole in your ship. A recent example is Bayer, AG's acquisition of Monsanto, whose Roundup weed killer has of late become a prime target for the attorneys of those claiming that Roundup™ caused their cancers. *The Wall Street Journal* reported that as of their April 2019 article, this resulted in a 35% decline in Bayer's value since the first verdict in the cases.[234] A failure of due diligence?

A more common reason for the combination's failing to thrive is conflict between the cultures of the two businesses. To mitigate that, you need processes:

- For assessing culture fit, and to ferret out and face other red-flag issues beforehand.
- For making the combined company *feel as one.*

Leveraging Assets

Know-How and Intellectual Property

In 1990, IBM's licensing royalties from its intellectual-property portfolio were $30 million. Then IBM decided to take better advantage of that portfolio. By 2003, licensing royalties had grown to more than $1 billion, a 3,233% increase.[235] The resulting profit is roughly equivalent to what would have come from an additional $20 billion in product sales. In IBM's case, mining just its intellectual property's untapped potential could have compensated for a $20 billion sales decline, or 22% of IBM's $89 billion 2003 revenue. Who would have thought that just one element of IBM's untapped potential could offset a 22% drop in revenue?

An interesting question: *How had IBM thought about its intellectual-property portfolio through most of the 1980s?*

Teleflex, a U.S. conglomerate based in Pennsylvania, is a living example of another form of asset leverage: using what it knows to organically move into new lines of business. Expertise serves as entrée. Simply, "We know how to do *this* (better than most everyone else), and now it will let us do *that.*" Teleflex began making helical cable for aircraft in World War II, then used the knowledge gained to move into the automotive, marine, medical-device, and other industrial markets. Its developed expertise in noncorrosive cable coatings led the company into the turbo-engine business. And its skill in creating inner-cable linings led them into invasive disposables, such as catheters.[236]

After a decade of managing its portfolio of businesses, Teleflex has now become a pure play, exclusively focused on medical devices, mainly catheters, owing largely to its cable, cable-coatings, and linings beginnings.

Technology

Consider what leveraging technology, and the business innovations it can create, now enable. *Examples:*

- Technology: The web (for extending your business's geographic reach), and cloud computing (for lowering the cost of creating a new business)
- Tech-based business innovations: social media (for selling, marketing, branding, and creating and managing relationships).

Your Brand(s)

Would another business benefit from the promise behind your brands, without risking the brand's value to you? Can, or should, you license one of your brands to a complementary provider, as Disney licenses its Star Wars characters to the toy maker Hasbro?

Your Relationships

What people or organizations do you enjoy a relationship with, that involves helping one another? Is there a company whose capabilities would increase your sales, and theirs? For example, putting a fun-themed family restaurant in a shopping mall's food court could serve as a draw for the mall, and increase the restaurant's overall sales. Are there businesses that you could run a joint promotion with?

Affiliates, Resellers, and Partnerships

What can others sell for you? Where?

Your Sales Force—What Else Can They Sell?

IBM has had success with buying small software companies whose products its worldwide sales force can offer, once the products are integrated with the rest of its offerings. This boosts the acquired software's sales, while giving IBM's reps more ways to satisfy their customers' needs.

The strategy has worked to a point, but is impeded a bit, because the acquired software is in some cases clunky, might not lend itself to integration, or needs to maintain compatibility with the software's pre-acquisition versions, limiting the degree to which it can be changed.

In your business, are there complementary product-or-service accompaniments to what you now offer that will boost profits while making customers happier?

Financial Strength

You can sell more if you or a partner can finance it, without either of you losing your shirts. GE Capital has long been a factor in increasing the sales of what GE manufactures. Automakers and most other purveyors of high-priced items offer similar financing options, either through internal divisions or by paying a better-heeled financial-services company to assume the risk.

Nonproprietary Business Processes

Simple examples:

- How the phone is answered. Does the caller get the sense that your business believes that they're important? How strong is that sense?

- Ensuring that plans are executed. Is there a process that ensures that your best-laid plans don't go off the rails?

Your People

To what degree does your company's management style, mission, and culture bring out the passion, OK, *juice,* in your people? Is there more you can do there? What steps can you take to boost "take the hill" attitudes, willingness, and commitment?

Is there more you can do about attracting, hiring, developing, and retaining talent? Even though the wages of mediocre people are not generally high, they're costly, mainly in ways that are hard to capture and measure. Hire people with a hunger and passion about your business, pay them appropriately, and engage them.

How good is your business at attracting keepers? What's your business's value proposition *for its people?* How magnetic is its purpose, mission, and vision? Does your culture and reputation attract or repulse those you'd really want? To what degree?

How about retaining people? Have you challenged them with meaningful work? Are you actively encouraging them to grow?

What's your process for "taking the temperature" of your people and acting on the results?

Optimizing Your Portfolios

Of Offerings

This is about taking a hard look at the profitability and long-term potential of the products or services you now offer. (We will treat creating profit exceeding cost of capital in the next chapter, and we covered the cost aspect of profitability in Chapter 7, Cost Management.)

Create an up-to-date analysis of your offerings and figure out if you need to drop, phase out, sell, or dramatically upgrade any of your current offerings, and what would be the best new ones to add, and when.

Of Brands

Is each of your brands a fit with your overall business strategy, intended image, and the value-creation engine you want your owners to perceive? A classic brand in a growth-company's portfolio could well be a misfit.

When a large company acquires another, it's not unusual for them to consider shedding one of their brands, or the acquired brands, so only one, the "best," remains. "Best," of course has many dimensions, and is specific to the brands and companies involved, and the market at large.

Of Businesses

It's also important that you do the above portfolio exercise with business units. One reason is that you might be able to sell the unit, whereas the sale of an individual offering or a small brand might not be worth the trouble. Here you can look at the unit's historical wealth creation (see Chapter 14) and its prognosis.

Basically, you're looking to maximize the combined value of the company's business units over time.

To do so, you might need to shutter, fix, or sell the underperformers, as well as grab onto something with a bright future, affordably. Use the money from what you sell or shut down to fund that bright-future something.

Understand where the bulk of the business's profits come from. Does the 80/20 rule apply? If so, what should you do?

But weigh the business-unit's synergies, if any. Some say synergies are scarce. But a few, like Teleflex, above, and 3M[237], have built their companies on them.

The full-throated version of business-portfolio management is the core concern of conglomerates. In these multi-business, usually public, companies, how well the portfolio of businesses is managed leads to what's called the *conglomerate discount* (or premium) being reflected in the stock price. In most situations, some of these companies' businesses are doing well, while others are not earning their cost of capital. This has been called, with tongue in cheek, the "something's always in the tank" business design. But there are those conglomerates, like 3M, that at times "fire on all cylinders."

Executives have choices to make in dealing with underperforming businesses in their portfolios. First, resolve whether the underperformance is chronic, or linked to a situation that will pass in the near future. If it is transient, you might not need to confront the possibilities below, although a little fix-up might still prove worthwhile.

Then, try to determine whether the underperformance is due to a declining business (is your whole industry suffering?) or a poor business design, or having the wrong people in key roles. Both of the latter two can be tied to, "It's your business, not the whole industry."

If the underperformance is chronic, your options are:

- Fix the underperformer, which might require additional investment, might not create a return, and could be lost altogether.

- Sell it, ideally to a strategic buyer to whom it could be worth more than it is to your company, and get that increased worth reflected in the sale price.

- Shut it down, so at least you'll no longer have to fund it, throwing good money after bad.

The conglomerate discount comes about when no decision is made about the underperformers, creating an ongoing drag on earnings by funding the losers instead of being willing to cut them off, quickly. Or, it might make sense to simply focus on your best businesses, biggest brands, or highest-potential opportunities.[238]

The conglomerate *premium* comes about because of:

- Strong synergies, such as a business unit that will finance products you offer.
- Showing real discipline in capital allocation.
- Investing much more in winners, taking it from what might otherwise have gone to the losers.
- Shareable costs, like R&D.
- Acquiring businesses for which a healthy chunk of the costs they have in common with your business can be taken out. This is more rarely the case when the acquired firm is in an entirely different business than the one you're now in.

Plugging Revenue Leaks

Lost sales are a major, often obscure villain behind lackluster results. Here are three of the biggest.

Your Supply-and-Demand Chains

If you can't economically make enough of what you offer to meet demand, or if you run out of a hot seller, the related revenue just flies out the window. If you're not able to quickly react to sudden bursts of demand, you'll also lose sales due to near-term stock outs.

Then there's being stuck with stale offerings that are not selling—a cost, in addition to a revenue loss.

Doing a good job of managing both your supply-and-demand chains is essential to keep revenue flowing at maximum. The Spain-based fast-fashion firm Zara is renowned for both.

There's not enough space here to tackle either supply- or demand-chain management. You can find excellent information on the more complex supply-chain aspect in Simchi-Levi et al.,[239] and there's also substantial available consulting help. The key to demand-chain management is analyzing sales trends, say, daily, and creating the ability to replace an offering for which sales are tanking, or just heading down, very quickly.

Pricing

Because pricing can be such a powerful revenue drain, we devoted Chapter 6 to it.

Sales and Marketing Integration

Marketing's job is to create a line of qualified customers at the door, so the sales force can present an appropriate offer and close the sale. The two departments don't always work effectively with each other, which lowers the number of closed sales.

For example, the results of marketing's lead generation, qualification, and lead turnover to sales are sometimes viewed skeptically by the salespeople, who then don't give marketing's leads the attention needed to create sales, creating a self-fulfilling prophecy. An agreed-upon prospect-qualification and sales-turnover process, tracking what happens as a result (and jointly making improvements), the mindset that marketing and sales should operate with one goal (higher sales, and, if need be, a strong executive who oversees both departments) can help.[240]

Managing Quality

Creating and maintaining quality protects your brand, helps keep sales where they are now and into the future, and justifies your pricing. How complete and effective are your processes for protecting quality? There's an extensive body of literature on quality, and considerable available consulting help. However, you might not need to go all the way to the ultimate quality approach, Six Sigma.

Process—A Prosperity Enabler

Most groups of people, however well-intentioned, will, when left to their own devices, create chaos. You need an antidote to that—processes—so you can focus on making money and growing, rather than coping with that chaos. Having processes gives you the management bandwidth to actually pursue your biggest upsides, rather than being too worn down by the chaos to do much of anything. Processes make things easier, cheaper, more internally consistent, and repeatable.[241]

So you have the opportunity to have some. You could have one for most everything you do, including most of those in this chapter: making sage decisions, managing risk, optimizing your offerings and lines of business, managing quality, your pricing, supply-and-demand chains, collaborations with other businesses, and integrating sales and marketing.

An extreme example of this is that IBM has a *single* financial process for its operations, worldwide, all run from one central point. If IBM can do that, you can create a suite of processes, too.

There is, as you might recall, a brief discussion of process streamlining, with an emphasis on cost reduction, in Chapter 7, and process streamlining is also used as an example of an upside element you might pursue, in Chapter 14, up next.

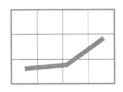

TAPPING YOUR UPSIDE:
Management Practices

Leading

1. Be honest: how enthusiastically are people following you?

_____

_____

2. Is there something you feel you need to do about your answer? What is it?

_____

_____

_____

3. Where do you want to take your business? Is it:

Clear to all? _____

Worth it? _____

Achievable? _____

Inspiring? _____

Long-term, will it continue to be a worthy goal? _____

Will it be bought into? (How enthusiastically?) _____

4. Is there alignment among the executive team around getting the business where you want to take it, and keeping it there?

_____

_____

5. Are any culture fixes needed to achieve this?

_____

_____

Making Sage Decisions

6. Many executives need to get better at making decisions. Do you?

_____

_____

7. If so, how, specifically will you and your team go about it?

_____

_____

_____

8. What is likely to be your next big, or bet-the-company, decision?

_____

_____

_____

9. **Based on what we've covered in this chapter, what will be different about how you approach that decision?**

_____

_____

_____

_____

10. **Does anything else about your decision-making processes need to change going forward?**

_____

_____

_____

_____

Managing Risk

11. **What, and who, specifically, are your disrupters, the technical or social developments, or the companies that could upend your business?**

_____

_____

_____

12. **Do you have one or more lookouts?**

Are they credible? _____

Are they heeded? _____

13. **Do you have a risk-management program?**

One with regularly scheduled reviews? _____

At the highest levels of the business? _____

14. **Rate your business's risk culture on the scale below.**

Highly risk-averse ⬅──────────────────➡ Reckless

Is that appropriate? _____

15. **Do you need, or have, a process for identifying, vetting, making, and integrating acquisitions?**

_____

_____

Leveraging Assets

16. **What assets can you leverage?**

_____

_____

_____

_____

What about intellectual property (patents, trademarks, know-how)? ____

_____

Technology? _____

_____

What technology enables:

- Social media? _____

- Online video and screencast marketing? _____

- Mass customization? _____

- Electronic tagging? _____

- Other _____

Brand(s)? _____

Relationships? _____

Affiliates/Resellers/Partnerships? _____

Your sales force? _____

Your financial strength? _____

Existing business processes? _____

Optimizing portfolios

17. **For offerings, brands, and businesses, do you conduct regular portfolio assessments?**

    a. What's covered in these?

    _____

    _____

    b. What measures and other information are used?

    _____

    _____

Before tackling the offering and brand assessments below, we suggest that you consider which of the two makes the most sense for your business. If you have one offering for each brand, use the offering assessment. If you have a number of products under an umbrella brand, then both of the next questions might apply. (If you have some lackluster offerings under the brand, start with the question just below.)

18. **Fill in what follows for *each* of the major product or service *offerings* in your business:**

Financial Aspects

a. % of firm's profits _____

b. % of firm's capital needed _____

c. % of firm's costs _____

d. Rank (leading product or service in the market, #2, laggard, etc.) _____

The Opportunity

e. Market size _____

f. Market growth rate _____

g. Market share _____

h. Market-share growth rate _____

i. The offering's remaining lifespan _____

j. Would it be worth significantly more to another firm? _____

k. Would affecting that transition be worth the trouble? _____

l. How integral is the offering to your firm's strategy? _____

Decision

_____ Continue as at present   _____ Emphasize

_____ De-emphasize   _____ Sell

_____ Shut down

19. **Fill in what follows for each of your major *brands*:**

Financial Aspects

a. % of firm's profits _____

b. Rank (leading product or service in the market, #2, laggard, etc.) _____

The Opportunity

c. Market size _____

d. Market growth rate _____

e. Market share _____

f. Market-share growth rate _____

g. Can the brand stand alone? _____

h. If so, would it be worth significantly more to another firm? _____

i. Would effecting that transition be worth the trouble? _____

j. How integral is the offering to your firm's strategy? _____

Decision

_____ Continue as at present   _____ Emphasize

_____ De-emphasize   _____ Sell

_____ Shut down

20. For each significant *business* in your portfolio...

Financial Aspects	Present	Projected
a. % of firm profits		
b. Economic profitability (see below)		
c. % of firm's capital required		
d. % of firm's costs		
e. Rank (leading business in the market, #2, laggard, etc.)		

Economic profits, covered in more detail in Chapter 14, are those earned after all costs, including the cost of capital, are taken into account. Economic profit shows how good the business is at making real money. One good measure of economic profit is economic margin, defined as operating profit, less a risk-weighted cost of capital, the result of which is divided by invested capital. That result, a ratio, is expressed as a percentage. If the percentage is greater than zero, the business is at least making some money. The higher the percentage, the better. If your economic margin is negative, you have an issue to confront. Also, there are other economic-profitability metrics, such as EVA: Economic Value Added, which some prefer. A brief survey of these metrics can be found on page 13 of the author's 2008 *Chief Executive* magazine article, "Leading Your Business to Maximum Results," posted with their permission at greatnumbers.com/Leading_Your_Business_to_Maximum_Results.pdf, pp 11–13.

The Opportunity

f. Combined market size _____

g. Revenue-weighted-average market-growth rate_____

h. Can the business stand alone? _____

i. Would it be worth significantly more to another firm? _____

j. What could it fetch? _____

k. Would effecting the transition be worth the trouble? _____

l. How integral is the offering to your firm's strategy? _____

_____

m. What would be the divestiture's impact on it? _____

_____

n. Are there any significant synergies with your other businesses? _____

_____

o. What would be the divestiture's impact on them? _____

_____

_____

Decision

_____ Continue as at present   _____ Emphasize

_____ De-emphasize   _____ Sell

_____ Shut down

21. Having reviewed the intended changes in your portfolios, what would be their net effects? (Working through several scenarios might prove helpful here.)

_____

_____

_____

_____

_____

_____

22. Plugging revenue leaks—where are they coming from?

	Leak Size	How We'll Address
a. Supply chain		
b. Demand chain		
c. Base-pricing level		
d. Multiprice strategy		
e. Sales and marketing integration		
f. Quality management		
g. Culture of pricing		

Processes

23. Where do you need some processes, or improvements to same?

_____

_____

What Are They?	Who Will Create Them?

UPSIDE ELEMENT ASSESSMENT: MANAGEMENT PRACTICES

Please enter your estimates for the *overall* gains and challenges you expect to derive from each of your management initiative(s) in the corresponding rows on the Upside Element Assessment Sheet, just before the last page.

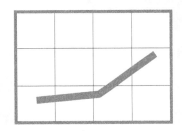

Part 4

Your Best Results Moves: *Insight-Based Management*

There are so many powerful ways to boost results that you won't be able to tackle them all, nor should you. Depending on the business you're in, some won't amount to much of anything, while others will make it rock. In a different business, an entirely different set of upside elements would make it rock.

Here you'll learn to use a set of tools for wisely choosing the realistic upside elements that, together, will produce the best possible results for your particular business. It's a template for doing so that we call *Insight-Based Management.* The idea is to first understand the type of performance (increased profit-margins or revenue growth) that your investors, senior management, or a prospective buyer of your business will value most. Then you can use the decision tool here to pick the realistic set of upside elements that will bring you the best possible results, and make your business the most valuable it can be.

Chapter 14

Discovering the Best Ways to Boost Results in Your Business—Insight-Based Management

The Classic Way to Try to Increase Results: Heat-Based Management

One of management's most enduring traditions has been the way CEOs, and those who lead large business units, try to get their direct reports to improve profits and boost revenue. You could call it *heat-based management*: the heat coming in the form of tough profit and revenue-growth targets doled out to the executives who run the company's individual businesses.

Most executives who've had P&L responsibility, particularly in public companies, have experienced heat-based management at the gut level. Their challenge is clear; how to meet it, anything but. There are the usual options: cut costs, squeeze suppliers (yet again), and exhort the sales force to still higher heights. But they did that last time, too.

I believe that heat-based management represents a yawning gap in management practice—that shortchanges both investors and executives. Because it lacks *a way* to get the increased results, the thought being, "You're smart, or you wouldn't be running your business. You'll figure out how to meet your targets." That doesn't seem to me to be the surest way for an executive to deliver the best possible results.

The other problem with results targets is that they're *limiting*. Meet them, or beat them by just a bit, and the executive with the target, and their business, "are done" until the next time the targets are set; and perhaps they're holding something in reserve for that next time. A better approach for CEOs setting goals, or for major investors wanting more, is, "Let's learn what your business's results potential *really* is."

If only there was a way to do that…

There is. It's rooted in the observation that what executives *choose to do* matters, *a lot*. Choosing patterns we've all seen: majoring in minors; swinging for too-distant fences; flailing—trying one thing, then another, in rapid succession; or just using "a hammer" on everything—one tool, like cost-cutting, yet again, and wondering why revenue's not growing.

Introducing... Insight-Based Management

In contrast, we'll now lay out an approach informed by the potential of the upside elements appropriate to the business, and by the underlying business's financial characteristics. It's one that will help you find the most powerful, and realistic, things you can do to *boost the value* of your business—your *best shots*.

Then you just have to make them happen. In short, the approach is to…

Find your best shots and take them!

The "Let's See" Tool (for Finding Those Best Shots)

In this chapter, we'll see *how* to find your best shots, by becoming clear about what determines the value of a business: how revenue and profit-margin growth figure into it, and how to choose the upside elements that will best boost it, given their potential and your realities.

Let's See

Let's See is an Excel spreadsheet for helping you find the best things you can do to increase profits, revenue, and the value of your business.

To do so, you'll need to enter some financial information. The tabs of the spreadsheet are integrated, so you only have to enter each data item once, and it will flow where needed. Its sequence of tabs will guide you.

- **Inputs:** Here you enter basic financial information about your business.

- **Goal Emphasis Advisor:** Use this tab to figure out which performance goal, revenue growth, or a profit-margin increase, will best increase your business's value, if met.

- **The Upside Calculator:** Here you'll enter the gains from the Upside Element Assessments sheet, that you used to record the percentage improvements you expected as you worked through Chapters 2–13.

- **The Chooser:** All of the above comes together on this tab, and you'll have, in one place, what you need to decide which upside elements to pursue. You'll combine The Upside Calculator's gains with reality: how much pursuing each upside element will cost, how hard it will be to pull off, and what resources it will require.

Getting *Let's See*:

You can download this book's tools and extras, including *Let's See*, from www.theupsidewithinreach.com.

The Value of a Business

The value of any business is what a willing buyer will pay for it. The fancy name for this is *enterprise value*: the amount of money it will take to buy all of the stock, and to pay off all of the debt. That value's often hard to know without receiving an offer to buy the business—even for a public company with a known stock price, a known number of shares outstanding, and known debt, because the value is only really determined when some entity offers to buy the company for a specific amount.

In most cases, what makes a business valuable are strong earnings now, and a strong outlook: high likelihood that those strong earnings will continue, and increase, into the future. Growth with little profitability is not terribly attractive, although there have been a few notable exceptions in the tech sector: YouTube and Instagram. Profitability without growth prospects puts the business at risk over the long term, because it becomes more vulnerable to disruptions in its profit engine. Clearly, having both increased profitability and revenue growth is much better.

One commonly accepted way to value a business is to use a stream of discounted cash flows (DCF) over a time period of interest. But a business's DCF valuation might be, and sometimes is, off by a lot. For several reasons:

- The business might have strategic value to a buyer, so it could be worth more than the DCF figures indicate. The additional value could include synergies that the buyer would create. Example: a startup software company with a hot technology would be much more valuable to a global IT company than it would be to most conglomerates.

- There can also be a significant contingent risk, such as new litigation, a sudden and unforeseen adverse regulatory development, or a game-changing technological threat to the business, making its value far lower than its DCF figure suggests.

But these are anomalies, and can't be used as a matter of course to manage the business.

Business Value and the Executive's Role

A P&L executive's *job* is to *make the business they run more valuable*—to get would-be buyers of the stock, or of the entire business, to feel justified in paying more for it.

What makes a business more valuable? The answer includes the fruits of the upside elements we've described, as well as sage financial, resource, and asset management. And if the business becomes more valuable, people will indeed pay more to own it.

Calculating the specific increase in business value that stems from a given increase in profits is, as they say, complicated—and inherently imprecise. It depends on, among other things: the degree to which the increased profits endure, the inherent riskiness of the business, its dependence on specific people or technologies, changing markets, tastes, and regulations.

Executives can't control all of those things. All they can do is to run the business so that it produces the best possible results, while avoiding unnecessary risks that could markedly reduce its value.

Measures of Value

There are two ways to gauge whether you as an executive are creating the most valuable business possible. We'll ask you to adopt one of them in working through this chapter.

The first measure of the value of the business stems from its operating results, as distinct from what the business owns, its liabilities and inherent risks, the quality of its management, and the other factors mentioned above. Operating-results-related value rises due to a combination of revenue growth and higher profit *margins* (profits divided by sales), in some proportion, which we'll get to in a moment. But as mentioned, that combination is only one element of the value of the overall business, so it doesn't directly translate into such things as an increased stock price (as if anything really does).

Pursuing operating-results-related value increases is more abstract than profit, the second type, below, which can be measured in monetary amounts. And being abstract, it might be harder for some people to wrap their heads around or get excited about. But pursuing it might prove more rewarding in terms of value gained.

That second, more tangible, performance measure is profit, the amount of money the business makes by growing revenue, lifting profit *margins* (how much revenue is left over after all costs, as a percentage of that revenue), or both. And to let the value of the business follow.

For this second type of goal, we'll use, as a measure, *economic profit:* cash flow from operations less a charge for the capital the business uses. Economic profit shows how good the business is at making real money—money exceeding *all* of its costs. Because the business is really not making money if it's paying out all of its operating income in the form of interest. It also could be diluting its shareholders' wealth with employee stock options.

The interest figure we'll use here is called the *weighted average cost of capital,* or WACC. It's the weighted total of its equity and debt, and varies by the business's inherent riskiness, and by industry, most often falling in the range of 4.1% to 10.8%. (By-industry averages for WACC can be found in a recent analysis by NYU Stern School of Business professor Aswath Damodaran.[242]) WACC is the minimum percentage return that investors expect in return for providing the company with their money. To be making real money, a business's operating income must exceed that capital cost. (As we'll see, both revenue growth and, obviously, profit-margin growth, contribute to the growth of economic profits by creating additional gross income in excess of fixed costs.)

Why the focus on operating results? It's less susceptible to accounting games than Earnings Before Interest and Taxes (EBIT) and its brethren, so it gives you a truer picture of how the underlying business is doing. You need that clarity before acting.

There are two useful measures of economic profit: Economic Margin (EM),[243] and Economic Value Added, or EVA*.[244] Each is used in its respective wealth-creation-assessment framework to measure the real value a business creates.

EM's the simplest: operating cash flow, less a risk-appropriate cost of capital or WACC, divided by invested capital. EM is a ratio. Positive EM (> 0%) implies wealth creation; negative EM, destruction.

EVA is net operating profit after taxes, less WACC, times the difference between total assets and *current* liabilities. (Often, a number of adjustments are

---

EVA is a service mark of Stern Value Management.

applied in arriving at a final figure.) EVA is a monetary amount, not a ratio. EVA *Margin*, however—EVA/Sales—shows economic profit per dollar of sales.

You can find readable explanations of both frameworks in the two articles just cited.

Grow Revenue or Profit Margins: Which Will Drive Value the Most?

Before you can pick your best shots, you'll first need to be clear on which type of results—increased profit margins or revenue growth—will be most valuable in the eyes of your investors, or the prospective buyers of your business. What type of performance do they *expect*? That strongly influences what they'll pay.

In some companies, investors clearly expect revenue growth and are less concerned about profit margins, as was the case with Google in its early days, and which is the case today with most tech start-ups. In others, like a manufacturer that serves established, slow-growth, or declining markets, investors want increased profit margins on what might be flat or flagging sales, which they see as the primary way to increase the company's value.

Which of these is more important in your business?

We'll present two ways to find out. The first applies to large- and mid-sized, usually public companies, and the second to any company; but the two might yield different results.

But First...

You'll need to enter a few numbers on *Let's See*'s Inputs tab (next diagram). This is so that its recommendations from here on reflect the financial characteristics of your unique business. (The Introduction tab of *Let's See* provides a bit more background.)

Given this information about your business, we can estimate what type of performance has the biggest influence on its value. *Which* performance goal should you emphasize?

To figure that out, we're going to use a *Let's See* tab called the GOAL EMPHA-SIS ADVISOR, an overview of which is on the next page. It provides two ways to estimate an appropriate performance-goal emphasis, both of which are explained in detail following this overview. Once you decide on the relative emphasis on revenue growth that your chosen estimation method provides, you can enter it in the shaded cell, next page. It will then be used in calculating the increases in business value that various upside elements can provide.

The Consensus-Expectations Approach

This is a way for public companies covered by security analysts to find their revenue-growth versus profit-margin-growth emphasis. It can also be used by large private companies, *if* there's a comparable public company covered by those analysts.

A public company should absolutely be clear on the stock market's expectations for both profit-margin gains and revenue growth. To learn what the expected goal emphasis is for your public company, you'll first need some data, then some judgment.

A major public company can use the relative values of security analysts' consensus expectations for both revenue and profit-margin growth, expressed as percentages, and recent stock-price moves in response to meeting or deviating from those expectations.

If you can find a recent quarter in which the company's results met analysts' consensus estimates for both organic revenue growth (adjusted for acquisitions and divestitures, if need be) and operating profit margins (adjusted for one-time items), and in which the stock price didn't move significantly after that earnings release, consider using those consensus growth rates to provide a results-goal emphasis.

For example, let's say that the consensus expectations were for 3% revenue growth and 1% profit-margin growth, and the stock price hardly budged after the results were announced. Dividing both figures by their sum, 4%, results in revenue growth seeming to represent 75% of the company's value, with profit-margin growth being the remaining 25%. You can use these as your relative-emphasis figures. In other words, in this example, it will boost your

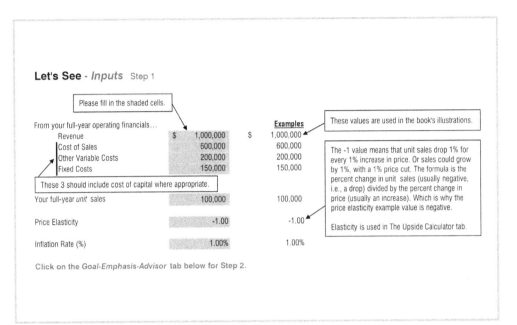

Let's See - *Inputs* Step 1

Please fill in the shaded cells.

From your full-year operating financials...

Revenue	$ 1,000,000	$ 1,000,000
Cost of Sales	600,000	600,000
Other Variable Costs	200,000	200,000
Fixed Costs	150,000	150,000

Examples

These values are used in the book's illustrations.

These 3 should include cost of capital where appropriate.

Your full-year *unit* sales   100,000   100,000

The -1 value means that unit sales drop 1% for every 1% increase in price. Or sales could grow by 1%, with a 1% price cut. The formula is the percent change in unit sales (usually negative, i.e., a drop) divided by the percent change in price (usually an increase). Which is why the price elasticity example value is negative.

Price Elasticity   -1.00   -1.00

Inflation Rate (%)   1.00%   1.00%

Elasticity is used in The Upside Calculator tab.

Click on the *Goal-Emphasis-Advisor* tab below for Step 2.

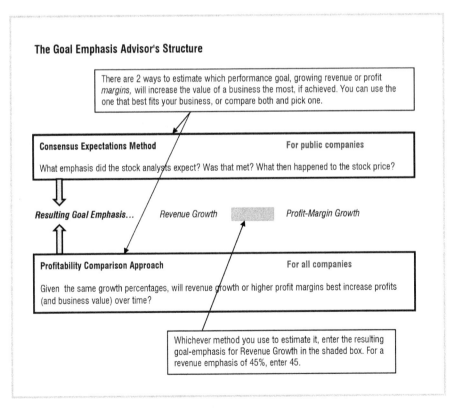

The Goal Emphasis Advisor's Structure

There are 2 ways to estimate which performance goal, growing revenue or profit *margins,* will increase the value of a business the most, if achieved. You can use the one that best fits your business, or compare both and pick one.

Consensus Expectations Method   **For public companies**

What emphasis did the stock analysts expect? Was that met? What then happened to the stock price?

Resulting Goal Emphasis...   *Revenue Growth*   *Profit-Margin Growth*

Profitability Comparison Approach   **For all companies**

Given the same growth percentages, will revenue growth or higher profit margins best increase profits (and business value) over time?

Whichever method you use to estimate it, enter the resulting goal-emphasis for Revenue Growth in the shaded box. For a revenue emphasis of 45%, enter 45.

company's value significantly more if you work on initiatives that will grow revenue by a percentage point, than it will if you try to lift profit margins by a point. At least that's what your investors would like to see.

If you're happy with that emphasis, you can enter its Revenue Growth percentage into cell E22, *Resulting Goal Emphasis,* in the GOAL EMPHASIS ADVISOR shown on page 302 (for a revenue-growth emphasis like 65%, enter 65). You can then move on to Let's See's UPSIDE CALCULATOR tab.

If the company didn't come close to meeting consensus estimates in any recent quarter, you can try the second approach, below, as can every other company, public or private.

The Profitability Comparison Approach

This option will work for all companies. Its *Base Summary Inputs* section ([B24:E29]* on page 302) will need to be populated with your data (here we show the Example data, though). Also, you should enter, in the *Assumptions* section ([G24:H29] on page 302), the lowest and highest growth rates [G29:H29] you want to analyze. (The same growth rates will be applied to both revenue and profit-margin improvements.)

On page 303, the middle-section of the GOAL EMPHASIS ADVISOR, there are two growth scenarios. The one on the left shows how profit will rise, based on increases in *profit margin,* over 1-, 2-, and 3-year periods. And it assumes, perhaps a big assumption, that the profit-margin increases on the left side will recur over the 3-year period. (That's certainly not a given.)

The section on the right on page 303, shows how profit would rise based on *revenue growth* over those 3 years. In the example, revenue growth results in higher profits in each of the three years.

Turning to page 304, the upper section of the range [B56:J60], *Inflation-adjusted **total** profits after n years,* summarizes the *present value* of the profit gains for both the profit-margin and revenue-growth scenarios after 1, 2, and 3 years.

Below that, [B62:J66] shows the additional profit that would come from *only the more worthwhile* goal emphasis.

---

*The notation [B26: E29] means, refer to the cell(s) inside the square brackets.

Finally, the bottom section, *Relative ability to create profit* [B68:J74], shows the expected business-value gains due to revenue increases [B71:J71]. The range [B72:J72] shows the value gains for profit-margin increases. [B73:J73] shows which one creates more profit in the 1-, 2-, and 3-year timeframes, and [B74:J74] reveals how much of a value difference there is.

Now, on row 69, choose the time frame that you want the performance goal to apply to (1, 2, or 3 years), and in your chosen time frame's pair of columns on row 70, which of the two gain percentages you want to shoot for. Enter the *Revenue* Gain, the bolded number, into the shaded cell [E22], see page 302.

For a 2% gain percentage in year 3, the example shows a revenue-gain of 52.8% in [I72]. If you chose revenue-growth as a goal, and 3 years as a timeframe, you would enter that as a decimal (.528) into cell [E22].

For the example business, after 3 years, with 2% annual increases of both revenue and profit margin, [I74] shows that 5.5% more profit arises from revenue growth than from profit-margin growth, based on inflation-adjusted profits up to that time. In other words, over 3 years, growing revenue by 2% is 5.5% more profitable than increasing profit margins by 2%. And using increases of 6% per year, revenue growth is 14.2% more profitable, [J74], than profit-margin growth over 3 years.

Let's See - Goal Emphasis Advisor Step 2

How will others, investors or potential buyers, put a value on your business? This is not about the accounting exercise called business valuation, although in some cases that can be useful. This exercise will help you figure out what type of future performance those with "the money" will value. On this sheet, you'll enter the relative importance of two performance goals that directly impact your business's value: revenue gains and profit-margin increases.

There are two ways to get a sense of this emphasis, see Chapter 14, pages xx-yy: the consensus of analysts' expectations, and the computed method, given below. You'll need to pick one.

Consensus Expectations Method

If you chose the consensus-expectations method, enter the relative weight analysts have given to revenue growth in cell E22 below. Entering a value of 1 means that revenue-growth is the only thing they're concerned with: an example would be a promising start-up. On the other hand, a value of 0 could be appropriate for a mature business in a declining market—the only thing analysts likely expect are profit-margin increases. A mix of the two

goals could also be appropriate: their assigned weights should (and will) total to 1.

If you decide to use the profitability-comparison approach below, it will suggest whether revenue-growth or a profit-margin increase is more important, and to what degree. Enter the **revenue** emphasis in cell E22.

Enter a value between 0 and 1

Calculated

Resulting Goal Emphasis...   *Revenue Growth:*   **65%**

Profit Margin: **35%**

Once you've entered a value for Revenue Growth, please click on the next tab (*The Upside Calculator*) for Step 3.

Profitability Comparison Approach

Base Summary Inputs

Revenue	$	1,000,000	Base fixed costs	150,000
Cost of sales		600,000	Base total costs	950,000
Other var. costs		200,000	Inflation rate	1.0%

Assumptions

Gain percentages applied to both Revenue and Profit Margin

Low	High
2.00%	6.00%

continues...

Profit-Margin Growth

Year 1	Base (Year 0)	2% Margin Gain	6% Margin Gain
Revenue	$ 1,000,000	$ 1,000,000	$ 1,000,000
Total Costs	950,000	949,000	947,000
Net Income	$ 50,000	$ 51,000	$ 53,000
Profit/Revenue (%)	5.00%	5.10%	5.30%

Cost cuts can be one-time. But if they recur...

Year 2	Base (Year 0)	2% Margin Gain	6% Margin Gain
Revenue	$ 1,000,000	$ 1,000,000	$ 1,000,000
Total Costs	950,000	947,980	943,820
Net Income	$ 50,000	$ 52,020	$ 56,180
Profit/Revenue (%)	5.00%	5.20%	5.62%

And if they recur, yet again...

Year 3	Base (Year 0)	2% Margin Gain	6% Margin Gain
Revenue	$ 1,000,000	$ 1,000,000	$ 1,000,000
Total Costs	950,000	946,940	940,449
Net Income	$ 50,000	$ 53,060	$ 59,551
Profit/Revenue (%)	5.00%	5.31%	5.96%

Revenue Growth

Year 1	Base (Year 0)	2% Sales Gain	6% Sales Gain
Revenue	$ 1,000,000	$ 1,020,000	$ 1,060,000
All variable costs	800,000	816,000	848,000
Fixed costs	150,000	150,000	150,000
Net Income	$ 50,000	$ 54,000	$ 62,000
Profit/Revenue (%)	5.00%	5.29%	5.85%

Year 2	Base (Year 0)	2% Sales Gain	6% Sales Gain
New Base Revenue	$ 1,000,000	$ 1,020,000	$ 1,060,000
Revenue	1,000,000	1,040,400	1,123,600
All variable costs	800,000	832,320	898,880
Fixed costs	150,000	150,000	150,000
Net Income	$ 50,000	$ 58,080	$ 74,720
Profit/Revenue (%)	5.00%	5.58%	6.65%

Year 3	Base (Year 0)	2% Sales Gain	6% Sales Gain
New Base Revenue	$ 1,000,000	$ 1,040,400	$ 1,123,600
Revenue	1,000,000	1,061,208	1,191,016
All variable costs	800,000	848,966	952,813
Fixed costs	150,000	150,000	150,000
Net Income	$ 50,000	$ 62,242	$ 88,203
Profit/Revenue (%)	5.00%	5.87%	7.41%

continues...

Inflation-adjusted total profits after *n* years

Due to Profit-Margin Growth

Year

Inflation-adjusted total profits after *n* years

n	Base (Year 0)	2% Margin Gain	6% Margin Gain
1	$ 49,505	$ 50,495	52,475
2	98,520	101,490	107,548
3	147,049	152,990	165,348

Additional profit due to profit-margin growth

Year

n	2% Margin Gain	6% Margin Gain
1	Cells at right will show	
2	as blank if lower than	
3	cols J-K.	

Due to Revenue Growth

Year

Inflation-adjusted total profits after *n* years

n	Base (Year 0)	2% Sales Gain	6% Sales Gain
1	$ 49,505	$ 53,465	61,386
2	98,520	110,401	134,634
3	147,049	170,812	220,243

Additional profit due to revenue growth

Year

n		2% Sales Gain	6% Sales Gain
1	Cells at right will show $	2,970	8,911
2	as blank if lower than	8,911	27,086
3	cols E-F.	17,822	54,895

Relative ability to create profit

		After 1 year		After 2 years		After 3 years	
		Expected Gain Percentages		Expected Gain Percentages		Expected Gain Percentages	
		2%	6%	2%	6%	2%	6%
Revenue (A)	= A / (A + B)	51.4%	53.9%	52.1%	55.6%	52.8%	57.1%
Profit Margin (B)	= B / (A + B)	48.6%	46.1%	47.9%	44.4%	47.2%	42.9%
Which Creates More Profit?		Revenue	Revenue	Revenue	Revenue	Revenue	Revenue
By How Much?		2.9%	7.8%	4.2%	11.2%	5.5%	14.2%

Whichever performance measure, Revenue Growth, or increase in Profit Margin, shows the largest percentage gain in your target time frame, 1, 2 or 3 years, is your most powerful profit driver. Enter the bolded **revenue** (not profit) percentage from row 72 for that target time frame, into cell **E22** above.

Results-Goal-Emphasis Methods and Management

Public companies can use both of the preceding approaches to figure out what will bring the biggest value increase. If the two agree, you have an additional validation. If not, digging into why could prove revealing. And sometimes management, or directors, know things about the company that would lead them to have a keener sense of what the revenue-versus-profit-margin-growth emphasis should be, "daring" the stock-market's assessment. Obviously, that's fine, if well-founded.

With results-emphasis data in hand, next comes judgment. What type of performance *should* you shoot for? What blend of prudence and ambition will best boost business value over the period you're planning for? For most companies, in most situations, a wise approach would be to profit your way into a solid financial position first, then grow revenue quickly. Because the more profitable you are, the faster you can grow without outstripping your available capital. A solid financial position can also serve as a shock absorber when something bad or unexpected happens.

There are, of course, exceptions. A start-up pursuing a promising new market, that avoided rapid growth, husbanding cash to bolster its financial strength, would likely miss its larger opportunity to become a dominant player.

But *decide on a goal emphasis;* you'll need it for the upcoming exercise: THE CHOOSER.

Whatever your final emphasis, enter the *revenue-growth* figure, *as a percentage,* into cell E22.

The Upside Calculator

On this worksheet, as mentioned, we'll insert the results gains you expect to get from each of the upside elements you analyzed, and recorded on the Upside Element Assessments sheet.

As preparation for that, we'll present four examples of upside-element gains, covering improved product design, more effective ads, business-process streamlining (which is not an upside element covered in this book, but it's a popular management practice), and the ever-popular cost cuts (in this case, people costs). As you'll see, some of these are more effective in boosting financial results than others. On the next eight pages, *there are shaded cells (rows 3–4 and 7–9) into which you can enter the changes you expect each upside element to bring about. (The unshaded cells in rows 5 and 6 are calculated, as are the rows below 10.)*

Harnessing Design

Suppose you're considering making a major improvement in the design of what you offer. Customers will pay more for something well-designed, even if it's not all the way to being, for some, an object of desire. Let's say that the improved design justifies an average price increase of 4% (cell [C3] in the worksheet at right *). And the more well-thought-out design will make more people want it, so sales volume will grow a net 6%. (Say 10% more want your offering [C4], but 4% [C5] now find that it's too expensive, yielding 6% [C6].) If you incorporate design for manufacturing into this effort, your production costs would decrease, but you might need to use higher-end components. So let's say that your per-unit Cost of Sales would come out 1% higher [C7].

You'd also have to pay for the design capability (2% in other variable costs [C8]). So the design-related revenue gain would be 10.2% [C21]: 1.04 (new average price: 1+[C3]) times 1.06 (new unit sales volume: 1+[C6]). The design-related profit gain would be 112.1% [C41] and the design-related profit-margin gain 92.4% [C45].

> The design-related figures just cited serve as a lesson—
> from Apple.

The resulting increase in the operating-results-related value of the business, if it pursued no other initiative, would depend on whether that value is more heavily influenced by revenue or profit-margin growth. But whatever the emphasis, you'd have at least a 10.2% increase in that value from the revenue gain, if investors didn't value the design-related profit-margin gain at all. And if all that investors cared about was profit-margin gain, you'd see a value increase of 92.4%. We'll see how these raw gains are combined with the Results-Goal-Emphasis figures, in the coming section on THE CHOOSER.

---

* *The **Harnessing Design** exhibit lays out the formulas used in the calculations, in column B.*

	A	B	C
1	**Harnessing Design**	Line IDs &	Product/Service
2		Formulas	Design to Die For
3	Change in Average Price (%)	A	4.0%
4	The Upside Element's Change in Units Sold (%)	B	10.0%
5	Price-Change-Induced Change in Units Sold (%)	C	-4.0%
6	Net Change in Units Sold (%)	D = B + C	6.0%
7	Per-Unit Change in Cost of Sales (%)	E	1.0%
8	Change in Other Variable Costs (%)	F	2.0%
9	Change in Fixed Costs (%)	G	0.0%
10			
11	Average Price ($)	H = N / K	$ 10.00
12	Change in Average Price ($)	I = H · A	0.40
13	Resulting Average Price ($)	J = H + I	$ 10.40
14			
15	No. of Units Sold	K	*100,000*
16	Change in No. of Units Sold	L = K · D	6,000
17	Resulting No. of Units Sold	M = K+L	106,000
18			
19	Base Revenue ($)	N	*$ 1,000,000*
20	Resulting Revenue ($)	O = J · M	$ 1,102,400
21	**Revenue Gain (%)**	P = (O - N) / N	**10.2%**
22			
23	Base Cost of Sales ($)	Q	*$ 600,000*
24	Change in Cost of Sales ($)	R=S - Q	42,360
25	Resulting Cost of Sales ($)	S = M · Q / K · (1 + E)	$ 642,360
26			
27	Base Other Variable Costs ($)	T	*$ 200,000*
28	Change in Other Variable Costs ($)	U = T · F	4,000
29	Resulting Other Variable Costs ($)	V = T+U	204,000
30			
31	Based Fixed Costs ($)	W	*$ 150,000*
32	Change in Fixed Costs ($)	X = W · G	-
33	Resulting Fixed Costs ($)	Y = W+X	150,000
34			
35	Base Total Costs ($)	Z =Q+T+W	$ 950,000
36	Resulting Total Costs ($)	a=S+V+Y	$ 996,360
37			
38	Base Profit ($)	b =N - Z	$ 50,000
39	Resulting Profit ($)	c =O - a	$ 106,040
40	Profit Gain ($)	d =c - b	$ 56,040
41	**Profit Gain (%)**	e =d / b	**112.1%**
42			
43	Original Profit Margin (%)	f =b / N	5.0%
44	Resulting Profit Margin (%)	g = c / O	9.6%
45	**Profit-Margin Gain (%)**	h =(g - f) / f	**92.4%**

More Effective Ads

Let's say that more effective ads lift sales volume by 8% [C6]. Those ads would not increase Cost of Goods Sold (COGS) [C7] as a percentage, but the COGS amount would rise with the increased sales. Also, the agency fees to create the ads would rise (research, new creative), classified as Other Variable Costs, by, say 3% [C8]. Let's also assume that you spend the same amount as before getting your more effective ads in front of people (media budget).

The ad-related revenue gain would be 8% [C21], with a profit gain of 52% [C41], and a profit-margin gain of 40.7% [C45]. This would yield an operating-results-related value gain of at least 8%, again depending on the relative influence of revenue and profit-margin growth. If the influence of Revenue Gain was 0, the operating results value increase would be the Profit Gain, or 52%.

	A	B	C
1	**More Effective Ads**	Line IDs &	Create *I Want That!*
2		Formulas	and Trigger the Sale
3	Change in Average Price (%)	A	0.0%
4	The Upside Element's Change in Units Sold (%)	B	8.0%
5	Price-Change-Induced Change in Units Sold (%)	C	0.0%
6	Net Change in Units Sold (%)	D = B + C	8.0%
7	Per-Unit Change in Cost of Sales (%)	E	0.0%
8	Change in Other Variable Costs (%)	F	3.0%
9	Change in Fixed Costs (%)	G	0.0%
10			
11	Average Price ($)	H = N / K	$ 10.00
12	Change in Average Price ($)	I = H · A	-
13	Resulting Average Price ($)	J = H + I	$ 10.00
14			
15	No. of Units Sold	K	*100,000*
16	Change in No. of Units Sold	L = K · D	8,000
17	Resulting No. of Units Sold	M = K+L	108,000
18			
19	Base Revenue ($)	N	*$ 1,000,000*
20	Resulting Revenue ($)	O = J · M	$ 1,080,000
21	**Revenue Gain (%)**	P = (O - N) / N	**8.0%**
22			
23	Base Cost of Sales ($)	Q	*$ 600,000*
24	Change in Cost of Sales ($)	R=S - Q	48,000
25	Resulting Cost of Sales ($)	S = M · Q / K · (1 + E)	$ 648,000
26			
27	Base Other Variable Costs ($)	T	*$ 200,000*
28	Change in Other Variable Costs ($)	U = T · F	6,000
29	Resulting Other Variable Costs ($)	V = T+U	206,000
30			
31	Based Fixed Costs ($)	W	*$ 150,000*
32	Change in Fixed Costs ($)	X = W · G	-
33	Resulting Fixed Costs ($)	Y = W+X	150,000
34			
35	Base Total Costs ($)	Z =Q+T+W	$ 950,000
36	Resulting Total Costs ($)	a=S+V+Y	$ 1,004,000
37			
38	Base Profit ($)	b =N - Z	$ 50,000
39	Resulting Profit ($)	c =O - a	$ 76,000
40	Profit Gain ($)	d =c - b	$ 26,000
41	**Profit Gain (%)**	e =d / b	**52.0%**
42			
43	Original Profit Margin (%)	f =b / N	5.0%
44	Resulting Profit Margin (%)	g = c / O	7.0%
45	**Profit-Margin Gain (%)**	h =(g - f) / f	**40.7%**

Streamlined Business Processes

Let's say chaos is rampant in your business and you could really use some sanity, and well-defined, streamlined, processes. What would be their impact on the value of your business?

Neither average price nor sales volume would change, but Cost of Sales could drop by 2% [C7]. And let's assume that over a 3-year horizon, the initial investment in processes would reduce Other Variable Costs by 4% [C8], with no effect on Fixed Costs [C9].

That would produce a 40% [C41] increase in both profit and profit margin, and an operating-results-related value gain somewhere between that and zero (no revenue gain). So if you pursued this, you might wind up trading uncertain increased business value for a higher level of management sanity. Which could free your team to pursue bigger game, but streamlining processes is a lot of work, and typically takes up significant management time.

	A	B	C
1	**Streamline Processes**	Line IDs &	Well-Crafted
2		Formulas	Business Processes
3	Change in Average Price (%)	A	0.0%
4	The Upside Element's Change in Units Sold (%)	B	0.0%
5	Price-Change-Induced Change in Units Sold (%)	C	0.0%
6	Net Change in Units Sold (%)	D = B + C	0.0%
7	Per-Unit Change in Cost of Sales (%)	E	-2.0%
8	Change in Other Variable Costs (%)	F	-4.0%
9	Change in Fixed Costs (%)	G	0.0%
10			
11	Average Price ($)	H = N / K	$ 10.00
12	Change in Average Price ($)	I = H · A	-
13	Resulting Average Price ($)	J = H + I	$ 10.00
14			
15	No. of Units Sold	K	*100,000*
16	Change in No. of Units Sold	L = K · D	-
17	Resulting No. of Units Sold	M = K+L	100,000
18			
19	Base Revenue ($)	N	*$ 1,000,000*
20	Resulting Revenue ($)	O = J · M	$ 1,000,000
21	**Revenue Gain (%)**	P = (O - N) / N	**0.0%**
22			
23	Base Cost of Sales ($)	Q	*$ 600,000*
24	Change in Cost of Sales ($)	R=S - Q	(12,000)
25	Resulting Cost of Sales ($)	S = M · Q / K · (1 + E)	$ 588,000
26			
27	Base Other Variable Costs ($)	T	*$ 200,000*
28	Change in Other Variable Costs ($)	U = T · F	(8,000)
29	Resulting Other Variable Costs ($)	V = T+U	192,000
30			
31	Based Fixed Costs ($)	W	*$ 150,000*
32	Change in Fixed Costs ($)	X = W · G	-
33	Resulting Fixed Costs ($)	Y = W+X	150,000
34			
35	Base Total Costs ($)	Z =Q+T+W	$ 950,000
36	Resulting Total Costs ($)	a=S+V+Y	$ 930,000
37			
38	Base Profit ($)	b =N - Z	$ 50,000
39	Resulting Profit ($)	c =O - a	$ 70,000
40	Profit Gain ($)	d =c - b	$ 20,000
41	**Profit Gain (%)**	e =d / b	**40.0%**
42			
43	Original Profit Margin (%)	f =b / N	5.0%
44	Resulting Profit Margin (%)	g = c / O	7.0%
45	**Profit-Margin Gain (%)**	h =(g - f) / f	**40.0%**

Cutting, Say, People Costs

Suppose, because of intense price competition, you have to cut costs, the major target being the cost of those who produce what you offer, and/or who serve customers.

Say the cuts let you reduce average price by 1% [C3], and as a result, unit sales grow by 1% [C5]. But because of the lower average price, revenue doesn't change [C21].

Due to the reduced head count, Cost of Sales [C7] falls by 2%, as do Other Variable Costs [C8], while Fixed Costs [C9] drop 1%.

The end result is that revenue [C21] is essentially unchanged, and both profit and profit margin rise by about 23% [C41 & C45], bringing with them an operating-results-related value gain between 0 and 23%.

Consider also the effect on workforce morale (and customer-facing people's attitudes) if the cost cuts are not made deftly, viewed as necessary, and seem fair to all.

The four upside elements we've just covered are shown side by side on the next page. The actual *Let's See* model has columns for all of the upside elements in the book.

The shaded rows 21, 41, and 45 show the potential gains the four upside elements can bring about. Notice how, in this example and for these upside elements, the gains vary dramatically. *Point: some upside elements can more powerfully boost results than others.*

	A	B	C
1	**Cutting, Say, People Costs**		Cutting, Say,
2		Formula	People Costs
3	Change in Average Price (%)	A	-1.0%
4	The Upside Element's Change in Units Sold (%)	B	0.0%
5	Price-Change-Induced Change in Units Sold (%)	C	1.0%
6	Net Change in Units Sold (%)	D = B + C	1.0%
7	Per-Unit Change in Cost of Sales (%)	E	-2.0%
8	Change in Other Variable Costs (%)	F	-2.0%
9	Change in Fixed Costs (%)	G	-1.0%
10			
11	Average Price ($)	H = N / K	$ 10.00
12	Change in Average Price ($)	I = H · A	(0.10)
13	Resulting Average Price ($)	J = H + I	$ 9.90
14			
15	No. of Units Sold	K	*100,000*
16	Change in No. of Units Sold	L = K · D	1,000
17	Resulting No. of Units Sold	M = K+L	101,000
18			
19	Base Revenue ($)	N	*$ 1,000,000*
20	Resulting Revenue ($)	O = J · M	$ 999,900
21	**Revenue Gain (%)**	P = (O - N) / N	**0.0%**
22			
23	Base Cost of Sales ($)	Q	*$ 600,000*
24	Change in Cost of Sales ($)	R = S - Q	(6,120)
25	Resulting Cost of Sales ($)	S = M · Q / K · (1 + E)	$ 593,880
26			
27	Base Other Variable Costs ($)	T	*$ 200,000*
28	Change in Other Variable Costs ($)	U = T · F	(4,000)
29	Resulting Other Variable Costs ($)	V = T+U	196,000
30			
31	Based Fixed Costs ($)	W	*$ 150,000*
32	Change in Fixed Costs ($)	X = W · G	(1,500)
33	Resulting Fixed Costs ($)	Y = W+X	148,500
34			
35	Base Total Costs ($)	Z = Q+T+W	$ 950,000
36	Resulting Total Costs ($)	a = S+V+Y	$ 938,380
37			
38	Base Profit ($)	b = N - Z	$ 50,000
39	Resulting Profit ($)	c = O - a	$ 61,520
40	Profit Gain ($)	d = c - b	$ 11,520
41	**Profit Gain (%)**	e = d / b	**23.0%**
42			
43	Original Profit Margin (%)	f = b / N	5.0%
44	Resulting Profit Margin (%)	g = c / O	6.2%
45	**Profit-Margin Gain (%)**	h = (g - f) / f	**23.1%**

	A	B	C	D	E
1	Upside Elements Compared	Product/Service Design to Die For	Create *I Want That!* and Trigger the Sale	Well-Crafted Business Processes	Cutting, Say, People Costs
2					
3	Change in Average Price (%)	4.0%	0.0%	0.0%	-1.0%
4	The Upside Element's Change in Units Sold (%)	10.0%	8.0%	0.0%	0.0%
5	Price-Change-Induced Change in Units Sold (%)	-4.0%	0.0%	0.0%	1.0%
6	Net Change in Units Sold (%)	6.0%	8.0%	0.0%	1.0%
7	Per-Unit Change in Cost of Sales (%)	1.0%	0.0%	-2.0%	-2.0%
8	Change in Other Variable Costs (%)	2.0%	3.0%	-4.0%	-2.0%
9	Change in Fixed Costs (%)	0.0%	0.0%	0.0%	-1.0%
10					
11	Average Price ($)	$ 10.00	$ 10.00	$ 10.00	$ 10.00
12	Change in Average Price ($)	0.40	-	-	(0.10)
13	Resulting Average Price ($)	$ 10.40	$ 10.00	$ 10.00	$ 9.90
14					
15	No. of Units Sold	100,000	100,000	100,000	100,000
16	Change in No. of Units Sold	6,000	8,000	-	1,000
17	Resulting No. of Units Sold	106,000	108,000	100,000	101,000
18					
19	Base Revenue ($)	$ 1,000,000	$ 1,000,000	$ 1,000,000	$ 1,000,000
20	Resulting Revenue ($)	$ 1,102,400	$ 1,080,000	$ 1,000,000	$ 999,900
21	**Revenue Gain (%)**	10.2%	8.0%	0.0%	0.0%
22					
23	Base Cost of Sales ($)	$ 600,000	$ 600,000	$ 600,000	$ 600,000
24	Change in Cost of Sales ($)	42,360	48,000	(12,000)	(6,120)
25	Resulting Cost of Sales ($)	$ 642,360	$ 648,000	$ 588,000	$ 593,880
26					
27	Base Other Variable Costs ($)	$ 200,000	$ 200,000	$ 200,000	$ 200,000
28	Change in Other Variable Costs ($)	4,000	6,000	(8,000)	(4,000)
29	Resulting Other Variable Costs ($)	204,000	206,000	192,000	196,000
30					
31	Based Fixed Costs ($)	$ 150,000	$ 150,000	$ 150,000	$ 150,000
32	Change in Fixed Costs ($)	-	-	-	(1,500)
33	Resulting Fixed Costs ($)	150,000	150,000	150,000	148,500
34					
35	Base Total Costs ($)	$ 950,000	$ 950,000	$ 950,000	$ 950,000
36	Resulting Total Costs ($)	$ 996,360	$ 1,004,000	$ 930,000	$ 938,380
37					
38	Base Profit ($)	$ 50,000	$ 50,000	$ 50,000	$ 50,000
39	Resulting Profit ($)	$ 106,040	$ 76,000	$ 70,000	$ 61,520
40	Profit Gain ($)	$ 56,040	$ 26,000	$ 20,000	$ 11,520
41	**Profit Gain (%)**	112.1%	52.0%	40.0%	23.0%
42					
43	Original Profit Margin (%)	5.0%	5.0%	5.0%	5.0%
44	Resulting Profit Margin (%)	9.6%	7.0%	7.0%	6.2%
45	**Profit-Margin Gain (%)**	92.4%	40.7%	40.0%	23.1%

Now we'll add in the realities of your business, so you can make considered choices about which upside elements to pursue. This involves gathering information, and making estimates, both of which you've now done, then resolving resource-related conflicts, and deciding when to creatively work past perceived limits. Introducing THE CHOOSER...

The Chooser: Picking the Best Things You Can Do to Boost Results and Business Value

THE CHOOSER is the capstone tool in *Let's See,* where all of your efforts come together, and your best shots for boosting results reveal themselves. THE CHOOSER will help you find the handful of upside elements that are both realistic and that will boost your results the most. To do that, it combines the results gains you've already determined, with each upside element's other characteristics: its capital and expense-budget consumption, how risky pursuing the element seems, the likelihood you can make it happen, and the demands it imposes on scarce resources such as management time and product-development staff (these can be changed, and added to, as described in Appendix B).

How to Approach Choosing Your Best Shots

Now you know:

- How much more value you can potentially get out of each upside element you analyzed.

- Whether it will be more worthwhile to focus on growing revenue, or improving profit margins, and each goal's relative power to make your business more valuable.

What's left to do is to *decide* what to do: which upside elements you will, in fact, work to tap. This might be simple, depending on your situation.

Your Situation	What to Do
There's only one upside element that you feel is worth pursuing.	Just analyze it in THE CHOOSER, so that you're fully aware of its costs, risks, chance of success, the demands it will put on you and your people's time, and your scarce resources. If none of those indicates problems, that upside element is your best shot.
Your results need to be better, but they don't need to be the best they can possibly be.	Do the exercise above with just the upside elements you feel best about, and choose your best shots from them. But don't choose more best shots than you can handle (three or four would be about right).
The people expecting you to improve results (including yourself) have made clear that nothing but getting the best possible results and value increases is essential.	Do the entire CHOOSER exercise.

While simple once you understand it, THE CHOOSER can seem like a bit much, visually. So once again we'll cruise into it. The next screenshot shows its overall structure. The upside elements are listed down the left side. Your revenue-goal emphasis and the upside elements' results gains will be automatically filled in from prior tabs. You'll need to fill in the Characteristics columns, and the limits row at the bottom, controlling how much money and resources you can devote to improving results. In the Chosen Upside Elements column, you can indicate that you'd like to pursue an upside element by entering any character in it. That will cause its row to be highlighted in green, and the content of the columns to its right to be taken into account: the results gains, budget impacts, and resource consumption will be reflected in the totals at bottom. Then you'll be able to see whether your upside-element choices violate any limits.

The Chooser's Structure

Upside Elements	Chosen Upside Elements	Revenue-Goal Emphasis %		Characteristics			
		Results Gains (from *The Upside Calculator*)		Capital & Expense-Budget Impacts	Risk	Chance of Success	Resource Demands (can be customized)
		Profit Gain	Value Gain				
	X						
	X						
...	X						
	Chosen Element Totals						
	Limits						
	Over/Under Limit Indicators						

The capital and expense budgets above require some explanation…

Some of your upside initiatives might cost little to nothing, such as better leveraging your assets, or getting sales and marketing to work as one, both addressed in Chapter 13. You'll need to fund others using what we'll call your *improvement* budgets: for both capital and expense.

You obviously now have both types of budgets; they pay for what you're already doing, or planning to do. Funding for your improvement efforts will need to come from somewhere: new sources, or funds that were previously meant for other purposes.

In order to make reality-based decisions in THE CHOOSER, you'll need to settle on the total *improvement* budgets you'll have for both expense and capital.

Cruising in closer, the annotated screenshot on page 319 will help to make its various sections clear. Please take a few moments to review the annotations.

The Chooser, unadorned, is shown on page 320. We've entered sample data in the columns, which you'll replace with your own, almost all of which necessarily involve estimates.

Concerning the accuracy of those estimates, do the best you can for now, and be at peace with it. Management in general, including the exercise you're about to do, is far from an exact science. It's an art. Doing THE CHOOSER exercise will: bring possibilities into focus, help you see blockers that you'll need to work around, and provide perspectives on what's really important to your business's performance. If, in the course of the exercise, you find one or two estimates that seem to need refining, again, try your best to do so. Perhaps ooching (page 264 in Chapter 13) will provide a way tighten them up.

At root, you're trying to create an informed judgment about the best ways to increase results—from incomplete information. If you get it mostly right, you'll be a hero. If you analyze all of the information to the nth degree, there's no reason to think that you'll get it any more right.

Instead, using what follows, come up with the few upside elements that seem to promise the highest results gains and that you can realistically pursue. Then do so, observe the results, and tune, or change your plan or the upside elements you chose, as your encounter with reality suggests.

Let's See – The Chooser Step 4

To choose an element, enter something in this column. It will highlight.

The percentage gain in business value that the element will deliver. The total for the selected elements is at bottom.

Both budget figures should be in monetary amounts (thousands, millions).

These 2 resources are in short supply. Enter the percentage of the resource that pursuing the upside element will require. You can change them and add new ones–see Appendix B.

The estimated revenue and profit-margin gain percentages you expect the upside element to produce (from The Upside Calculator).

For more on the element, see Chapter…

Rate risk on a scale, such as 0 (none) to 9 (extreme risk), with individual, or aggregate limits.

Rate the chances of actually realizing each upside element's estimated gains. Use 0 for "slam dunk," 9 for "long shot," again with individual or aggregate limits.

These "jackpot" figures show the maximum likely gains, not the total gains, even though they are the sums of the selected-upside-elements' gains. This is because some of the gains might be counted more than once in totalling them. For example, if you were to choose strengthening your brand, and making your ads more effective, the revenue gain from getting more people to buy your product could be attributable to either upside element. In that case, if the individual gains were totalled, the brand and the ad's contributions to higher revenue would be counted twice.

These figures show the amounts by which the selected upside elements exceed the limits you set, or don't. If you've exceeded one or more limits, shown by "over," you should unselect one or more of the elements, or raise the exceeded limits.

These figures represent your realities. However, if you find that some limits will keep you from pursuing upside elements with large gains, it might be worth exploring ways to raise one or more of the limits.

From the Goal_Emphasis_Advisor's results.

Relative Value of Gains in…. & Characteristics

Upside Element	Chap.	Pick	Profit Gain (%)	Revenue 65.0% Gain %	Profit Margin 35.0% Gain %	Operating-Results-Related Value Gain (%)	Consumption of Improvement-Expense Budget (000)	Consumption of Improvement-Capital Budget (000)	Risk	Likelihood	Available Management Time	Available Product Development
Create Zealous Customers	2		11.4	5.0	6.1	5.4	100	8	1	7	15%	0%
Knock	3	x	63.8	6.1	54.0	22.8	500	0	2	4	15%	30%
Comp	4	x	73.8	6.1	63.8			0	3	3	10%	0%
Create	5		52.0	8.0	40.7			0	2	4	20%	0%
Pricing	6		77.8	6.1	67.6	8.1	100	0	2	3	20%	0%
Deftly Manage Costs	7		23.0	0.0	23.1			0	1	4	35%	10%
Detect and Seize Plum Opportuni	8		23.0	5.0	17.1	9.3	500					35%
Player in Growing Hungry Market	9		20.1	8.0	11.2	9.1	2,000					15%
High Profit/Growth Business Des	10		69.8	6.1	60.1	25.0	200					20%
Product/Service Design to Die For	11	x	112.1	10.2	92.4	39.0	500					50%
Fabulo			6.1	4.0	2.0	3.3	250	0	1	3	15%	0%
Create			107.1	10.2	87.8	37.4	800	1,000	4	3	20%	40%
New S			132.2	12.4	106.6	45.4	3,000	0	5	3	5%	40%
Levera			36.0				0)	0	3	3	15%	0%
Optimi			7.1				0)	0				
Hone S		x	69.2				0	0				
Respon			21.1				0	0				
Market			32.0				0	0				
Offer S			26.6	4.0	21.7	10.2	2,000	500	0	6	10%	40%
Well-Crafted Business Processes	13		40.0	0.0	40.0	14.0	2,000	2,000		4	5%	10%
Limits							**3,000**	**2,500**	**11**		**100%**	**100%**
Amount over or under (-) limit							(900) Under	0 Under	-1 Under	N/A	-50% Under	-20% Under

Approximate Profit Gain 318.4%

Approximate Value Gain 112.8%

* This analysis, geared toward improving operating results, does not include proceeds from the sale of product lines, brands, or businesses.

Let's See - The Chooser Step 4

From the Goal_Emphasis_Advisor's results.

Upside Element	Chap.	Pick	Profit Gain (%)	Revenue (65.0%) Gain %	Profit Margin (35.0%) Gain %	Operating-Results-Related Value Gain (%)	Consumption of Improvement-Expense Budget (000)	Consumption of Improvement-Capital Budget (000)	Risk	Likeli-hood	Available Management Time	Product Development Time
Create Zealous Customers	2		11.4	5.0	6.1	5.4	100	0	1	7	15%	0%
Knock-'Em-Dead Value Propositions	3	x	63.3	6.1	54.0	22.8	500	0	2	4	15%	30%
Compelling Brand Promise	4	x	73.8	6.1	63.8	26.3	100	0	3	3	10%	0%
Create I Want That!, and the Sale	5		52.0	8.0	40.7	19.5	100	0	2	4	20%	0%
Pricing Captures the Whole Market	6		77.8	6.1	67.6	27.6	100	0	2	3	20%	0%
Deftly Manage Costs	7		23.0	0.0	23.1	8.1	100	0	1	4	35%	10%
Detect and Seize Plum Opportunities	8		23.0	5.0	17.1	9.3	500	0	6	4	30%	35%
Player in Growing Hungry Markets	9		20.1	8.0	11.2	9.1	2,000	0	5	5	25%	15%
High Profit/Growth Business Design	10		69.8	6.1	60.1	25.0	200	0	4	4	30%	20%
Product/Service Design to Die For	11	x	112.1	10.2	92.4	39.0	500	1,000	3	4	20%	50%
Fabulous Customer Experiences	11		6.1	4.0	2.0	3.3	250	0	1	3	15%	0%
Create/Strengthen "Hit-Record" Machine	11		107.1	10.2	87.8	37.4	800	1,000	4	3	20%	40%
New Solutions to Worthy Probems	12		132.2	12.4	106.6	45.4	3,000	0	5	3	5%	40%
Leverage Our Assets	13		36.0	4.0	30.8	13.4	0	0	1	3	15%	0%
Optimize Product, Brand & Business Portfolios *	13		7.1	-10.4	19.5	0.1	(1,500)	0	1	2	40%	0%
Hone Supply Chain	13	x	69.2	5.0	61.1	24.7	1,000	1,500	2	3	5%	0%
Responsive Demand Chain	13		21.1	6.0	14.2	8.9	2,000	0	1	3	10%	0%
Marketing & Sales, Working as One	13		32.0	3.0	28.2	11.8	0	0	0	4	5%	0%
Offer Superior Quality	13		26.6	4.0	21.7	10.2	2,000	500	1	6	10%	40%
Well-Crafted Business Processes	13		40.0	0.0	40.0	14.0	2,000	0	2	4	5%	10%
Limits							3,000	2,500	11		100%	100%
Amount over or under (-) limit							(900)	0	-1		-50%	-20%
							Under	Under Under	Under	N/A	Under	Under

Approximate Profit Gain 318.4%

Approximate Value Gain 112.8%

* This analysis, geared toward improving operating results, does not include proceeds from the sale of product lines, brands, or businesses.

Using The Chooser

As mentioned, you can work with either of two ways of scoring how the upside elements you decide to pursue should be measured: profit gain as a percentage, or the more abstract, but well-founded, weighted combination of revenue growth and higher profit-margins that we've called Operating Results Related Value, atop THE CHOOSER.

On page 319, column D shows the first of these, profit gain. Columns E through G show the components of, and the resulting, Operating Results Related Value gains, with cells E3 and F3 holding the relative importance of revenue versus profit-margin growth that you determined earlier on the GOAL EMPHASIS ADVISOR tab. The cells beneath them contain estimates of the percentage gains that the corresponding upside element will produce in terms of revenue growth and profit-margin growth.

Notice that none of the gain figures we've used are extreme. And one, E21, is negative, because a divestiture might well decrease ongoing revenue. Also, a more comprehensive pricing approach might decrease profit *margins,* but substantially boost *the amount of* profit, if revenue grows.

Column G shows the percentage gain in Operating-Results-Related Value that would come from pursuing the upside elements. The increase is the result of combining the revenue and profit-margin gains in columns E and F, using the weights in cells E3 and F3.

There being no free lunch, we also have to consider the impact on the business that pursuing the upside element will create: its near-term expense and capital costs (columns H and I), the associated risks (J), the likelihood that you can pull off the initiative (column K), and the upside element's use of various scarce resources (L, M, and others you can add).

The expense and capital budget consumption figures can be subject to overall limits, entered in THE CHOOSER's cells H27 and I27.

In column J, rate risk on a scale, such as 0 (none) to 9 (extreme risk), using aggregate limits in cell J27, or just avoid picking an upside element with a risk above a rating that seems to be acceptable.

You can use the same approach with likelihood (column K), the chance that you'll be able to make the upside element happen *and* realize its potential. Use *low* ratings for those you can easily make happen, and for which the results are pretty well guaranteed, and *high* ratings, where realizing the upside-element's potential is, well, a stretch. Notice that here, there are no aggregate limits. Also, recall that without gumption, we would not have gone to the moon.

Interpreting the Profit-and-Revenue-Gain Totals

The profit and the revenue gains shown by THE CHOOSER in cells D29 and G30 are the *maximum* likely gains, but they might not be the *total* gains, even though they are the sums of the selected-upside-elements' gains. This is because some of the gains might be counted more than once by totaling them. For example, if you were to choose both strengthening your brand, and making your ads more effective, the revenue gain from getting more people to buy your product could be attributable to *either* upside element. In that case, if the individual gains were added, the brand and the ad's contributions to higher revenue would be counted twice, which is obviously wrong. This happens in only a few cases; the results gains of other upside elements don't overlap, so adding them is fine. The point is that you should be aware of these possible overlaps, so you don't kid yourself in choosing which elements you'll pursue.

Customizing Let's See

The live *Let's See* model comes with four additional upside elements that you can customize, i.e., making them specific to your business, both in THE UPSIDE CALCULATOR, and as rows in THE CHOOSER. THE CHOOSER's actual model also has four scarce-resource columns you can customize. For additional customization, please see Appendix B – Customizing *Let's See*.

Adjusting the Limits

If you exceed a capital (or expense) limit by picking a high-gain set of upside elements, you might be able to move funds from expense to capital (or vice versa) to make things work, or just scrounge up more funding.

Usage of the scarce resources in columns L, M, and any others you add, should be entered as the percentage of the resource that pursuing the upside element will require, using overall limits of 100% (or less, to have something in reserve). If you find that some limits keep you from pursuing upside elements with large gains, it might be worth exploring ways to raise one or more of those limits.

The Grand Finale—How to Pick Your Best Shots!

This is where you get to flex your result muscles! You'll play with the possibilities that THE CHOOSER presents and select the set of upside elements to tackle that are both realistic, and that will bring the biggest gains, if you pull them off.

To do this, begin by looking at your upside elements just in terms of your gain measure—the resulting profit or operating-results-related value increases—and focus on those that, together, will provide the biggest increase. See whether you can creatively work around any exceeded limits that will prevent you from tackling them. You can also experiment with *combinations* of upside elements that together will provide a slightly lower gain, but that don't violate any of your limits, appear too risky, or are too much of a stretch to pull off. And don't pick more upside elements than you can realistically manage, like 3 or 4.

Finally, look at the jackpots in cell D29 or G30, depending on your chosen gain measure, and consider the implications of that gain for you, your business, your people, and your investors…

A New Road to Prosperity

Instead of stressing out about how you'll even meet your latest performance targets, you should now be able to create a deep, informed sense of just how to do so. Out of all the things you could do to improve results, what handful will *really* increase the value of your business?

Having said that, please bear in mind that Insight-Based Management IS. AN. ART., and will be.

<hr>

In the next chapter, we'll focus on pulling the upside elements you choose to tackle into a prosperity design for your business, integrating them into your existing plans, and figuring out who'll do what, and when. But first, you'll need to pick those best shots!

TAPPING YOUR UPSIDE:
Finding Your Best Shots

This chapter's exercise is to fill in and work with *Let's See,* for your business, or your entire company. I know, it's work. It's also *your job as an executive*—its core.

Before you begin, please visit www.theupsidewithinreach.com, and choose Download the book's tools and extras. Click the *Let's See* link and agree to its license terms. Then compare the version number you might have downloaded earlier (Inputs tab) with the website's current version. Use the latest version of *Let's See.*

1. **To get started, fill in the Inputs worksheet (page 299).**

2. **Use the *Goal Emphasis Advisor* worksheet to figure out how people will value your business, as described on pages 298–301.**

   If you've decided to use the Consensus Expectations Approach on pages 298–300, enter the importance of *revenue* growth to the overall value of your business in cell E22. Otherwise, use the Profitability Comparison Approach on pages 300–301, by entering your estimates of the low- and high-gain percentages you want to explore in its upper-right section. Then review the relative contributions of revenue and profit-margin growth from the outlined area at the bottom of the Profitability-Comparison-Approach section. Enter the importance of *revenue* growth from that analysis in cell E22.

3. **In *The Upside Calculator* worksheet of *Let's See* (like the excerpt shown on page 314), enter the values from the *Upside-Element Assessments* worksheet that you completed as you went through the chapters (or make your estimates now if you didn't).**

4. The downloadable version of *Let's See* comes with 4 customizable upside elements, and 4 customizable scarce-resource constraints. Beyond that, you can modify *Let's See,* adding any additional upside elements you'd like to consider, or any additional resources you want taken into account, in choosing the upside elements you'll pursue. But this needs to be done in such a way that you don't break anything (formulas) or that what you add ends up being ignored. Full instructions for making changes are in Appendix B.

5. Move to *The Chooser* worksheet (page 320).

   If you used very rough, or H-M-L, estimates for capital or expense-budget consumption by the upside elements, this would be a good time to refine them, or to have someone do so. Then add any appropriate restrictions in the Limits row at the bottom.

6. Enter a character in column C beside each of the upside elements you feel will bring the highest increases in business value and that are realistic.

7. This is where *making wise choices* begins.

   If you're not exceeding any of the limits you set, you might select additional upside elements until one or more of the cells in the limits row shows *Over,* then drop the selection that cuts increased value least, or that will best remedy the over-limit condition(s).

8. Now that you've put in all the effort needed to complete *The Chooser's* estimates, please spend some quiet time experimenting with the set of possibilities you've assembled. Let them speak to you.

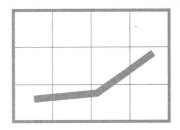

Part 5

Your Prosperity Design

You've now given your upside a thorough going over, and have
a clear idea of the initiatives you want to tackle. Now we'll work
through pulling those initiatives into a *prosperity design* for your
business—a plan laying out which elements of your upside you're
going to work on when, and how those initiatives will be integrated
into your existing business and plans. The design will by its nature
be a living, breathing creation, but capturing the starting version
will serve as a springboard.

"It is a hard rule of life, and I believe a healthy one, that no great
plan is ever carried out without meeting and overcoming endless
obstacles that come up to try the skill of a man's hand, the quality
of his courage, and the endurance of his faith." (Offered with
apologies to women, to whom this applies equally, if not more so.)
—*Donald Douglas (1892–1981), Founder,*
Douglas Aircraft Company, later McDonnell Douglas

Chapter 15

Creating Your Prosperity Design

In this final chapter we'll work on making the upside elements you've decided to pursue, and what you were already planning to do, into an executable whole, including who will do what, in the various time frames you've chosen. We'll call that plan your *Prosperity Design.*

It answers the question:

> *How, specifically, is our business going to make a*
> *remarkable amount of money, and build enduring wealth*
> *for us and our investors, over the next 5 to 10 years?*

Obviously, every business needs a Prosperity Design. Almost no business has one. Now *yours* can.

If you've worked through the entire book, use the best shots you chose in Chapter 14 as the actions you'll pursue. If you just cherry-picked a few upside-element chapters that seemed most relevant, analyze them in THE CHOOSER in Chapter 14 to make sure that you don't overlook something about your choices that you might later come to regret. Scrutinize their potential gains, their costs and resource demands, and the odds that you can successfully reap the gains that your choices promise.

Those choices will then need to be meshed with your business's existing plans, so that you don't create chaos, and so that your people aren't working on two different initiatives (one of which you're already pursuing), that will have roughly *the same effect* on your financials, when pursuing only one of them would produce the same results.

Finally, please recognize that pulling together a full-blown Prosperity Design will be a major executive, and business-wide, commitment.

What You'll Need, Before You Begin:

1. You've chosen, or are on the verge of choosing, your best shots (previous chapter).

2. From the *Tapping Your Upside* exercises for each of those best shots, you'll need the lists of what has to be done to realize their potential. You'll also need a list of the initiatives in your business's existing plans, and the resources already committed to them, that your Prosperity Design will have to mesh with.

3. It's crucial that the importance of creating a Prosperity Design is recognized across the highest level, and other appropriate levels, of your organization, so it won't get sidelined or sandbagged by things urgent, but not as important. Because this effort really is different—it can make the company prosper! And key to its success is senior leadership's enthusiastic and wholehearted commitment, and proactive support. Your Prosperity Design should be Job 1 or 2 for your business. After all, improving results is *why* P&L executives have jobs.

4. You'll need to get everyone in your business fired up about this. It's vital to the business's prosperity—and it will be fun, as you'll see. It's critical that it's not viewed as the "salvation of the month," or something similar, because it's a lot of hard work, and disillusionment could cause the effort to sag.

5. Everyone has to have, or be given, the bandwidth needed to create and realize their parts of the design.

6. You'll need to identify an overall Prosperity Design czar, usually the head of the business or the company. And you'll have to select and enroll the people who'll own each best-shot element's realization.

7. You'll need a process for ensuring the Prosperity Design's timely execution; the same one you use for the other critical things in your business that just have to happen.

8. Each element of the Prosperity Design's realization requires a somewhat unique skill set. The skills applicable to each best-shot element are listed in the two tables that follow. (Please note that the lists should serve only as a starting point: the entries are my *opinions*.)

The Skills Needed to Create a Prosperity Design—1 of 2
(read down each of your best-shot columns)

BEST-SHOT SKILLS	Inciting Customer Passion	Honing Your Value Proposition	Strengthening Brand Promise and Power	Creating *I Want That!* and Triggering the Sale	Pricing	Deftly Managing Costs	Detecting and Seizing Opportunities	Finding, and Serving, Hungry Markets
Ready grasp of what's possible	Y	Y	Y	Y	Y	Y	Y	Y
Making things happen, across the organization	Y	Y	Y		Y	Y	Y	Y
Leading teams	Y	Y	Y		Y	Y	Y	Y
Selling a vision; motivating	Y	Y	Y	Y	Y	Y	Y	Y
Creativity	Y	Y	Y	Y	Y	Y	Y	Y
Good sense of what's realistic	Y	Y	Y	Y	Y	Y	Y	Y
Making sage decisions	Y	Y	Y	Y	Y	Y	Y	Y
Able to execute tough decisions	Y	Y	Y		Y	Y	Y	Y
Persuasive writing	Y	Y	Y	Y	Y		Y	Y
Design sense	Y	Y	Y	Y	Y			
Financial acumen					Y	Y	Y	Y
Analyzing data	Y	Y	Y	Y	Y	Y	Y	Y

The Skills Needed to Create a Prosperity Design—2 of 2
(read down each of your best-shot columns)

BEST-SHOT SKILLS	Crafting a Powerful Business Design	Product and Service Design to Die For	Innovating	Managing Risk	Leveraging Assets	Portfolios	Plug Revenue Leaks	Quality	Process	Overall Prosperity Design
				Management Practices						
Ready grasp of what's possible	Y	Y	Y	Y	Y	Y	Y	Y	Y	Y
Making things happen, across the organization	Y	Y	Y	Y	Y	Y	Y	Y	Y	Y
Leading teams	Y	Y	Y	Y	Y	Y	Y	Y	Y	Y
Selling a vision; motivating	Y	Y	Y	Y	Y	Y	Y	Y	Y	Y
Creativity	Y	Y	Y	Y	Y	Y	Y	Y	Y	Y
Good sense of what's realistic	Y	Y	Y	Y	Y	Y	Y	Y	Y	Y
Making sage decisions	Y	Y	Y	Y	Y	Y	Y	Y	Y	Y
Able to execute tough decisions	Y	Y	Y	Y	Y	Y	Y	Y	Y	Y
Persuasive writing	Y	Y	Y	Y	Y	Y	Y	Y	Y	Y
Design sense	Y	Y	Y	Y	Y	Y		Y	Y	Y
Financial acumen	Y		Y	Y	Y	Y	Y	Y	Y	Y
Analyzing data	Y	Y	Y	Y	Y	Y	Y	Y	Y	Y

TAPPING YOUR UPSIDE

Creating Your Prosperity Design

1. If you're not going to personally lead the effort, appoint a Prosperity Design czar to direct the design's creation and implementation. Who is that?

   _____

   _____

   _____

2. For each of your best shots from Chapter 14, understand when it should be kicked off and when it should start to contribute to results.

No.	Best Shot	Begin Work on It By	Expect Results By
1.			
2.			
3.			
4.			
5.			

3. For each best shot, assess what you're going to need in the way of: someone to own making it so (if you're going to delegate it), what current initiatives it needs to mesh with, what skills and resources it will need, and what organizational alignments and agreements you will need.

Best Shot No.	Owner's (initials)	Related Current Initiatives	Skills and Resources Needed	Organizations Involved	Agreements Needed
1.					
2.					
3.					
4.					
5.					

The Most Important Thing

Begin. Today, if you can. You, and those who are counting on you, deserve it. I wish you wisdom, perseverance, luck, and a healthy dollop of prosperity!

"Once you see it, it's obvious."
—*Mathematician's joke*

Afterword

As should now be clear, you can very likely make your results rise. In other words, you have *a way* to prosper. What about other executives you know? Could this approach help them?

And would it become even more powerful if it incorporated the best ideas of those other executives, some of whom are facing the same results challenges you are?

My intent with this book is to spawn a movement: to create a community of executives who are both adept at tapping their upsides and passionate about contributing to the body of knowledge on how to do so.

Using the book's approach, and those that evolve from it, we can advance the practice of management, raising prosperity worldwide.

I welcome your suggestions!

I'd also welcome knowing of any needed corrections, for which there's a corrections and updates section on the website below.

Specifics

Everything will be on the book's website: www.theupsidewithinreach.com. There you'll find:

- The link for downloading the book's tools and extras, including the *Let's See* Excel workbook. The extras also include the worksheet for the *Tapping Your Upside* exercise that ends Chapter 3. You'll need to create an account (email address, and first name—both private) and a non-identifying username to receive them.

- Support for using *Let's See.*

- The (moderated) *Better Results* discussion forum. Answers will be public. You can choose to be notified of new posts.

- The *There's More!* blog that you can subscribe to.

- A contact form.

Marketing Reading List

Below is a list of the major works related to the chapter "Creating 'I Want That!' and Triggering the Sale" which are not referenced directly in that chapter's notes. The author has read, and recommends, each of the works listed (alphabetically, by author, in each section below).

Marketing in General

Harry Beckwith, *Selling the Invisible: A Field Guide to Modern Marketing* (services marketing), Grand Central Publishing, Reprint edition, 2012.

Seth Godin, *Unleashing the IdeaVirus: Stop marketing AT people! Turn your ideas into epidemics by helping your customers do the marketing for you,* Hachette Books, Reprint edition, 2001.

_____, *Permission Marketing: Turning Strangers into Friends and Friends into Customers,* Simon & Schuster, 1999.

Mitchell Goozé with Jane Broida Drake, *It's Not Rocket Science: Using Marketing to Build a Sustainable Business,* The Institute for Marketing and Innovation, 1997.

Dr. Lynella Grant, *The Business Card Book: What Your Business Card Reveals about You and How to Fix It* (a simple, near-complete, course in marketing), Off the Page Press, 1998.

Sam Hill and Glenn Rifkin, *Radical Marketing: From Harvard to Harley, Lessons from Ten That Broke the Rules and Made It Big,* Harper Business, Reprint edition, 2000.

Jay Conrad Levinson, *Guerilla Marketing: Secrets for Making Big Profits from Your Small Business,* Houghton Mifflin, 4th ed., 2007.

Al Ries and Jack Trout, *The 22 Immutable Laws of Marketing: Violate Them at Your Own Risk,* HarperBusiness, 1993.

Message Making

Jonah Berger, *Contagious: Why Things Catch On*, Simon & Schuster, Reprint edition, 2016.

Robert B. Cialdini, *Influence: Science and Practice,* 5th ed., Allyn and Bacon, 2008.

Chip and Dan Heath, *Made to Stick: Why Some Ideas Survive and Others Die,* Random House, 2007.

Ted Nicholas, *Magic Words That Grow Your Business,* youtube.com/watch?v=1ddULx4sdjE.

Al Ries and Jack Trout, *Positioning: The Battle for Your Mind,* McGraw-Hill Education, 3rd ed., 2001.

Roy H. Williams, *The Wizard of Ads: Turning Words into Magic and Dreamers into Millionaires* (the first of three volumes), Bard Press, 1998.

Advertising (Presenting Your Message)

Geoff Ayling, *Rapid Response Advertising,* Business and Professional Publishing Pty Limited, 1999.

John Caples, Revised by Fred E. Hahn, *Tested Advertising Methods,* 5th ed., Prentice Hall, 1998.

Robert L. Collier, *The Robert Collier Letter Book,* Martino Fine Books, 2018.

Claude Hopkins, *My Life in Advertising,* CreateSpace Independent Publishing Platform, 2012.

_____, *Scientific Advertising,* CreateSpace Independent Publishing Platform, 2012.

Howie Jacobson and Kristie McDonald, *Google Adwords for Dummies,* 3rd ed., Wiley, 2007.

Perry Marshall, Mike Rhodes, and Bryan Todd, *Ultimate Guide to Google Adwords: How to Access 100 Million People in 10 Minutes,* 5th ed., Entrepreneur Press, 2017.

Emanuel Rosen, *The Anatomy of Buzz: How to Create Word of Mouth Marketing,* Crown Business, 2002.

Worthwhile Marketing-Related Newsletters

MarketingSherpa: https://marketingsherpa.com/newsletters.

Revenue Production Update, from The Customer Manufacturing Group. Newsletter signup at customermfg.com/cmsupdates/

Appendix B

How to Modify Let's See

Note that the downloadable version of *Let's See* includes four customizable upside elements, and four customizable scarce-resource constraints. The point is that you might not *need* to do any additional customization.

These instructions assume that you are starting with the original version of *Let's See*. We can provide no assurance and take no responsibility for how to modify any other versions.

Before You Begin (this is critical)

Please make a backup copy of *Let's See*, one that contains the data you've entered into it thus far. Then if something goes wrong, you'll at least be able to start over, with another fresh and up-to-date copy. Also make backups after any significant change you make.

Adding an Upside Element (do this first if you're going to do it at all)

The spreadsheet-cell references below all refer to the downloadable version of *Let's See*, with its customizable upside elements and resource constraints.

1. You'll need to unprotect THE UPSIDE CALCULATOR and THE CHOOSER worksheets. (Obviously, you'll need to be very careful after you do.) To do so, for each of them, on Excel's Review tab, click Unprotect Sheet, then type the password, which is Let'sSee (without a separating space).

2. In THE UPSIDE CALCULATOR worksheet, insert the new upside-element columns to the *left* of column AK.

3. Copy column AJ into the newly added columns.

4. In row 4 (only), change the headings of the newly added columns to describe their upside elements, and delete the text in row 3.

5. Now, on THE CHOOSER worksheet, above row 30, insert the same number of rows that you just added as columns.

6. Copy the *entire* row 29 (click the number 29 to the left of column A to select it) into the empty rows you just inserted.

7. Copy your new column headings from THE UPSIDE CALCULATOR's row 4, in left-to-right order, into the newly inserted rows in THE CHOOSER's column A, in the same order, working from top to bottom (or copy all the new headings, then click in the first empty column-A cell you just created, and choose Excel's Paste > Transpose option). That will fill in the new headings in column A. Left-align them; remove the underlines.

8. Return to THE UPSIDE CALCULATOR, and enter the changes you expect for the new columns in rows 5, 6, and 9–11 (the yellow cells), just as you did for the original upside elements. (Make sure that the percentage values look realistic, i.e., 4%, not 400%.)

9. Now you're going to make the gains in THE UPSIDE CALCULATOR appear in THE CHOOSER. (You'll need to repeat this process for *every new column* in THE UPSIDE CALCULATOR.) The process can best be understood with an example...

10. In THE CHOOSER, go to cell D30, the Profit Gain for the first of your added Upside Elements. Type an = sign, then 100*, then switch to THE UPSIDE CALCULATOR, select cell AK43, the Profit you expect from the first added Upside Element, and press Enter.

11. You'll be returned to THE CHOOSER. Your first added Upside Element's Profit Gain should appear in THE CHOOSER's cell D30.

12. Now, in THE CHOOSER's cell E30, again type an = sign, then 100*, go to THE UPSIDE CALCULATOR, select cell AK23, and press Enter.

13. Back in THE CHOOSER, you should see your new element's Revenue Gain in cell E30.

14. One last time, in THE CHOOSER's cell F30, again type an = sign, then 100*, go to THE UPSIDE CALCULATOR, select cell AK47, and press Enter.

15. Back in THE CHOOSER, you should see your new element's Profit-Margin Gain in cell F30.

16. As mentioned, repeat this process for any other upside elements you've added.

17. In THE CHOOSER, fill in the Characteristics columns, starting in Column H, for the newly added upside elements.

18. If you're not going to add any Scarce Resources (see below), you can proceed to choose the upside elements you're going to pursue, *after again protecting both* THE UPSIDE CALCULATOR and THE CHOOSER. (If you *don't* use the password shown earlier, please write the new one down somewhere you'll always be able to find it, *because neither we, nor Microsoft, can help you retrieve it.*)

Adding a Scarce Resource (in The Chooser)

1. If you don't need one or more of the original scarce-resource columns, L and M, that THE CHOOSER provides, you can reuse them by changing their titles in the (merged) cells L3:L6 and M4:M6.

2. Or, if you don't need one, or both, of the original Scarce-Resource columns, and have no other scarce resources to substitute, you can leave their resource consumptions blank in rows 7 through the last of your upside rows, which was, originally, and might still be, row 30.

3. If you need to keep the original Scarce-Resource columns, and want to add others, add as many new scarce-resource columns as you need between the two original scarce-resource columns (L and M), by highlighting column M, right-clicking, and choosing Insert the needed number of times.

4. Insert the Scarce-Resource headings starting in cell M3 and moving to the immediate right for the remaining new columns.

5. Copy cells L7:L33 (or higher, if you added new upside elements) into your newly added columns, and fill in the percentage estimates.

Acknowledgments

It took a village. Indeed.

We'll begin by thanking the authors, who've contributed substantially to the body of knowledge we've drawn on: Harry Beckwith, Ken Blanchard, Robert Bloom, Ram Charan, the late Craig Christensen, Doris Christopher, Gary Cokins, Jim Collins, the late Thomas L. Collins, Geoff Colvin, Robin Cooper, Stephen Covey, Bradley Gale, Malcolm Gladwell, Seth Godin, Gary Hamel, Paul Hawken, Chip and Dan Heath, Jeremy and Tony Hope, Robert Kaplan, W. Chan Kim, Robert Kiyosaki, Steve Krug, Carol Loomis, Roger Lowenstein, the late Nathaniel Mass, Renée Mauborgne, Flint McGlaughlin, Bethany McLean, Ted Nicholas, Joe Nocera, Daniel Obrycki, Rick Ott, Michael Porter, the late C. K. Prahalad, Frederick Reichheld, Al Ries, Simon Sinek, Adrian Slywotzky, Bennett Stewart, Dan Thomas, Jack Trout, Richard White, and Roy Williams.

Vistage is an organization for CEOs which I was a member of for many years. I want to thank the group chairs, who've helped further and sharpen these ideas: John Howman, Rief Kanan, and Ginnie McDevitt, and the particularly insightful Vistage speakers: Mitch Goozé, Pat Murray, and Dan Wertenberg.

My sincere appreciation to those who've helped shape the content, and graciously given their help and input: Dawn Bladzinski, Mike Burdi, Daniel Burstein, the late J.P. Donlon, Jane Friedman, Steve Harrison, Susan Harrow, Christina Hills, Robert Middleton, Isabel Parlett, Bennett Stewart, Stu Tartarone, and Josh Weston.

In particular, here, I want to recognize the flame keepers—those who've helped even more: Ann Convery, Roger Jackson, Ken McCarthy, Monica McCready, Keith Miklas, Jennifer Pellet, Tom Redman, Dan Roam, Susan Scott, Chris Shaver, Mark Sickles, Raj Varadarajan, and Mike Yoder.

I had the wonderful experience, in the process of obtaining the permissions needed for some of the book's material, to find a number of people, and companies, whose spirit of generosity was heartening: Basic Books; Chief Executive's Marshall and Wayne Cooper, and J.P. Donlon; Trident Design's Chris

Hawker and Lisa Woodward; American Girl's Susan Jevens; Perry Marshall &
Associates; Suzzy Roche; Harvard Business School's Kevin Sharer; and Chief
Marketer's Beth Negus Viveiros.

The book itself would not exist without the efforts of Beverly Bearden and
Dotty Eberhardt, who organized the mountain of material. Special thanks to
Raj Varadarajan, who rigorously dug through Chapter 14, providing clarity and
corrections. Hearty applause to the team that crafted the book itself: Natalie
Horbachevsky for her strong, wise hand in content and line editing, Lois Smith,
copy editor par excellence, Mary Schuck, whose design insight shaped the cover,
Domini Dragoone, the book's crackerjack interior designer, and Rachel Kuhn,
ace indexer, for seeing essences. Each of you have proved a delight to work with
and I'll always be grateful.

I would welcome knowing about any mistakes: please see the Afterword for
how to do so.

Endnotes

Introduction

1. Annie Gasparo and Vipal Monga, "3G Capital, Once a Disrupter, Is Reeling," *The Wall Street Journal*, February 23–24, 2019, A1, A12.

   Annie Gasparo, "Kraft Heinz's Promise Turns Sour," *The Wall Street Journal*, February 23–24, 2019, B3.

   Aaron Back and Carol Ryan, "The Lessons from Kraft's Sudden Fall," *The Wall Street Journal*, February 23–24, 2019, B12.

   Julie Creswell and David Yaffe-Bellany, "How 2 Great Brands Merged Into a Mess," *The New York Times*, September 24, 2019, B1, B4.

2. Kevin Roose, "Best Buy's Secrets for Thriving in the Age of Amazon," *The New York Times*, September 19, 2017, B1–B2.

3. Here are the details behind the performances of Best Buy and Kraft Heinz under Mr. Joly and Mr. Hees.

   Best Buy's Mr. Joly served as its CEO from 2012 until April 15, 2019.

   Mr. Hees, of Brazil's 3G Capital, was appointed CEO of Heinz on March 24, 2015, and on March 25, 2015, Heinz announced its agreement to merge with Kraft Foods, with Mr. Hees to serve as its CEO. The merger closed on July 2, 2015. Mr. Hees' tenure as CEO ended on April 22, 2019.

   The comparison below was based on the quarterly periods ending on September 30, 2015 (Kraft-Heinz' first reported quarterly results after the two companies merged) and March 31, 2019.

Enterprise Value ($B)*	9/30/2015	3/31/2019
Kraft Heinz	94.00	69.99
Best Buy	10.90	18.44

   * Sources: Yahoo Finance, which notes that its data is derived from multiple sources, or they calculate it themselves, and the Kraft Heinz website.

Chapter 1: Leading Your Business to Better Results

4. *Harvard Business Review*, January–February 2015, 124. HBR Reprint R1501L.

5. Carol S. Dweck, *Mindset, The New Psychology of Success: How We Can Learn to Fulfill Our Potential*, Ballantine Books, 2008.

6. Simon Sinek, *Start With Why*, Portfolio/Penguin, 2011.

7. Thomas W. Malnight, Ivy Buche, and Charles Dhanaraj, "Put Purpose at the Core of Your Strategy," *Harvard Business Review*, September–October 2019, HBR Reprint R1905D

8. Katrina Gardner, Speech to the Smith College Freshman Convocation, September 1999.

Chapter 2: The (Relatively) Quick and Easy Stuff

9. Frederick F. Reichheld, *The Loyalty Effect: The Hidden Force Behind Growth, Profits and Lasting Value*, Harvard Business School Press, Revised edition, 2001.

10. Ibid., 33.

11. Mitchell Goozé, "What Is Customer Loyalty All About?," *Revenue Production Update* newsletter, November 2019, customermfg.com.

12. Ginia Bellafonte, "Wegmans Has Come to Brooklyn. Why Are New Yorkers Losing Their Minds?," *The New York Times*, https://www.nytimes.com/2019/10/24/nyregion/wegmans-brooklyn.html.

    Amelia Nierenberg, "Wegmans Opens in Brooklyn; Fans Wait in the Rain, and Rejoice," *The New York Times*, https://www.nytimes.com/2019/10/27/dining/wegmans-new-york-city-navy-yard.html.

    Jesse Wegman, "Wegmans Feels Like Family, Even if It Isn't Mine" *The New York Times*, https://www.nytimes.com/2019/10/28/opinion/wegmans-brooklyn-opening.html.

13. Simon Sinek, in *Start With Why*, cited in Chapter 1, provides a worthwhile insight into the biological underpinnings of true loyalty, 74.

14. Frederick Reichheld with Rob Markey, *The Ultimate Question 2.0: How Net Promoter Companies Thrive in a Customer-Driven World*, Harvard Business School Press, 2011.

15. Ken Blanchard and Sheldon Bowles, *Raving Fans: A Revolutionary Approach to Customer Service*, William Morrow, 1993.

16. Jonathan P. Hicks, "Sales Practices at Dell Draw New York Suit," *The New York Times*, May 17, 2007, C5.

    "Cuomo Announces Dell Will Pay $4 Million for Defrauding New York Consumers," New York State Attorney General's Office Press Release, September 15, 2009.

17. Source: https://www.websiteiq.com/domain/mugglenet.com.

18. Thomas Gibbons-Neff and Helene Cooper, "Cases Spiral Aboard an Aircraft Carrier, and a Commander Pleads for Help," *The New York Times*, April 1, 2020, A1.

Helene Cooper, Thomas Gibbons-Neff, Eric Schmitt, and Emily Cochrane, "Navy Captain Is Dismissed After Seeking Help for Crew," *The New York Times*, April 3, 2020, A15.

Helene Cooper, Thomas Gibbons-Neff, and Eric Schmitt, "Sailors Cheer On Boss They Feel Sacrificed His Career for Their Safety," *The New York Times*, April 4, 2020, A15.

Tweed Roosevelt, "Captain Crozier Is a Hero," *The New York Times*, April 4, 2020, A23.

19. Thomas Gibbons-Neff, Eric Schmitt, Helene Cooper, and John Ismay, " 'There Will Be Losses': How a Captain's Plea Exposed a Rift in the Military," *The New York Times*, April 13, 2020, A1.

20. David Segal (The Haggler), "A Preferred Guest Gets the Cold Shoulder," *The New York Times*, February 15, 2015, BU5.

Chapter 3: Honing Your Value Proposition—So More People *Buy*

21. Michael J. Lanning, *Delivering Profitable Value*, Basic Books, Revised edition, 2000.

22. Clayton M. Christensen, Taddy Hall, Karen Dillon, and David S. Duncan, *Competing Against Luck*, Harper Business, 2016.

23. Patricia Sellers, "P&G: Teaching an Old Dog New Tricks," *Fortune*, May 31, 2004. A. G. Lafley's reference to the customer's experience of the product is on page 178.

24. James W. Cortada, "Building the System/360 Mainframe Nearly Destroyed IBM," *IEEE Spectrum*, https://spectrum.ieee.org/tech-history/silicon-revolution/building-the-system360 -mainframe-nearly-destroyed-ibm, April 5, 2019. (This article is excerpted from Mr. Cortada's 2019 book, *IBM: The Rise and Fall and Reinvention of a Global Icon*, MIT Press.)

25. Jim Rendon, "From a Store With 300,000 Titles, a Big Music Lesson," *The New York Times*, July 20, 2003, Sunday Business, 5.

26. Jeff Bertolucci, "Technology's Most (and Least) Reliable Brands," *PC World*, January 2008, 115–124.

Jeff Bertolucci, "Reliability Report Card: Grading Tech's Biggest Brands," *PC World*, February 2009, 82–92.

Jeff Bertolucci, "The Tech Brands You Can Trust," *PC World*, January 2011, 83–94.

Eric Griffith, "Annual Reader Satisfaction Survey," *PC Magazine*, October 16, 2007, 56–63.

Eric Griffith and Sascha Segan, "Readers' Choice Awards," *PC Magazine*, September 2008, 66–72.

Eric Griffith et al., "Readers' Choice Awards," *PC Magazine* (Digital Edition), November 2009, 48–65.

Ben Gottesman, "Readers' Choice Awards," *PC Magazine* (Digital Edition), October 2010, 30–43.

27. Lanning, op. cit., Chapters 8–14.

28. Christensen et al., 74.

29. Ibid., 90.

30. Rita Gunther McGrath, "Old Habits Die Hard, But They Do Die," *Harvard Business Review*, January–February 2017, 54–57.

31. Adrian J. Slywotzky, with Karl Weber, *Demand: Creating What People Love Before They Know They Want It*, Crown Business, 2011, 40–42, 55–91.

32. W. Chan Kim and Renée Mauborgne, *Blue Ocean Shift*, Hachette Books, 2017, 146.

33. W. Chan Kim and Renée Mauborgne, "Value Innovation: The Strategic Logic of High Growth," *Harvard Business Review*, January–February 1997, 102–112, reprinted in its July–August 2004 issue.

34. James C. Anderson, James A. Narus, and Wouter van Rossum, "Customer Value Propositions in Business Markets," *Harvard Business Review*, March 2006, 91–99.

35. W. Chan Kim and Renée Mauborgne, *Blue Ocean Strategy*, Harvard Business School Publishing, Expanded edition, 2015.

36. Slywotzky, op. cit., 34–54.

37. Charles E. Lucier, Leslie H. Moeller, and Raymond Held, "10x Value: The Engine Powering Long-Term Shareholder Returns," *strategy+business*, July 1, 1997 (Third Quarter 1997/Issue 8), 21–28.

38. Ronald B. Leiber, "Storytelling: A New Way to Get Close to Your Customer," *Fortune*, February 3, 1997, 102.

39. Tucker Westerbrook, "10 Things You Didn't Know About L.L. Bean," *Town&Country*, March 24, 2015.

40. Lanning, op. cit., 298.

41. Adam Bryant, "Feedback in Heaping Helpings, An Interview with Amgen's CEO, Kevin W. Sharer," Corner Office, *The New York Times*, March 29, 2009.

42. Lanning, op. cit., 296.

43. Ibid.

44. Lanning, op. cit., 296–301.

45. Lanning, op. cit., 298.

Chapter 4: Strenghtening Your Brand's Promise and Power

46. Sinek, *Start With Why*, 54–55.

47. Perry Yeldham, "The Real Definition of a Brand," (Mr. Yeldham is the Founder and Creative Director of 21Thirteen Design): Websites that Connect - 21thirteen.com, cited in Rick Frishman's *Sunday Tips* newsletter, April 30, 2017.

48. Roy H. Williams, "Name Recognition Isn't Branding," *Monday Morning Memo From the Wizard of Ads*, March 22, 2004.

49. Kevin Helliker, "In Natural Foods, a Big Name's No Big Help," *The Wall Street Journal*, June 7, 2002, B1.

50. Glenn Rifkin, "How Snap-on Tools Ratchets Its Brand," *strategy+business*, First Quarter 1998, 51–58.

51. Charlotte Beers, "Building Brands Worthy of Devotion," *Leader to Leader*, Winter 1998, 39–42.

52. Natasha Singer, "Drug Maker Seen as Uncooperative on Inquiry," *The New York Times*, June 10, 2010, B1.

_____, "Drug Maker Cited on Quality Issues," *The New York Times*, November 26, 2010, B1.

_____, "Johnson & Johnson Recalls More Products," *The New York Times*, January 14, 2011.

Natasha Singer and Reed Abelson, "Can Johnson & Johnson Get Its Act Together?" *The New York Times*, January 16, 2011, BU1.

"Changing Attitudes Toward J&J," *The New York Times*, January 16, 2011.

Katie Thomas, "New Recalls by Johnson & Johnson Raise Concern About Quality Control Improvements," *The New York Times*, September 12, 2013.

53. Barry Meier, "Maker Aware of 40% Failure in Hip Implant," *The New York Times*, January 23, 2013, A1.

_____, "Maker Hid Data About Design Flaw in Hip Implant, Records Show," *The New York Times*, January 26, 2013, B1.

_____, "Implant Risk Was Assessed Inadequately, Court Is Told," *The New York Times*, February 1, 2013, B3.

_____, "Johnson & Johnson Said to Agree to $4 Billion Settlement Over Hip Implants," *The New York Times*, November 13, 2013, B1.

54. Susan Berfield, Jef Feeley, and Margaret Cronin Fisk, "Johnson & Johnson Has a Baby Powder Problem: More than 1,000 women are suing the company for covering up cancer risk," *Bloomberg Business Week*, March 31, 2016, 52–59.

Anne Steele and Jonathan D. Rockoff, "J&J Loses Suit Tying Cancer to Baby Powder," *The Wall Street Journal*, May 6, 2017.

Roni Caryn Rabin and Tiffany Hsu, "Baby Powder, a Carcinogen and Red Flags," *The New York Times*, December 15, 2018, A1.

Chris Kirkham (Reuters), "Johnson & Johnson Subpoenaed by DOJ, SEC Over Baby Powder Safety Concerns," *HuffPost*, February 21, 2019.

Tiffany Hsu and Roni Caryn Rabin, "Talcum Powder Will Be Pulled Off the Market," *The New York Times*, May 19, 2020, A1.

55. Stephen Gandel, "New York files $2 billion lawsuit against Johnson & Johnson for its alleged role in opioid epidemic," CBS News, September 17, 2020, https://www.cbsnews.com/news/johnson-johnson-opioid-epidemic-new-york-lawsuit-2-billion/

56. Joe Nocera, "The First Thing We Do, Let's Pay All the Lawyers," *Bloomberg Business Week*, December 17, 2018, 76.

Sheila Kaplan and Matthew Goldstein, "F.D.A. Orders Pelvic Mesh, Tied to Injuries, Off Market," *The New York Times*, April 17, 2019, B1.

57. Sewell Chan and Louise Story, "S.E.C. Settling Its Complaints With Goldman," *The New York Times*, July 16, 2010, A1.

58. Larry Ackerman, "Secrets of the Corporate Brand: Why Do Companies Fall Short of Exploiting Their Hidden Potential?" *Across the Board*, January 1998, 33–36.

59. Al Ehrbar, "Breakaway Brands: How Ten Companies, Making Products from Drills to Waffles, Took Good Brands and Made Them Much, Much Better," *Fortune*, October 31, 2005, 153–162, esp. 156.

60. Perry Marshall, Confessions of a Big-Ass Marketing Guy, https://www.perrymarshall.com/marketing/big-ass-fans/confessions/. The whole story, including an audio interview with Big Ass Fans' marketing person at the time, Bill Buell, and an email series, is available at the link just cited.

61. Mitch Goozé, "Branding: Making a Name for Yourself. Is Your Brand Just a Name or Something of Value?", https://customermanufacturing.com/resources/white-papers/brands-branding. From there, click on: Branding: Making A Name For Yourself. (You'll need to provide your name and email address.), 2001–2002.

62. Two good general references on branding are: David Aaker, *Building Strong Brands*, The Free Press, 1995, and Al Ries and Laura Ries, *The 22 Immutable Laws of Branding: How to Build a Product or Service into a World-Class Brand*, Harper Business, 2002.

63. Neal E. Boudette, "BMW's CEO Just Says 'No' to Protect Brand," *The Wall Street Journal*, November 26, 2003, B1.

64. Susan Berfield, Jef Feeley, and Margaret Cronin Fisk, "More than 1,000 women accuse Johnson & Johnson of covering up the risks of Baby Powder," *Bloomberg Business Week*, April 4–10, 2016, 54–59.

65. Nanette Byrnes, Robert Berner, Wendy Zellner, and William Symonds, "Branding: Five New Lessons," *Business Week*, February 14, 2005, 26–28.

66. Vijay Vishwanath and Jonathan Mark, "Your Brand's Best Strategy," *Harvard Business Review*, May–June 1997, 123–129. This is about how to manage brands in various categories in the consumer-products space.

67. Linda Grant, "Where Did the Snap, Crackle & Pop Go?" *Fortune*, August 4, 1997, 223–226.

68. Julie Deardorff, "Gone, But Not Forgotten: When a Product Is Discontinued, Consumers Feel the Pain," *The Star Ledger* (NJ), March 16, 2014, Section 3, 3.

69. Tanzina Vega, "Mothers Will Get the Glory in P.&G.'s Campaign," *The New York Times*, April 17, 2012, B3.

70. Andrew Adam Newman, "Direct Approach to Disaster Relief From Procter & Gamble," *The New York Times*, June 3, 2011.

71. https://www.businesswire.com/news/home/20190323005003/en/
Procter-Gamble-Brings-Relief-Residents-Affected-
Nebraska.

Chapter 5: Creating "I Want That!" and Triggering the Sale

72. Rick Ott, *Creating Demand: Move the Masses to Buy Your Product, Service, or Idea*, 2nd ed., Ocean View Communications, 1999, 47–65.

73. Ibid., 67–81.

74. Jonah Berger, *The Catalyst: How to Change Anyone's Mind*, Simon & Schuster, 2020.

75. Michael McCarthy, "God May Forgive Ads That Offend, but Customers Probably Won't," *The New York Times*, December 14, 2015, B6.

76. Bryan and Jeffrey Eisenberg with Lisa T. Davis, *Call to Action: Secret Formulas to Improve Online Results*, Nelson Business, 2006.

77. Jonah Berger, *Contagious: Why Things Catch On*, Simon & Schuster, Reprint edition, 2016.

78. Emanuel Rosen, *The Anatomy of Buzz: How to Create Word of Mouth Marketing*, Crown Business, 2002.

79. Dan Roam, *Show and Tell: How Everybody Can Make Extraordinary Presentations*, Portfolio/Penguin, 2016.

Chapter 6: Pricing Perspectives With Legs

80. Janice Revell, "The Price Is Not Always Right," *Fortune*, May 14, 2001, 240.

81. Yasmin Ghehremani, "But for You, I'll Charge an Additional 10%," *CFO Magazine*, June 1, 2008.

82. Rafi Mohammed, *The 1% Windfall: How Successful Companies Use Price to Profit and Grow*, Harper Business, 2010.

83. Rafi Mohammed, *The Art of Pricing: How to Find the Hidden Profits to Grow Your Business*, Crown, 2005.

84. Rafi Mohammed, "The Good-Better-Best Approach to Pricing," *Harvard Business Review*, September–October 2018, 106–115

85. Mohammed, *The Art of Pricing*, 78.

86. Amy Merrick, "Retailers Try to Get Leg Up on Markdowns With New Software," *The Wall Street Journal*, August 7, 2001, A1.

87. The first example was adapted from William Poundstone's *Priceless: The Myth of Fair Value (and How to Take Advantage of It)*, Hill and Wang, 2010.

88. Dan Ariely, *Predictably Irrational*, HarperCollins, 2008, 3–4.

89. Thomas T. Nagle, "Pricing Strategies: Where Companies Go Wrong Again...Again," *Bottom Line/Business*, September 15, 1995, 5.

90. Leonard L. Berry and Manjit S. Yadav, "Capture and Communicate Value in the Pricing of Services," *Sloan Management Review*, Summer 1996, 41–51.

91. Richard Perez-Pena, "Extra! Extra! Now the Post Doesn't Cost That Extra 25 Cents," *The New York Times*, May 10, 2007.

92. Mohammed, *The Art of Pricing*, 183–185.

93. Ariely, 183–184.

94. Linda Tischler, "The Price Is Right," *Fast Company*, November 2003, 83.

95. Nick Zubco, "Are Your Prices Right?," *Industry Week*, January, 2009.

96. Virginia Postrel, Economic Scene, *The New York Times*, January 3, 2002, C2.

97. Ruth La Ferla, "When High Price Is the Allure," *The New York Times*, August 9, 2007, G1, G5.

98. Christina Binkley, "The Psychology of the $14,000 Handbag," *The Wall Street Journal*, August 9, 2007, D8.

99. Charles Fishman, "Which Price is Right?," *Fast Company*, March 2003, 92–101.

100. Kusum L. Ailawada and Paul W. Farris, "How Companies Can Get Smart About Raising Prices," *The Wall Street Journal*, July 22, 2013, R1–R2.

101. Frank V. Cespedes, Elliot B. Ross, and Benson P. Shapiro, "Seven Mistakes of Poor Pricers," *The Wall Street Journal*, May 24, 2010.

102. Jennifer Bayot, "Fees Hidden in Plain Sight, Companies Add to Bottom Line," *The New York Times*, December 28, 2002, A1.

103. "Using Targeted Pricing Carefully," *Chief Executive: CEO Wire*, April 1, 2003.

104. Miguel Bustillo and Ann Zimmerman, "Phone-Wielding Shoppers Strike Fear Into Retailers," *The Wall Street Journal*, December 16, 2010, A1.

105. Indrajit Sinha, "Cost Transparency: The Net's Real Threat to Prices and Brands," *Harvard Business Review*, March–April 2000, 43–50, *Harvard Business Review* Reprint R00210.

106. Jill Griffin, "Best Buy's Turnaround: You Can't Make This Stuff Up," *Forbes*, July, 27, 2018.

107. Justin Bariso, "Amazon Almost Killed Best Buy. Then Best Buy Did Something Completely Brilliant," *Inc.*, March 4, 2019.

108. John McPartlin, "The Price You Pay," *CFO-IT*, Spring 2004.

109. www.zilliant.com.

110. Faith Keenan, "The Price Is Really Right," *BusinessWeek*, March 31, 2003, 62–67.

111. John Shipman and Paul Vigna, "Protecting Profits at a Price," *The Wall Street Journal*, January 24, 2011.

112. Daniel Burstein, "Pricing Strategy: 7 factors marketers can leverage to increase sales," MarketingSherpa newsletter: https://www.marketingsherpa.com/article/how-to/pricing-strategy-7-factors?utm_source=MS-list&utm_medium=email&utm_content=newsletter&utm_campaign=b2b2c, October 21–November 4, 2019.

113. Akshay R. Rao, Mark E. Bergen, and Scott Davis, "How to Fight a Price War," *Harvard Business Review*, March–April 2000, 107–116, HBR Reprint R00208.

114. Manmohan S. Sodhi and Navdeep S. Sodhi, "Six Sigma Pricing," *Harvard Business Review*, May 2005, 135–142, HBR Reprint R0505H.

Chapter 7: Deftly Managing Costs

115. Steven Rosenbush, "A Novel Ship Extends Shell's Reach," *The Wall Street Journal*, January 3, 2013.

116. Halliburton, 2010 Annual Report.

117. John D. Stoll, "What's on Kraft's Menu Beyond Cuts?" *The Wall Street Journal*, April 24, 2019, B6.

   Heather Haddon, "New Kraft CEO Targets 'Dusty' Brands," *The Wall Street Journal*, April 23, 2019, B1.

   Michael Rapoport, "Kraft Heinz Tailored Results in Spotlight," *The Wall Street Journal*, March 6, 2019, B5.

   Nicole Friedman, "Kraft Tests Buffett and 3G Ties," *The Wall Street Journal*, February 26, 2019, B3.

   Nicole Friedman, "Big Kraft Investment Bites Berkshire," *The Wall Street Journal*, February 25, 2019, B1.

   Annie Gasparro and Vipal Monga, "3G Capital, Once a Disrupter, Is Reeling," *The Wall Street Journal*, February 23–24, 2019, A1.

Annie Gasparro, "Kraft Heinz's Promise Turns Sour," *The Wall Street Journal*, February 23–24, 2019, B3.

Aaron Back and Carol Ryan, "The Lessons From Kraft's Sudden Fall," *The Wall Street Journal*, February 23–24, 2019, B14.

Reuters, "Kraft Heinz Reveals S.E.C. Accounting Inquiry," *The New York Times*, February 22, 2019, B6.

Heather Haddon, "Kraft Heinz Pays Price for Snubbing Retailers," *The Wall Street Journal*, February 22, 2019, B1.

Annie Gasparro, "Kraft Swings to Loss, Shares Plunge," *The Wall Street Journal*, February 21, 2019.

Aaron Back, "Kraft Heinz Still Needs to Show It Can Post Sales Growth," *The Wall Street Journal*, August 6, 2018, B10.

118. These are some of the more salient works on zero-based budgeting. The Investopedia reference briefly lays out the pros and cons. More on the pros is in the McKinsey citations, while Mahler's *HBR* article provides the cons.

Investopedia, "What are the advantages and disadvantages of zero-based budgeting in accounting?,"https://www.investopedia.com/ask/answers/051515/what-are-advantages-and-disadvantages-zerobased-budgeting-accounting.asp, May 15, 2015.

Matt Fitzpatrick and Kyle Hawke, "The return of zero-base budgeting," https://www.mckinsey.com/business-functions/strategy-and-corporate-finance/our-insights/the-return-of-zero-base-budgeting, August 2015.

Shaun Callaghan, Kyle Hawke, and Carey Mignerey, "Five myths (and realities) about zero-based budgeting," https://www.mckinsey.com/business-functions/strategy-and-corporate-finance/our-insights-five-myths-and-realities-about-zero-based-budgeting, October 2014.

Daniel Mahler, "Zero-Based Budgeting Is Not a Wonder Diet for Companies," *Harvard Business Review*, June 30, 2016.

Stefan Househam, Carey Mignerey, and Rob Pepper, "Zero-based budgeting then and now: Technology remakes the ZBB rules," https://operations-extranet.mckinsey.com/article/zero-based-budgeting-then-and-now-technology-remakes-the-zbb-rules, March 21, 2017.

Kyle Hawke, Matt Jochim, Carey Mignerey, and Allison Watson, "Five new truths about zero-based budgeting," https://www.mckinsey.com/business-functions/operations/our-insights/five-new-truths-about-zero-based-budgeting, August 2017.

119. The author has read each of those listed below—they're excellent. They're alphabetical, by author.

Gary Cokins, Alan Stratton, and Jack Helbling, *An ABC Manager's Primer*, McGraw-Hill, 1992.

Douglas T. Hicks, *Activity-Based Costing: Making It Work for Small and Mid-Sized Companies*, 2nd ed., Wiley, 1999.

Tony Hope and Jeremy Hope, *Transforming the Bottom Line: Managing Performance with Real Numbers*, Harvard Business School Press, 1995–1996.

Robert S. Kaplan and Robin Cooper, *Cost & Effect: Using Integrated Cost Systems to Drive Profitability and Performance*, Harvard Business School Press, 1998.

Mohan Nair, *Activity-Based Information Systems: An Executive's Guide to Implementation*, Wiley, 1999.

120. Michael Hammer and Lisa W. Hershman, *Faster Cheaper Better: The 9 Levers for Transforming How Work Gets Done*, Crown Business, 2010.

121. James Womack, Daniel T. Jones, and Daniel Roos, *The Machine That Changed the World: The Story of Lean Production—Toyota's Secret Weapon in the Global Car Wars That Is Now Revolutionizing World Industry*, Free Press, 2007 (Reprint edition), originally published in 1990.

122. David Simchi-Levi, Philip Kaminsky, and Edith Simchi-Levi, *Managing the Supply Chain: The Definitive Guide for the Business Professional*, McGraw-Hill, 2004.

123. Tom Copeland, "Cutting Costs Without Drawing Blood," *Harvard Business Review*, September–October 2000, 155–164, HBR Reprint R00503.

Chapter 8: Detecting and Seizing Opportunities

124. Clayton M. Christensen, Taddy Hall, Karen Dillon, and David S. Duncan, *Competing Against Luck*, Harper Business, 2016.

125. Slywotzky, *Demand*, Chapter 2.

126. Kim and Mauborgne, *Blue Ocean Shift*, 146.

127. Richard M. White, *The Entrepreneur's Manual*, originally published in 1977 and again available: Churchill & Dunn, Ltd; Reprinted edition, 2014.

128. Peter F. Drucker, *Innovation and Entrepreneurship: Practice and Principles*, Harper Business; Reprint edition, 2006, and "The Discipline of Innovation," *Harvard Business Review*, August 2002, 95–102.

129. Mark W. Johnson, *Seizing the White Space: Business Model Innovation for Growth and Renewal*, Harvard Business Review Press, 2010, Chapter 2 and 127–134.

Chapter 9: Finding and Serving Growing Markets

130. Denny Hatch, "Are You Surrounding Your Market? The Marketing Genius of American Girl," *Target Marketing*, February 12, 2008.

131. https://www.tomsguide.com/us/-tmobile-vs-verizon,review-5133.html.

132. Danielle Beurteaux, "Tailoring Durability and Fit for Women Who Wrangle and Weld," *The New York Times*, October 20, 2016, B4.

133. Mark W. Johnson, *Seizing the White Space: Business Model Innovation for Growth and Renewal*, *Harvard Business Review* Press, 2010.

134. Clayton M. Christensen, Taddy Hall, Karen Dillon, and David S. Duncan, *Competing Against Luck*, Harper Business, 2016.

135. Richard White, *The Entrepreneur's Manual*, originally published in 1977 and again available from Amazon and others: Churchill & Dunn, Ltd; Reprinted edition (November 18, 2014).

136. Kim and Mauborgne, *Blue Ocean Shift*.

137. Michael E. Porter, "The Five Competitive Forces That Shape Strategy," *Harvard Business Review*, Updated January 2008, 79–93, especially 89. Also From Porter, *Competitive Strategy: Techniques for Analyzing Industries and Competitors*, Free Press, 1998.

138. Kim and Mauborgne, *Blue Ocean Strategy*.

139. Al Ries and Jack Trout, *Positioning: The Battle for Your Mind*, McGraw-Hill Education, 3rd edition, 2001.

140. Andy Cunningham, *get to Aha!*, McGraw-Hill Education, 2018.

Chapter 10: Crafting a Powerful Business Design

141. Robert T. Kiyosaki and Sharon L. Lechter, *Before You Quit Your Job: 10 Real-Life Lessons Every Entrepreneur Should Know About Building a Multimillion-Dollar Business*, Warner Business, 2005, 20.

142. The author contributed to *Chief Executive*'s Wealth Creation Index for the eight years (2008–2015) it was published. The articles included analyses of why the best and, in some years, the worst, wealth creators were ranked as they were. For 10 of the highest-ranked companies, among the reasons for its ranking was their business's design. The next-highest reason, product and service design, applied to only 7 of the highest ranked. For 11 of the lowest ranked, a poor business design was among the reasons; while poor economic-margin management (Chapter 14) applied to only 5. The articles are available on *Chief Executive*'s website: chiefexecutive.net, and, with permission, on the author's site: greatnumbers.com.

143. Andrea Ovans, "What Is a Business Model?" *Harvard Business Review*, January 23, 2015.

144. Alex Osterwalder, Yves Pigneur, and Alan Smith, *Business Model Generation*, self-published, 2010.

145. Charles E. Lucier, Leslie H. Moeller, and Raymond Held, "10x Value: The Engine Powering Long-Term Shareholder Returns," *strategy+business*, July 1, 1997 (Third Quarter 1997 / Issue 8).

146. Base numbers for MOABG 1, the Product Business (in thousands)

Units Sold	Revenue	Variable Cost	Total Cost	Profit
100	$100	$75	$175	$ -75
200	$200	$150	$250	$ -50
300	$300	$225	$325	$ -25
400	$400	$300	$400	$0
500	$500	$375	$475	$25
600	$600	$450	$550	$50
700	$700	$525	$625	$75
800	$800	$600	$700	$100
900	$900	$675	$775	$125
1,000	$1,000	$750	$850	$150

147. Numbers for MOABG 2, the Base Business With a 10¢ Drop in Variable Costs

Units Sold	Revenue	Variable Cost	Total Cost	Profit
100	$100	$65	$165	$ -65
200	$200	$130	$230	$ -30
300	$300	$195	$295	$5
400	$400	$260	$360	$40
500	$500	$325	$425	$75
600	$600	$390	$490	$110
700	$700	$455	$555	$145
800	$800	$520	$620	$180

Units Sold	Revenue	Variable Cost	Total Cost	Profit
900	$900	$585	$685	$215
1,000	$1,000	$650	$750	$250

Note that both units sold and all financial figures are in thousands.

148. Numbers for MOABG 3, the Base Business With a 25% Drop in Fixed Costs.

Units Sold	Revenue	Variable Cost	Total Cost	Profit
100	$100	$75	$150	$ -50
200	$200	$150	$225	$ -25
300	$300	$225	$300	$0
400	$400	$300	$375	$25
500	$500	$375	$450	$50
600	$600	$450	$525	$75
700	$700	$525	$600	$100
800	$800	$600	$675	$125
900	$900	$675	$750	$150
1,000	$1,000	$750	$825	$175

Note that both units sold and all financial figures are in thousands.

149. Numbers for MOABG 4: the Base Business With Both a 25% Drop in Fixed Costs and 10% Per Unit Lower Variable Costs.

Units Sold	Revenue	Variable Cost	Total Cost	Profit
100	$100	$65	$140	$ -40
200	$200	$130	$205	$ -5
300	$300	$195	$270	$30
400	$400	$260	$335	$65
500	$500	$325	$400	$100
600	$600	$390	$465	$135

Units Sold	Revenue	Variable Cost	Total Cost	Profit
700	$700	$455	$530	$170
800	$800	$520	$595	$205
900	$900	$585	$660	$240
1,000	$1,000	$650	$725	$275

Note that both units sold and all financial figures are in thousands.

150. Ram Charan and Noel M. Tichy, *Every Business Is a Growth Business*, Times Books (Random House), 1998, 47–59.

151. Michael E. Porter, "The Five Competitive Forces That Shape Strategy," *Harvard Business Review*, updated January 2008, 79–93, esp. 90 (Shaping Industry Structure), or page 1 in HBR Reprint R0801E. Also from Porter, *Competitive Strategy: Techniques for Analyzing Industries and Competitors*, Free Press, 1998.

152. David Kirkpatrick, "Houston, We Have Some Problems: The World's Leading PC Maker [Compaq] Faces Texas-size Challenges [Dell]. Can Compaq Continue to Soar?" *Fortune*, June 23, 1997, 102–103.

153. J.P. Donlon, Bennett Stewart, and Drew Morris, "Wealth Creation Index," *Chief Executive*, November/December, 2015, 28–33.

154. Brent Bowers, "Paying Entrepreneurs to Find the Right Business," *The New York Times*, March 12, 2009, page B5.

155. Mark W. Johnson, Clayton M. Christensen, and Henning Kagermann, "Reinventing Your Business Model," *Harvard Business Review*, December 2008, 50–59.

156. Mark W. Johnson, *Seizing the White Space: Business Model Innovation for Growth and Renewal*, *Harvard Business Review* Press, 2010, Chapter 2 and 127–134.

Chapter 11: Product and Service Design to Die For

157. Bruce Nussbaum, "A Decade of Design," *Business Week*, November 29, 1999.

158. A video interview with the chair's late designer, Niels Diffrient, on the HumanScale website, well captures the essence of the approach: https://www.humanscale.com/resources/watch-listen-learn/index.cfm#videoTop, then click on the *Studio Insights: Diffrient Smart* photo of Mr. Diffrient.

159. Steve Krug, *Don't Make Me Think, Revisited: A Common Sense Approach to Web and Mobile Usability*, 3rd ed., New Riders Publishing, 2014.

160. trident-design.com.

161. Farhad Manjoo, "The iPhone Continues to Break Tech's Rules," *The New York Times*, September 10, 2015, B1.

162. Mark Maremont, "Gillette Is Finally Revealing Its Vision of the Razor's Future," *The Wall Street Journal*, April 14, 1998, A1.

163. Tim Brown and Roger Martin, "Design for Action: How to Use Design Thinking to Make Great Things Actually Happen," *Harvard Business Review*, September 2015, 56–64.

164. Jon Kolko, "Design Thinking Comes of Age," *Harvard Business Review*, September 2015, 66–71.

165. Nicole Perlroth, "Solving Problems for Real World, Using Design: Program at Stanford Makes a Global Impact," *The New York Times*, December 30, 2013, B3.

166. Steve Lohr, "Setting Free the Squares: IBM Is Challenging Its Stodgy Reputation by Hiring Thousands of Designers and Turning Them Loose on Conventional Thinking," *The New York Times*, November 15, 2015, BU1.

167. Marnie Harnell, "Who Made That?," *The New York Times* Magazine, June 9, 2013, 28, and Life Savers' company history.

168. Sam Grobart, "Apple Chiefs Discuss Strategy, Market Share—and the New iPhones," *Bloomberg BusinessWeek*, September 19, 2013, 61–64.

169. Carol Matlack, "Electrolux's Holy Trinity for Hit Products," *Bloomberg BusinessWeek*, Oct. 31, 2013, 55–56.

Chapter 12: Innovation: The Why and How of Solving Worthy Problems

170. Peter Drucker, "The Discipline of Innovation," *Harvard Business Review*, May–June, 1985.

171. W. Chan Kim and Renée Mauborgne, "Value Innovation: The Strategic Logic of High Growth," *Harvard Business Review*, 1997, HBR Reprint R0407P.

172. Kim and Mauborgne, *Blue Ocean Strategy*.

173. Jon Gertner, "The World's 50 Most Innovative Companies: No. 50," *Fast Company*, March 2014, 142–148.

174. Jessica Weiss, "The World's 50 Most Innovative Companies: No. 41," *Fast Company*, March 2014, 127.

175. Harold Evans, *They Made America*, Little, Brown, 2004.

176. Clayton M. Christensen, *The Innovator's Dilemma: When New Technologies Cause Great Firms to Fail*, Harvard Business Review Press, HBR Reprint edition, 2016.

177. Scott Thurm and Ben Fox Rubin, "Sycamore: From $45 Billion to Zilch," *The Wall Street Journal*, February 2–3, 2013, B1.

178. John Bussey, "The Anti-Kodak: How a U.S. Firm Innovates and Thrives," *The Wall Street Journal*, January 13, 2012, B1, B4.

179. https://www.milliken.com/en-us/industries/building-construction-and-infrastructure.

180. Robert Berner, Nanette Byrnes, and Wendy Zellner, "P&G Has Rivals in a Ringer," *BusinessWeek*, October 4, 2004, 74.

181. Carol Matlack, "Electrolux's Holy Trinity for Hit Products," *Bloomberg BusinessWeek*, Oct. 31, 2013, 55–56.

182. Nicole LaPorte, "In the School of Innovation, Less Is Often More," *The New York Times*, November 6, 2011, BU4.

183. Jessica Bruder, "You're the Boss; Inventor, Age 13, Hires Marketers for a Cure for Hiccups," *The New York Times*, May 3, 2012 (online). See also the print version with inventor and product pictures, "A 13-Year-Old Enlists M.B.A. Students to Build Her Start-Up," May 1, 2012.

184. safetynailer.com.

185. Hannah Bloch, "A 'Smart Syringe' That Can't Spread Disease," *The Wall Street Journal*, April 25–26, 2015.

186. Jan Chipchase, with Simon Steinhardt, *Hidden in Plain Sight: How to Create Extraordinary Products for Tomorrow's Customers*, Harper Business, 2013.

187. https://www.sandiegouniontribune.com/news/science/sd-me-aging-place-20170630-story.html.

188. Jim Manzi, *Uncontrolled: The Surprising Power of Trial and Error for Business*, Basic Books, 2012.

189. Gary Klein, "Performing a Project Premortem," *Harvard Business Review*, September 2007, 18–19.

190. Matt Ridley, "Don't Look for Innovations Before Their Time," *The Wall Street Journal*, September 16–17, 2012.

191. Tom Kelley, with Jonathan Littman, *The Art of Innovation*, Profile Books, 2001.

192. Peter Drucker, *The Effective Executive*, Harper Collins, 2006, 116.

193. Robert B. Tucker, *Driving Growth Through Innovation*, 2nd ed., Berrett-Koehler, 2008.

194. Alan G. Robinson and Sam Stern, *Corporate Creativity: How Innovation and Improvement Actually Happen*, Berrett-Koehler, 1997.

195. Peter Drucker, "The Discipline of Innovation," *Harvard Business Review*, May-June, 1985.

196. John Bussey, "Myths of the Big R&D Budget," *The Wall Street Journal*, June 15, 2012, B1–B2.

197. A.G. Lafley and Ram Charan, *The Game Changer: How You Can Drive Revenue and Profit Growth with Innovation*, Crown Business, 2008.

198. Adam Bryant, "Want to Innovate? Get Ready to Kiss Some Frogs," *The New York Times*, April 5, 2013, B2.

199. Nick Bilton, "Innovation Isn't Easy, Especially for an Industry Giant," *The New York Times*, April 6, 2012, B6.

200. Clayton M. Christensen, "Innovation Killers: How Financial Tools Destroy Your Capacity to Do New Things," *Harvard Business Review*, January 2008, 98–105.

Chapter 13: Management Practices for Delivering the Upside

201. Dale Buss, "Love Your People," *Chief Executive*, January/February 2020, 34–39.

202. Sinek, *Start With Why*, 37.

203. Sinek, *Start With Why*, 72–73.

204. Sinek, *Start With Why*, Chapter 12, especially page 185.

205. Vanessa Fuhrmans, "New Ben & Jerry's CEO Plans to Stir Social Activism," *The Wall Street Journal*, August 16, 2018, B5.

206. Harry McCracken, "Microsoft Rewrites the Code," *Fast Company*, October 2017, 51.

207. Megan Murphy, An interview with Satya Nadella, CEO, Microsoft, *Bloomberg Business Week*, December 25, 2017, 46–50.

208. Ibid.

209. McCracken, "Microsoft Rewrites the Code," 98.

210. Murphy, Nadella interview, 48.

211. Satya Nadella, Greg Shaw, and Jill Tracie Nichols, *Hit Refresh: The Quest to Rediscover Microsoft's Soul and Imagine a Better Future for Everyone*, HarperBusiness, 2017.

212. Notes 213–215 and 218–222 below are drawn from *Fortune* Magazine's June 27, 2005, 75th Anniversary Special Issue, "How to Make Great Decisions," the introduction to which, by Jerry Useem, is on 55–56.

213. Corey Hajim, "Sam Walton explores the final frontier," op. cit., 82.

214. Jerry Useem, "Ford offers $5 a day," op. cit., 65.

215. Cait Murphy, "Pan Am flies the ocean blue," op. cit., 68–70.

216. Corey Hajim, "Thomas Watson Jr. does a 360," op. cit., 74–75.

217. Cortada, "Building the System/360 Mainframe."

218. Cortada, *IBM*.

219. Kate Bonamici, "Grove fires himself," op. cit., 84.

220. Bonamici, "Ruth Handler bets Mattel on the Mouseketeers," op. cit., 72.

221. Stephanie N. Mehta, "Jerry Levin decides he doesn't need a collar," op. cit., 86.

222. _____, "Ma Bell gives away her babies," op. cit., 82–84.

223. Malcolm Gladwell, *Blink: The Power of Thinking Without Thinking*, Little, Brown, 2005.

224. Chip and Dan Heath, *Decisive: How to Make Better Choices in Life and Work*, Crown Business, 2013, 25.

225. Malcolm Gladwell, *Blink: The Power of Thinking Without Thinking*, Back Bay Books, 2007—this, the paperback edition, includes the cited Afterword on 266.

226. Ram Charan, "How Amazon Does It," *Chief Executive*, November/December 2019, 24–30, and Ram Charan and Julia Yang, *The Amazon Management System*, Ideapress Publishing, 2019.

227. Heath and Heath, *Decisive*, 23–29.

228. Daniel Kahneman, *Thinking Fast and Slow*, Farrar, Straus and Giroux, 2013.

229. Heath and Heath, *Decisive*, chapter 7.

230. Suzy Welch, *10/10/10: A Fast and Powerful Way to Get Unstuck in Love, at Work, and with Your Family*, Scribner, 2009.

231. Gladwell, *Blink*, 122.

232. Daniel Kahneman, Dan Lovallo, and Oliver Sibony, "A Structured Approach to Strategic Decisions," *Sloan Management Review*, March 4, 2019.

233. Paul Ziobro and Joann S. Lublin, "Ouster of Target Directors Is Urged," *The Wall Street Journal*, May 29, 2014.

234. Jacob Bunge and Ruth Bender, "Roundup, Best-Selling Weed Killer, Faces Reckoning," *The Wall Street Journal*, April 9, 2019, A1, A10.
"Shareholders Blast Bayer Over Monsanto Deal," *Reuters*, April 11, 2019.

235. Kathleen R. Allen, "Creating New Value From Intellectual Property," Leader to Leader, Winter 2003, 10–14.

236. Randy Myers, "A Case for Conglomerates," *CFO Magazine*, March 1, 2001.

237. Austen Hufford, "3M Sticks Together as Rivals Break Up," *The Wall Street Journal*, April 12, 2019, B3.

238. Rachel Abrams, "Procter & Gamble to Streamline Offerings, Dropping Up to 100 Brands," *The New York Times*, August 2, 2014, B3.

239. Simchi-Levi et al., *Managing the Supply Chain*.

240. Brian Carroll, "What's a Lead?" *Target Marketing*, November 2006, 28–34.

241. Hammer and Hershman, *Faster Cheaper Better*.

Chapter 14: Discovering the Best Ways to Boost Results in Your Business—Insight-Based Management

242. Aswath Damodaran, Cost of Capital by Sector (US), https://www.stern.nyu.edu/~adamodar/pc/datasets/wacc.xls. (As of this writing, the data was current as of January, 2022).

243. J.P. Donlon, Drew Morris, and Michael Burdi, "Wealth Creators Index," *Chief Executive Magazine*, November/December 2012, 56–61.

244. J.P. Donlon, Drew Morris, and Bennett Stewart, "Wealth Creation Index," *Chief Executive Magazine*, November/December 2014, 37–43.

Index

F

Facebook
    business design, 191, 206
    network effects and, 203, 206
    unexpected success of, 162–163
    unique value proposition, 192
fairness, 149
fashionability, 150
Fastenal, 191, 192, 193, 205
Faust, Gerry, 252, 266
Firefox, 33
First Republic Bank, 103
Five Forces, Porter's, 202–205
fixed costs, 201
focus
    on appropriate markets, 178
    The Chooser tool for, 315–323
    in describing value, 57
    for opportunity choices, 162, 165
    for tapping upside, 19
Ford, 199, 257

G

Game Changer (Charan and Lafley), 241
Gardner, John. W., 231
gatekeepers, 49–50, 215
Gates, Bill, 254
General Electric, 271
get to Aha! (Cunningham), 186
Gillette razors, 212, 233
Gladwell, Malcolm, 260, 266
Goal Emphasis Advisor, 298–304
goals
    alignment around, 253
    clarity about, 15–16, 186, 252
    combined marketing/sales, 275
    deciding on, 305
    Goal Emphasis Advisor, 299–304
    in heat-based management, 291–292

    increasing profit margins, 295
    pricing and market share, 121–122
    revenue vs. profit margin, 297–305
Goldman Sachs, 80
Google
    as asset-light business, 200
    business design, 191
    as an enabler, 33
    measuring ad effects via, 112
    network effects, 203
    revenue focus of, 297
    value proposition, 192
    values of, 265
Goozé, Mitch, 25
Gore-Tex, 242
growth
    and business value, 294
    market, 182
    revenue vs. profit margin, 297–305, 322

H

habits, buying, 78, 201–202
Halliburton, 145
Handler, Ruth, 259
Harley-Davidson, 31, 77, 84
Harvard Business Review, 18, 57, 60, 193, 201
hassles
    maps of customer, 55, 161
    pricing for services, 133
    in product instructions, 220–222
Hatch, Denny, 186
heat-based management, 291–292
Heath, Chip and Dan, 262, 265
Hees, Bernardo, 3–4, 346
Hewlett-Packard, 34, 48, 79
HumanScale chairs, 212
hungry markets, 177–178

problem-solving
  by becoming the customer, 60–61
  as business' intention, 256
  business opportunities as, 160
  customers' role in, 51
  empathy for, 214
  via "hit records," 215
  innovative co-production, 238
  for new markets, 181
  products, 47
  value proposition as, 54–55
  see also innovation
process
  assessing business, 286
  for brand delivery, 88
  for business acquisitions, 268–269
  cost management, 147
  decision-making, 261–267
  dynamic assessment of, 148
  employee assessment, 271–272
  for innovation, 213, 240, 242
  marketing/sales, 97
  new business, 208
  nonproprietary business, 271
  opportunity assessment, 160, 165
  as prosperity enabler, 276
  Six Sigma, 136
  streamlining, 147, 148, 310–311
  of tapping upsides, 17
  upside initiatives and current, 330
  value delivery, 54, 64
Procter & Gamble
  customer enabling by, 33
  emotional ad campaigns by, 91–92
  innovation by, 235
  value delivery by, 65–66
production facility control, 151
products and services
  activity-based costing of, 146–147
  attractors to, 99–100
  brands of, 80–81

compared with competitors, 97
customers' role in new, 51
cutting marginal offerings, 144
designing, 213, 306–307
discontinuing, 88–89
early adopters of, 239
fashionability and timing, 150
to fill market gaps, 179–180
instructions for use of, 216
inventory, 152, 197, 203
longevity of, 204
most profitable, 200, 202–205
optimizing portfolio of, 272
pricing strategies, 123–126
R&D, 151
sales of complementary, 270
service pricing, 133–134
substitutes for, 184
Tapping Your Upside exercises, 223–225
value engineering of, 128–129
value-proposition choices, 62–63
profit margins
  in business design, 195–199, 208
  and business synergy, 204
  and business value, 294, 295–296
  cost cutting to improve, 143
  defined, 195
  five forces influencing, 183–184, 200,
    202–205
  fixed costs and, 199–200
  fixing drains on, 132–133, 152
  measuring, 296
  pricing and, 119–123
  vs. revenue goals, 19, 297–305, 315
  value proposition to increase, 49, 63
profitability comparisons, 300–304
prospective customers
  advertising to, 97–99
  brand resonance with, 77
  creating zealous, 25, 37
  emotional loyalty in, 27

system for, xvii–xviii
tapping upside gaps for, 5
tools for, 2–3
via *The Upside Within Reach*, 9–10, 12–13
retailers
in distribution chain, 51
dynamic pricing by, 126, 133
and perceived value, 134–135
returns, financial, 66, 198
revenue
activities to boost, 6, 200
in business design, 195
defined, 194
disrupters, 233–234
as function of value, 43
leaks, 30, 274–275, 286
loss from so-so brands, 78
pricing and, 119–123
vs. profit-margin goals, 19, 297–305, 315
via value proposition, 60
rewards programs, 25
Ries, Al, 186
risks
assessing, 144
being out of fashion, 150
to brand image, 87
of innovation, 236, 244
managing, 144, 267–269, 279–280
of not innovating, 234
of outsourcing, 151
and profitability, 204
value-reducing, 294
Road Rescue, 206
Robinson, Alan, 241
Roche, Margaret A., 211
Rometty, Virginia, 214
Rosetta Stone, 99
Roundup, 268
R.W. Auto Repair, 26

S

Safety Nailer, 237
sales
in business design, 194, 195–199
business to business, 51–52
of complementary products, 270
department, vs. marketing, 275
driving up, 200
of innovative products, 238–240
lost, 274
multi-party appeals for, 49–50
by partners, 270
pricing and profit leverage, 119–123
related entities to, 51–52
scalability of, 203
triggering, 112
of unfamiliar products, 51
value-delivery system for, 52
scalability, 203
security analysts, 298
Seizing the White Space (Johnson), 166, 180
selection, broad, 48
services. *see* products and services
Sharer, Kevin, 64
Shell/Noble drilling, 144
showrooming, 132
Shrage, Michael, 241
shrimp farming, 235–236
simplicity, 235–236
Sinek, Simon, 18, 253
Six Sigma, 136, 148, 276
Slywotzky, Adrian, 9, 55, 161
Smart LEDs, 232
smartphones, 47, 212
Sodhi, Manmohan and Navdeep, 136
Southwest Airlines, 47, 79, 192, 253
stage-gate planning, 243
Starbucks, 48, 200
Start With Why (Sinek), 253

T-Mobile, 179
Together is Better (Sinek), 253
Trader Joe's, 25
transportation, 150
Trout, Jack, 186
trust
    of brands, 81
    customer/business, 28
    innovation via, 237
    by managers, 252
Tucker, Robert, 241
TurboTax, 205

U

Under Armour, 211
underserved markets, 179
unexpected events, 162–163
Uniqlo
    customer care by, 26
    hassle-solutions by, 161
    product design, 211, 213
    value proposition, 47
Upside Calculator, 305–314
Upside Element Assessment Sheet,
  384–385
upside elements
    advertising, 97
    best shots, 8, 292–293, 323
    brands, 78, 89
    business design, 193–194
    choosing, 15–16, 315–323
    cost management, 143
    creating zealous customers, 25
    design and innovation, 213
    design for implementing, 329–333
    detecting/seizing opportunities, 213
    executive's role in, 18
    extracting potential from, 16
    finding/serving hungry markets, 177
    innovation, 231

Let's See additions, 341–343
    management, 251
    map of, 6–8
    pricing, 119
    product/service designs, 217–220
    Upside Element Assessment Sheet,
      384-385
    value-proposition delivery, 43
Upside Map, 6–8
The Upside Within Reach (Morris)
    audience for, 4
    benefits of, 9–10
    community served by, 337
    experts' ideas in, 9
    online support/tools for, 337–338
    results-boosting system of, xvii–xviii
    structure of book, 10–12
    tips for using, 12–13
U.S. Steel, 243

V

value
    best shots to increase, 292, 315–323
    of brands, 78
    of a business, 294
    context as determining, 126–129
    curves, 56–57, 185–186
    documentation of, 102
    engineering, 128–129
    as "get"/"pay" balance, 45–46
    of operating results, 295, 321
    perceived, 122, 128–129, 134–135
    price as statement of, 128–129
    relative, 127
    revenue vs. profit-margin growth,
      297–305
    value-delivery system, 52, 53–58, 63
value propositions
    of Big Ass Fans, 84–85
    in brand development, 82
    in business design, 194

About the Author

Drew Morris is the founder and CEO of Great Numbers! LLC, which teaches executives and their teams a new way to boost their profits, revenue, and their business's value, based on over 25 years of research and managing.

He was invited by *Chief Executive* magazine to lead its CEO Roundtable on leveraging intangible assets, like brands, and patents, and to co-create the Wealth Creation Index it published annually from 2008 to 2015.

Earlier, Drew started what became a midsize consulting firm and sold it to a public company after serving as its CEO for 22 years.

He holds a PhD in Systems Engineering from what is now NYU's Tandon School of Engineering, with a concentration in optimization (getting the best-possible outcomes).

Upside Element Assessments

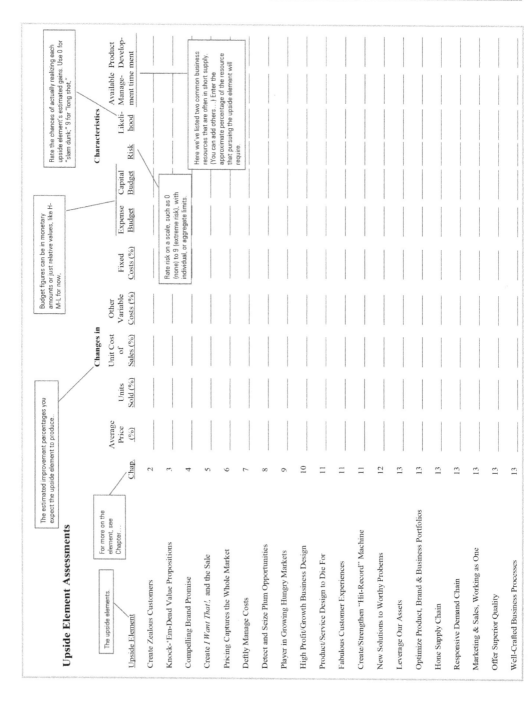

Upside-Element Assessments

Upside Element	Chap.	Changes in					Characteristics					
		Average Price (%)	Units Sold (%)	Unit Cost of Sales (%)	Other Variable Costs (%)	Fixed Costs (%)	Expense Budget	Capital Budget	Risk	Likeli-hood	Available Manage-ment	Product Develop-ment
Create Zealous Customers	2											
Knock-'Em-Dead Value Propositions	3											
Compelling Brand Promise	4											
Create *I Want That!*, and the Sale	5											
Pricing Captures the Whole Market	6											
Deftly Manage Costs	7											
Detect and Seize Plum Opportunities	8											
Player in Growing Hungry Markets	9											
High Profit/Growth Business Design	10											
Product/Service Design to Die For	11											
Fabulous Customer Experiences	11											
Create/Strengthen "Hit-Record" Machine	11											
New Solutions to Worthy Problems	12											
Leverage Our Assets	13											
Optimize Product, Brand, & Business Portfolios	13											
Hone Supply Chain	13											
Responsive Demand Chain	13											
Marketing & Sales, Working as One	13											
Offer Superior Quality	13											
Well-Crafted Business Processes	13